THE Ghosts BEHIND HIM

THE
Ghosts
BEHIND HIM

Doris Ray

CAITLIN PRESS

Published by
CAITLIN PRESS
Box 2387, Stn.B
Prince George, BC V2N 2S6

Cover design by Roger Handling, Terra Firma Graphic Design
Cover artwork by Bruce Ray. The original was part of a
    high-school C ommercial Arts project in 1981.
Page design and production by Eye Design Inc.

Caitlin Press acknowledges the financial support of
the Canada Council for the Arts for our publishing
program. Similarly, we acknowledge the support of
the Arts Council of British Columbia.

THE CANADA COUNCIL | LE CONSEIL DES ARTS
FOR THE ARTS | DU CANADA
SINCE 1957 | DEPUIS 1957

Canadian Cataloguing in Publication Data

Ray, Doris, 1938-
  The ghosts behind him

  ISBN 0-920576-77-X

  1. Ray, Bruce. 2. Schizophrenics–Biography. 3. Mental Health Services–British Columbia.
4. Mental Health Laws–Canada I. Title
RC464.R39R39 1999   616.89'82'0092   C99–910610–4

This book is dedicated to the memory of
the many young men and women who have died
tragically as a direct result of a mental illness.
Forty percent of royalties from sales will be deposited to
The Victims of Mental Illnesses Memorial Fund
established by the author in June of 1999.

ACKNOWLEDGMENTS

First and foremost I need to express my heartfelt appreciation and love to members of my family: to Phoenix for her many hours of word processing, editing and re-editing of the first six chapters and for her contributions of writings and poetry. Thank you to Cathy for printing out large blocks of manuscript material on her computer, and to Darwin for bringing home a word processor when I so desperately needed one.

To Bruce for contributing to my research, and for the use of his writings, poetry and the book cover illustration. To Fern for her poetry and insights, and to my husband Leon for being strong enough for me to lean on.

A huge thank you to Cynthia Wilson and Melanie Callahan of Caitlin Press for taking a chance on a somewhat flawed manuscript, and who instigated, spurred and inspired me into a vastly improved re-write.

Special thanks to Bruce's other parents Ed and Connie Ray of Fort Fraser, for their recollections and their insights. Also to the following people who provided me with their time and invaluable contributions: Jim Draper of Parksville; Sharon Selinger; Stephen D. Taylor; Noreen Flanagan (and other staff members of the *Nanaimo Daily Free Press*); Ching Blas-Muego; Gail Asselin; Mildred Trembley; Louis Devoin; Judy Wittingham; Annemarie Manke; Staff Director Dr. A. Robin Hutchinson Medical Coordinator, the Records Room staff of Nanaimo Regional General Hospital and J.P. Bechdholt Superintendent of RCMP of Nanaimo; Psychiatrist Dr. Robin Routledge of Duncan; Lucy Waters of BCSS Richmond; June Pryor, Nancy Davis, Nancy Panagabko (of Acute and Specialized Programs, Ministry of Health) and Debbi Rupert (Secretary to Chief Coroner) of Victoria; Diane Neilsen and Lisa Rae (of Community Legal Assistance Society); FPI Chaplain Tim

Fretheim, Mary Acheson (Legal Counsel for FPI), FPI Director Michael J. Quinn and FPI Coordinator Clem Poquiz of Port Coquitlam; Andrea Nash, Acting Registrar of the BC Review Board, New Westminster; Chris Basnett and Kim Dixon (of BCSS branch office) and Ian Kluge of Prince George; Marg de Lange of Aldergrove, BC; the Secretary of the NSA of The Baha'is of Canada; Reginald Newkirk of Thornhill, Ont. and Dr. Joyce Burland, director of the Family-to-Family education program, National Alliance for the Mentally Ill (USA).

Other people who offered valuable assistance were: Dr. Alan Gow, Angus Davis, Hazel Mitton, Gina (Dougan) Smith, Jeanette Brophy, my dear friend Joyce Fraser who passed away much too soon, Elaine Storey, Wendy Galvin, Carol Carson, Judy Mooney, Gerry Irwin and Pat Fallat –all of whom are past or present residents of the Fraser Lake area; June Moulton of Burns Lake; Peter Ommundsen of Castlegar; Anne Bowles of Victoria; Bejay Kenney and Mary Lou Nordstrom of Nanaimo and Margo Button of Nanoose Bay, BC.

Where indicated with an asterisk names have been changed to protect the privacy of the individual.

CHAPTER ONE

What was "IT"
(Toronto 1984)

"I walked along life's lonely road
until I met a lonely man
a gentle glint was in his eye
as he hinted at "IT"
What was "IT"
I asked of him..."

From a poem entitled "IT"
written by Bruce Ray in 1984

One of life's ironic contradictions is that as we approach what is supposed to be the age of attaining wisdom, our recollection of past events becomes less clear. But memories associated with uncomfortable emotions such as fear, horror and guilt are ones that we are least likely to forget. Perhaps the pain is part of the teaching process. What hurts the most is what needs to be remembered. And what is remembered needs to be shared.

It has become a twentieth century cliché that almost every adult is able to recall the details of what he or she was doing on November 22, 1963, when the news broadcast about the assassination of US President

John F. Kennedy was flashed around the world. I do. I listened to the shocking report on our battery-powered radio and, as we did not have a telephone, left my sleeping six-month-old son alone for a few minutes while I ran across the road to confirm the news with my sister-in-law. I returned home before the baby awoke.

Twenty-one years later that baby became psychotic and attempted to dive through a window of his upstairs Toronto apartment. I was preparing supper in the late afternoon of September 25, 1984 –"Black Tuesday" as Bruce later referred to it–when I received the telephone call from his landlady who assured me he was only slightly injured. Her matter-of-fact tone of voice stirred up similar feelings of disbelief and horror, as had that news release so long ago.

Little did I know then that this was merely the beginning. That as the years passed by I would come to dread the ringing of the telephone, and that one day it would relay the ultimate message that my son had committed an unspeakable act of violence.

Bruce had been a planned baby. I had carefully chosen his birth month as a likely time to produce a son and heir for my husband. I wasn't sure about the old adage: that every woman has a pattern to her conceptions, with alternate months throughout the year being surefire "girl" or "boy" months, but I took no chances. My two daughters had been born in April and August; so according to formula, May should have been my month for a change of sex. It worked wonderfully and we welcomed our son into the world on May 5th, 1963.

His birth had not been an easy one. The nearest hospital at Williams Lake, BC was almost a hundred miles of rough road away, and I had already made the trek in once with false labour pains. The doctor decided to initiate a procedure that would bring on labour when it was convenient for all. The baby was reluctant to arrive on that particular day but the doctor was in charge; as so many other doctors would be in charge during his adult years.

Bruce was a healthy baby though as were his older sisters, Debbie, six and Cathy, five. We lived in a newly bulldozed rural subdivision near the tiny community of Eagle Creek, east of the town of 100 Mile House. The subdivision was created to accommodate a number of sawmill camp buildings which had been hauled down from a temporary bush camp to a more permanent location. Two or three of these buildings were then attached to one another, like Lego blocks, to make fairly comfortable homes for young families. Ours had electricity, running water and an inside bathroom, the ultimate in modern living to me, accustomed to living in the bush.

My husband Ed worked for the sawmill company that provided these amenities for its employees. Our neighbors were almost all, in one way or another, related to us and many had children the same ages as our own. I and the mothers of Bruce's cousins–Bonnie and Teresa who were all born within weeks of one another, sometimes took turns baby-sitting all three babies providing each of us with some respite from time to time.

I recall my sister-in-law Hazel's hilarious assessment of one afternoon's baby-sitting session when the babies were at the crawling stage of development: "The girls screamed all afternoon," she had related. "But Bruce was quiet–especially when he was destroying the house!"

Bruce was extremely curious about the mechanics of how all things worked. He was also intent on learning the fastest way to get from wherever he happened to be to wherever he wanted to be. He could climb before he could walk, and as soon as he was capable of propelling himself along on two feet, was inclined to explore all the dangers of the outside world.

When Bruce was about three months old I experienced a very strange perception that I remember quite clearly. My baby lay in his crib and–just for a moment–I fancied I saw a mature intelligence and even wisdom, reflected in his eyes. It was as if the two of us had slipped into an entirely different dimension. I fully expected my infant son to utter words of profound significance to me. Perhaps if I had been able to comprehend that silent message, I would have been better prepared to deal with the series of unforeseen circumstances, and horrific events that would commence a little more than twenty-one years in the future.

As it was, my stomach did frantic flip flops that beautiful September afternoon in 1984, as I listened to the voice of the woman who said she was my son's landlady. She had identified herself on the phone as Mary Swick*, explaining that she had found my phone number while searching through the pigsty that was my son's apartment. Earlier that afternoon Mary and several of her tenants had been playing cards in one of the downstairs rooms of the two-storey apartment building. Someone spotted a television set lying outside on the lawn and everyone filed outdoors to investigate. It was then that they heard the sound of glass breaking, and looked up to see Bruce's half-naked torso hanging out of an upstairs window.

Mary Swick and the people whom she referred to as her witnesses rushed upstairs to Bruce's suite. When they opened the door an incredible disarray of dirty dishes, books and ashtrays overflowing with cigarette butts met their eyes. In one corner of the living room, a brass-colored television stand lay overturned; the disconnected cable cord dangled nearby.

Bruce's body hung suspended half out of a large double-paned window, his toes barely touching the carpet. He was completely naked except for a torn black and white striped shirt. They watched silently as his body began to collapse, very slowly, toward the floor. His flesh appeared to be embedded with numerous shards of glass. Mary was amazed to learn later that he had received only one minor scratch.

Shakily, Bruce pulled himself to his feet. He began muttering strange disjointed phrases, fragments from the books of Chinese philosophy and esoteric religions that he had been devouring for the past few weeks. When he noticed the onlookers he became hostile. "You are all going to die," he proclaimed to his fearful audience. "By spontaneous combustion," he added, causing them to relax somewhat.

Someone finally called an ambulance. By the time it arrived, Bruce was docile. As attendants led him downstairs, Mary Swick heard him whisper, "Now I can go home to Fraser Lake," the name of the small community in the northern interior of BC where my family and I had moved in 1972.

Mary told me Bruce had appeared to be depressed for approximately four months. The other tenants had been worried about him, she said. Before that he was quite sociable. He and Mary even smoked a few joints of marijuana together from time to time. One of the witnesses to the incident that afternoon suggested Bruce's behavior was much like someone having a bad trip on LSD. Mary had combed through Bruce's apartment, searching for evidence of his having recently used drugs, but found none. She ended our conversation by informing me that Bruce was in East Toronto General Hospital. If I phoned in the morning, she suggested, a doctor would likely fill me in on his condition.

My hands trembled as I hung up the phone. I had suspected that something was wrong with Bruce's situation in Toronto. He'd had such high hopes when he left Fraser Lake nine months earlier, after having given up his job at a local sawmill. Bruce had worked hard since graduating from the Commercial Arts program at Victoria Composite High School in Edmonton in 1981. To further his commercial art studies, he'd had to earn some money. He returned home to Fraser Lake and for a year and a half traversed the distance to the sawmill site with my second husband Leon, who worked as a millwright on the same shift.

Bruce's father Ed and I had separated while Bruce was a toddler and less than a year later I fell in love with Leon. We now had a child of our own—a ten-year-old daughter named Fern. Ed continued to maintain a strong bond with his son, but because his real dad lived so far away on Vancouver Island, Leon had been the most visible father figure in Bruce's life.

Bruce's dream had been to attend an art school, preferably at the University of Ontario. He had applied there shortly after graduation and been turned down, possibly because he was not an Ontario resident. One of his teachers in Edmonton, a fellow by the name of Mark Randall*, had recently moved to Toronto. While still in school Bruce had drawn some illustrations for a book of poetry that Mark hoped to have published. When Bruce telephoned two years later, Mark assured him that he was indeed welcome to stay with him at his Toronto apartment—for awhile.

Bruce had managed to accumulate several thousand dollars in a savings account. He hoped to supplement that by finding a part-time job in Toronto. His plan was to attend night school classes in commercial art and build up his portfolio of drawings and paintings. He thought he would need an impressive portfolio to be accepted into the Commercial Arts Program at the University of Ontario. It sometimes turned down two thirds of applicants.

Before Bruce left home, his sisters surprised him with a going-away party. My gift to him had been a supply of stationery and postage stamps–a gentle hint for him to write. Although Bruce promised that he would, I had not received a single letter from him. And when we last talked on the telephone, he had sounded distant and uncommunicative. I rationalized that perhaps he preferred not to be tied to home and family. After all, he was twenty-one years old and no longer a child.

A few weeks previously, I'd had a strange dream in which Bruce's hair suddenly changed to a bright, almost psychedelic, orange in color. The following morning I jokingly mentioned it to Leon and Fern. Now, after learning a few details about what had happened to her half-brother in Toronto, my ten-year-old reminded me of that dream. "Mom," she said, "You must have been psychic!"

That night I did not dream at all because I could not sleep. I am an insomniac at the best of times, and all night long I reviewed what Mary Swick had told me. She said Bruce had been depressed for about four months. I thought I knew the definition of depression. When my marriage to Ed disintegrated and I realized there was no hope of reconciliation, I had been unable to sleep for five nights and lost about 15 pounds. But I had never contemplated suicide and certainly never would attempt it in the bizarre fashion that Bruce apparently had.

Four months earlier would have been around Bruce's twenty-first birthday. I remembered calling him at that time. He had laughingly mentioned a gift that some new friends had given him. It was a kind of initiation into adulthood. They took him into a bar where a strip-tease dancer put on a performance especially for him. When he told me later that the woman had a boyfriend, his voice had sounded strained. Perhaps that was the reason for his depression?

The next morning I called East Toronto General Hospital and was told the doctor had already completed his rounds and had left the facility. The woman I spoke to told me that Bruce was still in an acute psychotic state. He had confessed to using cocaine and heroin for a period of two years, she confided, but the doctor did not believe that was so. According to his medical report, there was no evidence that Bruce had used street drugs prior to the incident. She suggested I call back the next day, Thursday, at around 10 a.m. Eastern Time. I could then speak directly to Bruce's doctor.

The following morning I finally did get through to the doctor. He said Bruce was under sedation but was still in a psychotic state. It was definitely not a suicide attempt, the doctor assured me. In a few days Bruce would likely be well enough to be transferred out of the crisis ward into a public ward. When I asked him how long Bruce would be kept in the hospital, he replied, probably for some time.

That evening Mary Swick phoned again and I noticed an abrupt change from her previous attitude of friendly concern. She sounded reserved and formal as she stated that she wanted the family to take responsibility for Bruce. She did not want him back in his apartment after he was discharged from hospital. I was dumbfounded by her words and tone of voice. I told her what the doctor had said; that Bruce would be in the hospital for some time. What was she worried about, I wondered. Did she not think Bruce would become well after being treated in hospital?

The thought did cross my sleep-deprived mind that someone in our family should go out to Toronto. Leon and I had very little money though and he had to work. The thought of travelling alone that far on a Greyhound bus scared me half to death. I did not know a soul, other than Bruce, who resided east of the Alberta / Saskatchewan border. It was not as if it was an emergency, I rationalized. Whatever it was that had caused Bruce to throw his television set out the window and then attempt to hurl himself through that same broken pane of glass, was a malady that was not likely to reoccur. Leon and I had talked it over. Both of us were convinced it had something to do with street drugs, although the doctor had found no evidence that this was so.

I called my ex-husband Ed who now resided in the small city of Duncan on Vancouver Island. I filled him in on what Mary Swick had told me. Ed stated that neither he nor his wife Connie had the time or money to travel to Toronto. He sounded angry and a bit suspicious about the reasoning behind Mary Swick's sudden decision to evict Bruce before he had even been released from hospital. He wondered if Mary might have been the cause of whatever was wrong with our son. Bruce was quite naive and trusting. He had no idea what some people in a big city were capable of.

On Saturday morning when I called the hospital, I learned that Bruce had been transferred to a public ward and my call was put through directly to his room. To my surprise and joy, he sounded calm and rational. He had just been informed that he was not to leave the hospital floor, and the reality of his situation was beginning to sink in. He was amazed and pleased to have survived the incident without physical ill effects. Bruce said he recalled the ambulance ride, but after reaching the hospital, he had been placed in restraints. Terrified, not understanding what was happening, he had returned to a psychotic state. For the past three days his mind had been rollercoasting wildly back and forth between sublimely ecstatic, and horrifying degrading images. As he described some of these, I wondered if he was a bit disappointed to find himself back in the "real" world.

When I asked Bruce why he told the doctor he had used cocaine and heroin, he answered that he had just wanted to be agreeable. "It was what I thought he wanted to hear," he said sheepishly. In fact, the only street drugs he had used were marijuana and hashish. He admitted that he had smoked a lot of pot and it was "good stuff."

That night I mulled over what I knew about the effects of marijuana on the human nervous system. I once tried using marijuana years earlier and had experienced an unsettling reaction. My thoughts became extremely crisp and clear, almost as if they had a life of their own. Row upon row of my ruminations, composed with little effort on my part, formed psychedelic red and orange sentences that blazed across the landscape of my mind. I had a touch of gastritis and the colorful rows of words undulated back and forth in huge waves with each attack of indigestion. The indigestion was not severe but the visual effects had transformed it into a psychically painful experience. I recalled lying on someone's bed for what seemed like hours, anxiously waiting for the effects to wear off.

I also recalled reading a series of articles published in the *Reader's Digest* magazine, entitled "Marijuana Alert," but I could not remember in what issues. Oddly enough, when I went to look, I immediately picked out the relevant copies from the disorganized stacks of *Reader's Digests* in the hall cupboard. The articles I was looking for were published in the December 1980 issue and continued through January and February 1981. When I read the articles again, I learned that marijuana can trigger schizophrenia in some susceptible people, as well as cause other frightening health hazards. These opinions were expressed by a number of physicians and scientists, who had based their conclusions on actual case histories of patients.

When I spoke with Bruce's doctor on Monday morning, he suggested I call back on Wednesday; at that time, he said, he would be able to tell me more. I talked to Bruce and inquired if he had any money left in his bank account. He answered that he had exactly "one-forty-five." I took that to mean one hundred and forty-five dollars; what he actually meant was one dollar and forty-five cents. I debated with myself about whether to tell Bruce that his landlady wanted to evict him; then decided to save that piece of bad news until my next phone call on Wednesday morning. At that time we would also discuss how I could forward the money for his plane ticket home.

On Tuesday afternoon Bruce phoned from his friend Dave's home in Toronto. He had been discharged from the hospital that morning, one week from the time he was admitted.

Earlier in the day he had returned to his apartment where Mary Swick presented him with an eviction notice. She returned one month's rent, which was enough money for a plane ticket to Prince George. His suitcases were packed, he told me wearily, and tomorrow he would be home.

I felt a tremendous sense of relief. Bruce had everything under control after all! He sounded fatigued, but said that was probably from the medication. He was taking a drug called Haldol which had some side-effects. He had a second prescription of a drug called Cogentin which was supposed to counter those side-effects.

Bruce's sister Cathy, and her husband Darwin, offered to drive the one hundred and sixty kilometers to the Prince George airport to meet Bruce's plane. They were a few minutes late. Cathy told me later that they found him curled up in a chair looking totally wiped out.

When they arrived home and Bruce stepped from their car, I could hardly believe my eyes. His wide grin was the same, but that was the only thing about his appearance that had not changed. He looked nothing at all like my good-looking, muscular son who had left Fraser Lake only nine months earlier. His hair was long and greasy, his eyes protruded from their sockets and his clothes hung loosely from an emaciated body. "He must have been starving himself for some time to get that thin," I thought, mystified. He walked toward the house and I noticed that he stepped slowly and carefully, as if balancing himself along a tightrope.

Bruce's oldest sister Debbie and her three children arrived shortly. Together with Cathy, Darwin, their two children–and Fern who was not much older than her nieces and nephews–our small house was soon alive with laughter and loud conversation. With the exception of Leon who was on afternoon shift at the sawmill, everyone was there to welcome Bruce back home. It reminded me of the last family gathering at our home, shortly before Bruce left for Toronto. In fact as Bruce unpacked his suitcases, I noticed he had brought home the same rag doll that Debbie and Cathy had presented to him as a gift at his farewell party.

The doll which Bruce referred to as Vincent after the wildly eccentric Dutch artist, Vincent Van Gogh, had been hand-crafted by my two older daughters. Vincent was a long thin artist figure, complete with paint-daubed smock. It clutched a paintbrush in one hand and an artist's palette in the other. Debbie had painted its face with bloodshot eyes and a tongue hanging out of its mouth. As a finishing touch, she had added a mop of stringy red hair.

I wondered at the irony of it. Bruce had left behind in Toronto an apartment filled with pieces of furniture and many personal items, including most of his clothing. He had packed only his most valued possessions: his books, camera and photography equipment, a few art supplies, some clothes, and Vincent. I glanced morosely at the doll which was dangling from his suitcase. The words Mad Artist neatly printed on its rumpled smock, were clearly visible.

I berated myself for my less than optimistic musings. All Bruce need-ed, I told myself, was plenty of nutritious home-cooked meals to put some meat back on his bones. The medication he was on seemed to be helping his frame of mind. I sat back and watched as he joked with his sisters, nieces and nephews.

The only other quiet person in the room was Darwin. Besides the age difference, Bruce and Darwin were two very different individuals. Darwin was an outdoorsman, as was my husband, while Bruce preferred more esthetic activities such as reading, art and music.

As a youngster Bruce had enjoyed our frequent fishing trips and camping out. Upon reaching adolescence he had usually preferred to stay at home with his artist's sketch pad, his music and his books. I was relieved that, unlike his older sisters, he had not wished to attend social functions where he would be exposed to drugs and alcohol. Other than the minor hockey games that he enjoyed immensely, Bruce had tended to be a loner.

Their mutual passion for hockey was the one interest that Bruce and Darwin had in common. Both had played hockey when they were younger. Now they religiously watched all of the National Hockey League games on television.

The awkward part of having Bruce back home, I soon realized, was that our cabin with attached mobile home was just too small. The only space available for Bruce to sleep was an area off the kitchen that we used as a dining room. Leon and I moved an old bed chesterfield in there, and I hung up plastic drapes as a room divider, to give him at least an illusion of privacy. But with Leon on shiftwork and Fern going to school, our kitchen was often the busiest part of the house. Possibly the intermittent activity so close to his bed contributed to Bruce's near-ly constant fatigue. When Fern was in school, he often lay down to rest in her room.

Our small acreage was located eight kilometers from the nearest settlement, the village of Fraser Lake. A few years earlier when the nearby Endako Mine was in full operation, Fraser Lake had a popula-tion of about 1,800. Now because of an economic downturn in the price of molybdenum, the company had cut back to a bare minimum of employees. The mining and sawmill community located along Highway 16 between Vanderhoof and Burns Lake, was in a population decline.

The few families who resided in our rural neighborhood were either middle-aged, retired or young couples with small children. Bruce did not drive and no longer had a job to break his isolation. But his sisters were very supportive. Cathy and Debbie often drove out from town to pick him up. They were convinced that Bruce's problems were psycho-logical in nature, possibly caused by loneliness and low self-esteem.

Cathy trimmed his hair. Both she and Darwin welcomed him into their home and encouraged him to participate in activities with relatives and friends. Darwin's brother Jim and his wife Karen even offered him a place to stay when he was well enough to move back into town, to look for a job.

Bruce already had a special relationship with his sister Debbie, after having resided with her and her husband Gary for the two years he attended school in Edmonton. He had developed a strong bond with her three children during that time. When Debbie left Gary in 1983 and moved into a house in Fraser Lake, Bruce had moved in with her, paying for his room and board while he was working at the sawmill. Debbie now had a significant male friend, but she continued to enjoy her brother's company. She and her sister sometimes conversed with Bruce for hours over numerous cups of coffee while their children were at school.

At home Bruce's fatigue, or perhaps boredom, was often evident. My husband is an accomplished guitarist, having learned to play the instrument by ear in early childhood.

Bruce had picked up the guitar from time to time over the years and demonstrated that he too had an ear for music. At Leon's suggestion, Bruce began to teach himself to play the guitar and sing rock and roll songs. Darwin's brother Jim also played guitar and offered some pointers from time to time.

When Bruce first arrived home, he had a great craving for candy and sweets. He chain-smoked cigarettes but expressed a tremendous amount of guilt about his addiction to them, possibly because I had given up the noxious weed during the past year and was quite vocal about it.

After a few weeks Bruce overcame the appearance of balancing along a tightrope when he was walking. But he said he still felt as if a wind was constantly blowing through him. And whenever he closed his eyes he could see bright colours. Bruce's Aunt Vi, who is diabetic, told me she also sees colours when she closes her eyes. I remembered that several other family members suffered from diabetes, and that it was generally assumed to be an inherited illness. According to my medical encyclopedia, hypoglycemia which often precedes full-blown diabetes, can have symptoms that mimic mental illness.

During one of Bruce's visits to Dr. Alan Gow our long-time family doctor, I suggested a complete physical examination. I told Dr. Gow about the incidence of diabetes in the Ray family and my suspicion that it may have been a factor in Bruce's mental breakdown.

The examination did not indicate any evidence of diabetes. I must have appeared less than delighted with the results because Dr. Gow chided me in his charming Scottish accent, saying, "You wouldn't wish diabetes on the poor fellow, would you?" I felt abashed because deep down I wished that very thing–that Bruce's strange symptoms were caused by diabetes. It would have been a relief to put a familiar name to his problem to find out that he had something treatable and relatively common.

I had another fear that I had not yet acknowledged. My mother had suffered from anxiety attacks and at least one episode of severe depression. She never exhibited behavior as bizarre as Bruce's had been, but when I was eleven my father signed the papers to confine her to the Crease Clinic, which in those days was a part of the Essondale Mental Hospital at Port Coquitlam. He refused to sign the papers for her release for a period of three years. When she finally came home, she appeared to have fully recovered from whatever symptoms had plagued her.

I remembered the shame I had felt as an adolescent at having a mother who was mentally ill. I had experienced a lot of guilt too for having those feelings. If Bruce was also suffering from mental illness, I vowed to help him in every possible way, to become well.

CHAPTER TWO

The Devil is Illusion

*"One of the most striking images he recalled
was of the Earth gradually being covered over
with concrete and steel until it was completely
encased, like an egg in a shell. Then, when it
appeared no life was left, the shell cracked and
a thin green tendril escaped. It grew until the
entire covering fell away and the new green
living earth was free, Edenlike and pristine..."*

From the recollections of Bruce's sister Debbie,
regarding conversations with him about his experiences
while in a psychotic coma at East Toronto General Hospital.

During those long lonely days and nights in his Toronto apartment, Bruce had begun the habit of composing philosophical essays concerning social and spiritual issues that were troubling him. He chronicled these in a series of spiral-bound notebooks and brought them home for his sisters and me to read. One short epigram is ingrained in my memory: the phrase "The devil is illusion" appeared sporadically throughout his writings. In certain places it had even been penned in upper case letters and underlined.

Now that he was home Bruce continued to write in his notebooks. Several times a day I would notice him rise from his chair to lie upon one of the beds, seemingly in a meditative state. He appeared to derive the information he later wrote about from communications he received inside his own mind.

My son had his extroverted moments though. Over the next few months Bruce and I indulged in many interesting conversations. Eventually I was able to piece together the sequence of events that preceded his mental breakdown. He had arrived at Mark Randall's apartment on a cold, blustery Toronto day with approximately five thousand dollars in his wallet. Although he placed most of it in a savings account, he was unable to hang onto his money for very long. Mark did not have a steady job, and he and his friends smoked marijuana as often as they could afford to buy it. Bruce soon learned to enjoy their group pot-smoking sessions. His savings dwindled, as did his ambitions for getting a job and attending night school classes in commercial art.

Sometime in March, Bruce phoned to say he had moved into his own apartment. He had purchased all the essentials for living a bachelor's life. Debbie and I packed his big steel trunk with art supplies, photography equipment and his beloved books and shipped it to him at his new address. Bruce continued to smoke marijuana, both by himself, and in the company of his new friends. One event that he especially enjoyed was when he attended a Bruce Springsteen rock music concert; the fact that he was stoned, he told me, added an extra dimension to the pleasure he felt listening to his favourite performer.

Sometimes Bruce and his friends would drink beer and smoke marijuana at the same time. They referred to this combination as "using the gas and the brakes." The two substances apparently affected the state of inebriation of the user in entirely different ways.

The reason he did not write letters or telephone home, Bruce explained, was that he had been ashamed of the way he was squandering his money. When his bank account became depleted, he subsisted for several weeks on nothing but tomato sandwiches and a raw-grain cereal called muesli. Mark finally persuaded Bruce to apply for unemployment insurance benefits.

Bruce's infatuation with Dale Olson* the exotic dancer, began the night she invited him on-stage to act as a passive partner in her performance of the evening. To celebrate his twenty-first birthday, Mark and his friends had taken Bruce to the nightclub. The seductive scenario with Dale had been a pre-arranged gift upon his having attained adulthood. Later that night when he and Mark were drinking beer and smoking pot, Dale arrived at Bruce's apartment to join the party. She was so beautiful it was almost as if an angel had visited his home. Dale was stoned on LSD and Bruce was stoned on marijuana, but it was obvious to him that she liked him a lot.

He called her several times after that. One night she even consented to go to a movie with him. But as it turned out, Bruce was too stoned to go anywhere. When next he called her, she told him not to bother phoning anymore; she said she already had a boyfriend. When Bruce realized that the blonde, blue-eyed Dale Olson would not become a part of his life, he did the next best thing. He sketched a portrait in pastel crayons of the woman whose lovely features were etched in his memory.

Bruce gradually began to isolate himself from everyone, although he confessed later that he was often lonely. One night he noticed that some cockroaches had invaded his apartment. He actually experienced pleasure from learning of their companionship. The money from his unemployment insurance cheques was not enough to cover his expenses. To pay the rent, Bruce decided to wean himself cold turkey off cigarettes and marijuana, as well as the numerous cups of coffee that he consumed daily. But he soon found himself unable to fall asleep at night. During the weeks preceding his breakdown, Bruce spent much of his time reading. Often several books at a time; huge books on metaphysics, philosophy and various religions. His thirst for knowledge became more and more compulsive. He began practicing self-hypnosis, at first in hopes of expanding his artistic ability. Later during these sessions, he experimented with ways to unlock the mysteries of what the well-known philosopher Carl Jung had referred to as "the collective unconscious."

Jung's theory was that we, as humans, have buried within our subconscious minds all the knowledge ever obtained throughout the course of mankind's history. The trick was in learning how to access it. Bruce would lie down upon his bed in a self-induced trance. During these times he would affirm repeatedly, "I am open and receptive."

As time passed Bruce came to believe that the other tenants in his apartment building had the ability to read minds. Also that they were trying to influence him by placing their thoughts inside his head. He isolated himself even further from his neighbors and from his friends.

One morning Bruce looked outside his living room window and noticed some unusual yellow lights in the sky. When he glanced at a familiar tree, he could hear voices coming from its leaves. The spirits of his dead ancestors began to stir themselves inside of him. He listened with great interest to the wisdom of their collected advice. Bruce was acting upon that advice the day he threw his television set out the window.

The black and white striped shirt he wore that day was symbolic of a hockey referee's uniform, which in Bruce's state of mind, signified the ultimate in power and authority. He believed he had been given the ability to fly through the air for great distances in order to carry out an important mission. That mission had been to pass along certain messages that the spirits of his ancestors had entrusted to him, to people in all parts of the world.

Bruce often discussed the hallucinations that he had experienced while in a psychotic coma at East Toronto General Hospital. His sister Debbie was interested in listening to her brother's vivid, detailed accounts:

> "Bruce's hallucinations were so lifelike it was impossible for him to know they were not real. He said he was alternately brought to states of exaltation (where he entered beautiful Eden-like worlds and was given lessons relating to other dimensions of existence) and later, when he was punished cruelly for all the suffering in the world which he was told by the "conductors" of his cosmic tour, was all his fault. At one point he imploded inwardly until he became a "black hole." Bruce recalled that he no longer existed. He was nothingness—nowhere at all. That, he told me with a shudder, was the most horrifying experience of all. During calmer periods he was shown visions of wondrous beauty on a television-like screen that was over his head.

"Many of these images he recounted caught my imagination and intrigued me. I wondered if Bruce's hallucinations might not be entirely delusional but "real" experiences of sorts, on planes of existence unknown to science."

I was also intrigued by Bruce's hallucinations, especially one which, he said, was in the form of a memory of a time when he was only two years old. The spirits informed him that the recollection was not a false memory. It was of an event that had actually occurred in 1965.

Bruce asked me if something significant had happened to his grandmother that year. I replied that his father's mother had passed away in October 1965. But his hallucination, he said, had to do with my mother. Bruce recalled a chair cover with a pattern on it that reminded him of "the bubbling pits of Hell." He saw broken glass everywhere in the room. A woman who resembled my mother, he later thought it may have been my mother's mother whom none of us had known, put shards of glass up his rectum. He told me he now knew what it was like to be raped.

I was horrified by Bruce's account of that hallucination. I phoned Dr. Gow to ask if he thought it possible that my son's memory of the shards of glass scene could be a metaphor for what had actually been a rape. The doctor replied hesitantly, "That could very well be…"

I tried to recreate in my mind all of the events that had occurred in our family that year. I wondered how Bruce, as a small child, could possibly have been sexually assaulted without his father or I noting any evidence of it. The only way it could have happened, I decided, was if he had spent time with a baby-sitter.

My mother seldom baby-sat and I felt sure her appearance in his hallucination had little to do with what may have happened in real life. The children had stayed with baby-sitters for two periods of time during the fall of 1965: first, on Labour Day weekend when we had visited Ed's mother in hospital and a month later when she died. Try as I might, I could not recall who had baby-sat the children during those times.

I have a tendency to become obsessive about anything that concerns my children. I began to write down a number of scenarios that, by a huge stretch of the imagination, could have been factors in what may have happened to my son almost twenty years earlier. Weeks later I was still mulling over my theories, which I had chronicled on a sheet of paper. I finally showed them to Bruce who suggested quietly: "You're banging your head against a stone wall." He persuaded me to throw the paper into our wood-burning stove.

Bruce and I were frequent visitors at the public library in Fraser Lake. He enjoyed reading books about metaphysical experiences and had developed an interest in a recent phenomenon known as channeling. People who channelled did so while in a trance-like state of mind. An entity, usually claiming to be the spirit of someone who had once lived on earth, would speak through the vocal chords of the channeller. Numerous books had been written on the phenomena. They had been based upon personal interviews with these entities whose channellers remained in an unconscious state, oblivious to the entire exchange. I was as fascinated by these books as was Bruce.

During one of our library visits, Pat the librarian asked Bruce what he had been doing with his time, while in the "big city" of Toronto. Bruce, with a sheepish grin on his face, answered, "Smoking a lot of pot." She laughed until the tears came to her eyes because she thought he was joking. Bruce told me later that he couldn't tell a lie, because of his compulsive honesty. I could relate to that. As a child I had usually blurted out the truth although it sometimes meant a spanking.

Cathy felt that Bruce would do well to talk to Pastor Weibe* who was the minister of her church, and receive counselling from a Christian perspective to help him resolve his religious conflicts. Bruce had gone to Sunday school a few times while growing up in Fraser Lake, but we had never been a church-going family. Cathy now attended services at the Lakeview Bible Chapel where Darwin's parents and many of their friends were members.

Bruce could not relate to Pastor Wiebe and his views, and some of the counselling sessions upset him instead of giving him peace of mind. Pastor Wiebe's assertion that "the heart is the root of all evil," a biblical quotation, bothered Bruce a lot. I have since learned that people who suffer from mental disorders are sometimes unable to comprehend abstract concepts. For example, they may not perceive that the well-known cliché "a rolling stone gathers no moss" actually alludes to people, not rocks. Bruce may have interpreted Pastor Weibe's reference to evil as being like a physical malignancy with roots that grow inside the organ that is the human heart.

I remembered my young neighbour, Tracy Heigh's quest for a religion when she was going to high school and her interest in the Baha'i Faith. One day I met Gina Dougan, a long time friend who is also a Baha'i. I told Gina about Bruce's interest in religion and that I felt he was not benefitting from the counselling sessions with Pastor Weibe. I asked Gina for information about the Baha'i Faith. She said Bahai's do not proselytize, but they are encouraged to teach the tenets of the faith to those who wish to learn.

Gina invited me and Bruce to a fireside gathering at the home of two high school teachers, Ian and Kirsti Kluge. A fireside, she explained, was an informal talk with a relevant Baha'i theme. The fireside that evening would focus on the tenet that "all religions are one." It would explain the founding of the Baha'i Faith for the benefit of Bruce and I and any other non-Baha'is who would attend.

Bruce already knew Ian Kluge who had taught English at the high school for a number of years. When Bruce was in grade ten, Mr. Kluge wrote a play, entitled "Tornrak" that was staged by a local theatre group. Bruce's art teacher, who was one of the actors, had delegated Bruce to draw the illustrations used as props in the play. Tornrak went on to receive high acclaim at various provincial competitions.

Bruce was perspiring and very nervous when we arrived at the Kluge residence. He and I are both shy at social functions, especially when there are people in attendance whom we do not know. The living room where the fireside was to be held was crowded with people. When Gina told Bruce that she too smoked cigarettes, he joined her in the kitchen for a smoke.

He seemed more relaxed after that and we both enjoyed the evening. Bruce later became an avid participant at the firesides. He joined the Baha'i Faith in early 1985.

One bright, sunny day my son experienced a visual hallucination as he entered the house. It appeared to him that the living room was filled with smoke. Obviously puzzled he queried me about the smoke, and I had to tell him that there wasn't any. A few days later, he bit into a piece of fruitcake that was in the refrigerator and said he could not eat it because it tasted salty. There was no way I could detect the taste of salt.

Weeks later Bruce confided in me about another incident that had caused him to question his own perceptions. He had tasted some Coca Cola from the refrigerator and, as he put it, "it tasted awful." When I informed him that the bottle actually contained a sample of a friend's very dry homemade wine, he was obviously relieved.

Bruce's condition seemed to stabilize, and for several weeks he took no medication. Then one day after another of his attempts at giving up smoking cigarettes, I noticed him sitting in a chair, obviously spaced out. He was staring straight ahead not at all tuned in to his surroundings. I took him to see Dr. Gow, who renewed the prescriptions for his medications.

My first real experience with the nightmarish quality of my son's illness occurred the evening when his eyes rolled up into their sockets and he began to talk strangely, praying and mumbling to himself. In a panic I phoned Dr. Gow, who was busy with an emergency at the clinic. The good doctor took time out to assure me that Bruce's symptoms were caused by too much of the Haldol medication. He said I should give Bruce more of the other drug, called Cogentin, to lessen these side-effects. I did that–but it did not seem to help.

All that night I sat close to my son as he lay on his bed trying to cope with his distress. He appeared to be in great emotional pain as well as suffering physically from the muscle spasms and rigidity that were, apparently, caused by the anti-psychotic medication. I was baffled and frightened as he coiled his body into a fetal position, his hands clasped tightly in prayer. I made him cups of Ovaltine and from time to time, mouthed a few prayerful words along with him. Every few hours I gave him another Cogentin pill. I was afraid of giving him too many because Dr. Gow had said they had a tendency to induce some serious side-effects of their own.

Leon had gone to work the following morning when I prepared to take Bruce to the medical clinic. The muscle rigidity had worsened during the night. It now affected his arms, which he held upright almost shoulder high. It was unusually cold for November, and my old car was reluctant to start. After I prayed frantically, it finally rumbled to life. I bundled Bruce up and led him toward the back seat where he would have plenty of room. I felt a twinge of claustrophobia from time to time, as I watched my son in the rear mirror on our way in to town. His arms rose as if they were on strings, and his eyes rolled up in their sockets until they bulged whitely. He sat stiff and still; his head inclined at an unnatural angle in the direction of the morning sun.

As I drove, the speedometer cable which had a habit of freezing up, began to scream loudly. I worried that in Bruce's state of mind he might not understand the cause of the noise. I babbled trivia at him, hoping to head off any distress he might have because of the dreadful noise that was emanating from the frozen cable.

Dr. Gow gave Bruce an injection of Cogentin to counteract the effects of the Haldol. But it took several hours before he began to improve. My son lay motionless on a cot at the medical clinic while I waited in a chair beside him. Apparently, the Cogentin should have been taken at the same time as the Haldol medication. It was more effective as a preventative than when it was taken later after the side-effects had already set in.

That night I could not sleep even though I was exhausted. Whenever I closed my eyes, I envisioned Bruce's eyeballs rolling up into their sockets. Tiny red blood vessels edged the glossy white orbs. My mind explained that it was merely the result of his overdosing on a powerful drug. But I was still deeply horrified by what had happened. Looking back, I realize I was experiencing symptoms of post traumatic stress syndrome.

The next morning I begged Leon to stay home from work even though we had been counting on every dollar from his upcoming pay-cheque. I clutched at him, shaking and crying hysterically. Bruce was fine, I managed to assure him, it was his wife who was the crazy one. Leon phoned his foreman, while I lay back on the bed and attempted to banish the image of my son's white eyeballs from my mind.

The medication had such dreadful side-effects that I could not blame Bruce for deciding not to take any. He insisted that he felt fine without it. But as the skies grew darker during our early northern winter, Bruce began spending more and more of his time lying on his back. He explained that he was using self-hypnosis to inspire himself to write. After these sessions he would rise from his bed to compose lengthy essays on such topics as man's place in the universe and social ethics. He also wrote poetry, some of it very good, I thought.

The books that Bruce now borrowed from the library were about people who entered "alternate realities" and experienced "altered perceptions." They used hallucinatory drugs such as LSD or mescaline to induce imaginative adventures inside their own minds. Leon and I wondered if Bruce was experiencing similar adventures, but without the use of drugs. The many hours he spent in prone, silent reverie reminded my husband of a documentary he had watched on television. It was about an age-old custom of certain Australian aborigines, who ritualistically drift into an extended somnolent state they refer to as "The Dreamtime."

I worried about Bruce's increasing interest in maintaining a dreamtime state of mind. If I asked him to help me with a chore, he would respond, only to retire immediately afterward to the most available bed. In winter we had few visitors, and I was away from home several afternoons a week, selling beauty products door-to-door. I wondered if he needed the stimulation that would have come from a more constant interaction with other people.

From time to time I noticed the rag doll Vincent where I had stored it in a linen closet shortly after Bruce arrived home. I would straighten out its gangly arms and legs, so that it appeared to be comfortable as it rested on a shelf with the sheets and pillowcases. Despite my pains it seemed that every few days or so, Vincent would once again be disarranged, with its legs wound around its neck and its head dangling at an unnatural angle. It became a puzzling obsession for me. I began to worry about the state of the doll's health almost as much as I worried about Bruce's.

Years later, Fern confessed that she and a neighbour's daughter used to sneak the doll out of the closet to be part of a frightening game the girls had invented. The doll represented Bruce's strange illness which they had no way of understanding. Whenever I found Vincent in a disarranged state in the closest, it was probably because the children had thrown it back up there in a state of imagination-induced terror.

One cold dark day when Bruce seemed particularly withdrawn, I impulsively threw Vincent into our wood-burning stove. As I watched my daughters' handiwork crumble into charcoal, I deeply regretted having destroyed the doll. Later I felt unaccountably relieved that it was gone.

Dr. Gow was a qualified hypnotherapist. In hopes of overcoming my now chronic insomnia, I began a series of weekly sessions with him. They were not what I had expected them to be. I desperately craved lessons on how to blot out my conscious mind with its persistent concerns that kept me awake at night. But rather than a shortcut to oblivion, the treatments taught me how to become receptive to my own advice. With Dr. Gow's coaching I was able to drift into a light hypnotic trance.

Later I recalled one of the admonitions that the doctor had recited to help me attain a calmer state of mine. "You will accept things as they are," he had urged. Dr. Gow well knew my obsession with the "whys" in my life.

CHAPTER THREE

The Blonde Shadow

"Then when sanity broke
Its shell upon the beach
Its Venus a blonde shadow
That carried its breadth upon sand."

From "The Blonde Shadow"
by Bruce Ray 1991

Bruce had done little in the way of artwork while he was in Toronto. One creative effort that he did bring home was the partly-finished pastel painting of a nude Dale Olson. In December, after Bruce prepared to move from our house into his old room in Debbie's basement, he was motivated into completing the project. Debbie liked the painting and for several months, displayed it in her living room. He later destroyed it.

It was around this time that Debbie was converting to vegetarianism. She also smoked marijuana. Her friend Rick, smoked a great deal of marijuana; the strong, sweet odour of it often lingered in the house. Despite my concerns about Bruce inhaling second hand marijuana smoke, he seemed happier and more energetic at Debbie's than he had been at home.

But before long it became obvious that he was slipping back into his familiar lethargy. More and more often, when I visited my son I found him in his bed. He said he was trying—once again—to give up smoking cigarettes. He also mentioned that he ate very little because Debbie's meatless meals did not appeal to him.

I was not always tactful about my misgivings when I spoke to my oldest daughter about her use of marijuana. Now I questioned her decision to serve only vegetarian food at mealtimes. One afternoon at our favorite coffee shop, Debbie and I commenced a subdued but heated debate on the subject of vegetarianism versus man's need for meat. I told her what Bruce had said, that he did not enjoy her meatless meals. Debbie responded that Bruce had been well aware of the changes in her menu since the last time that he boarded with her, when he asked to move back into her home.

My daughter admitted that she had second thoughts about having Bruce live with her. Now that his mental health was deteriorating, she found his presence to be strangely unsettling. Debbie has often displayed psychic tendencies and in recent weeks, she had sensed an ominous cloud hanging over the house. Although she felt guilty about leaving her brother alone, she had felt a desperate need to escape the pervasive, dark atmosphere as often as possible.

Later that same day when I visited Bruce, he appeared to be disoriented and confused. I asked him if he had taken any medication lately, but he could not even recall where he had placed the two vials of pills. Debbie wasn't home, so I took Bruce to Cathy and Darwin's trailer before returning to my older daughter's home to search for the medication.

Darwin's sister-in-law Karen was visiting with Cathy. Karen's bubbly personality and friendly disposition seemed to draw Bruce back into the real world for awhile. When I returned, he was laughing and joking with her.

Bruce took his medication, but admitted later that he had probably taken some earlier in the day. At ten o'clock that night, he acknowledged that he was not well, and I took him to the emergency clinic to meet with Dr. Gow. Bruce told the doctor and me that the main symptom of his distress was something he referred to as "mental confusion." He explained that it was like having three different sets of parents—all giving conflicting advice at the same time.

It was the first time I learned that the nature of his illness involved hearing voices inside his head. When they were under control, Bruce said, which was most of the time, he had no trouble assimilating what they had to say. But if he took too much of the Haldol or forgot to take the side-effect pills, they would babble all at once and it was very confusing.

Dr. Gow phoned a psychiatrist in Prince George and made the first of several appointments with Doctor S. for him. Bruce was anxious to speak to a mental health specialist and a few days later, armed with his notebooks, took the bus to Prince George. When he returned he seemed disappointed. The psychiatrist had a pronounced South African accent, Bruce said. Because of that he had been difficult to communicate with.

Dr. S's final assessment of Bruce's condition was that "the patient may be schizophrenic." Dr. Gow was not surprised. But I continued to believe that the disorder was caused by the marijuana Bruce had smoked in Toronto. I had read that the chemical ingredient in "pot" can linger in the fatty tissues of the brain and other organs for many months. I clung to the hope that when it was all out of his system, he would become well.

Debbie and I agreed it would be better if Bruce moved back home where I could monitor his medication needs. Dr. S's prognosis of possible schizophrenia had frightened him, and he became diligent about taking his pills on schedule.

Almost immediately he began to improve, so much so that he decided to look for a job. This was difficult; the molybdenum mine at Endako had shut down in 1982 and the sawmill was not hiring at the time. He filled out some application forms at small local businesses, but without any success.

Bruce claimed that he was not ashamed or embarrassed by the psychiatrist's tentative diagnosis. He made a point of telling everyone, including prospective employers, about his illness, explaining that he believed in being honest. In our small community where everyone knew everyone, most people knew about his symptoms anyway. I told him I did not think it necessary to mention the diagnosis to those who did not ask. "After all," I said, "psychiatrists have been wrong before."

Whatever the reasons, Bruce was unable to find a job. His unemployment insurance benefits ran out in January. I suggested to him that he apply for Social Assistance until such time as the economy improved. Reluctantly, he agreed to do so. Bruce's cousin Teresa, who was also on Social Assistance, and her two young children, had recently moved into a fairly large house in town. The rent was higher than she could comfortably afford. Teresa's mother Hazel suggested that Bruce could move in with his cousin and pay her room and board. It would help her out financially and give him the opportunity for more independence. There was room in Teresa's house for him to set up an artist's studio, and perhaps earn some money by painting portraits. That, Bruce was very eager to do.

Soon after he moved into his new home Bruce began painting portraits of family and friends, using the oil pastels that he had brought home from Toronto. He completed a good likeness of Karen and Jim Harder. Cathy later commissioned him to do one from a photograph, of Darwin and Jim's older brother Andy and his wife.

Every winter The College of New Caledonia in Prince George sponsored a community learning program at the high school. Local people were encouraged to participate in the teaching process by sharing their particular expertise. The co-ordinator Sylvia Cooper suggested that Bruce teach an art course. He agreed to, preparing a set of instructions on learning how to draw from a book entitled *Drawing on the Right Side of the Brain* by Betty Edwards. He made photocopies to be ready for students on registration night. As it turned out, only four people showed up and the course had to be cancelled. Many other courses had to be cancelled that year, likely because of the depressed state of the economy.

One happy after-effect of Bruce's mental breakdown in Toronto was the clearing up of the disfiguring acne that had plagued him for all of his teenage and early adult years. From puberty on, Bruce had lathered up with every kind of medicated soap in the drugstore and tried cutting out various foods from his diet–all to no avail. Dr. Gow had placed him on a long-term prescription of tetracycline, but the medication only slowed down the formation of pimples and boils.

In retrospect, some have suggested that symptoms of Bruce's mental illness may have manifested as long ago as puberty, when he began to isolate himself from social events where he would be forced to mingle with girls. But character and personality traits are not precursors of schizophrenia. It can strike both the extroverted and the introverted. Most likely Bruce isolated himself because of his chronic and severe acne.

But in the winter of 1985, Bruce's social life in Fraser Lake began to improve. He visited the Kluge household often to participate in the fireside discussions. Several other non-Baha'is were regular participants at these talks, which were usually interesting and stimulating. I attended the sessions too and was happy to see that Bruce was developing new friendships.

The young adults in Fraser Lake most often socialized in the local pub or at community dances where liquor was served. Bruce realized that he could not drink alcohol while he was on anti-psychotic medication. He told me he tried having a few beers once, and became very disoriented. He had also experienced mental confusion.

Bruce's school chum Kevin who worked at the sawmill, had saved enough money to buy a car. Kevin invited Bruce to accompany him on an excursion to the neighbouring village of Vanderhoof one evening. Bruce told me later he enjoyed himself immensely, dancing and socializing while drinking nothing stronger than 7-Up.

He decided to join the Baha'i Faith. Bruce understood and approved of the basic principals, such as the equality of men and women and the harmony of science and religion. But he did not seem interested in learning about the history of the religion and was reluctant to read any of the spiritual writings. He told me he had joined because he had "never met a Baha'i he didn't like." I was happy Bruce was a member because I thought it meant he would not smoke marijuana. The Faith forbids the use of alcohol and drugs for recreational purposes.

In February, Debbie began suffering from symptoms of acute depression. Dr. Gow prescribed an anti-depressant and informed her that, in order to alleviate her symptoms, it would take approximately three weeks to cross the blood-brain barrier and reach the glands it was supposed to. In her journal she penned the following: "The worst part about this depression is the feeling of aloneness it creates…the absolute conviction that I am alone in the world, that no one would miss me if I were gone…"

As Debbie's emotional health deteriorated, I became more and more adamant that both her and Bruce's symptoms were related to their use of marijuana. At the time I was ready to blame all the world's problems on the notorious weed. I clipped the *Reader's Digest* "Marijuana Alert" articles out, and gave them to Debbie to read. Smoking marijuana was too trivial an answer, my daughter sobbed, for why she had fallen into such a dark pit of emotional despondency. But Debbie's friend Rick read the articles with interest. Rick was a confirmed vegetarian who jogged every morning and appeared to be in excellent health. But lately, he told me, he was experiencing chest pains and his blood pressure was very high. The *Reader's Digest* articles related marijuana smoke to various health problems, including heart disease. Rick told me he was trying very hard to cut down on his use of pot.

I was not able to empathize with my daughter's emotional distress. Like my mother had been when she too suffered from depression, Debbie was entirely self-absorbed. She was not at all interested in the problems and aspirations of others. And to my dismay, she confided that her illness may have originated in childhood when she experienced trauma that I had been unaware of. She had repressed her emotions for all of those years. Now, the feelings were being released–all at once. Once again I felt as if I had been an unfit mother to my children. Debbie had not received the attention and comfort from me that she had desperately needed when she was a child. Now all I could feel was pain, on top of the pain I already was experiencing because of Bruce's illness. When I tried to relate to my oldest daughter as she cried out in her anguish, the words I spoke were often the wrong words and in the wrong tone of voice.

Bruce had become emotionally involved in Debbie's problems and like myself, felt inadequate because he was unable to help. One evening he and I were visiting when suddenly she lapsed into a state of hysterics and darted outside. I encouraged Bruce to follow her while I stayed behind with the children. I was worried that she might get into her car, and she appeared to be in no shape to drive.

But despite the surge of intense emotion that had driven her from the house, Debbie realized what she was doing. In the semi-darkness of the March evening she fled on foot toward Rick's tiny cabin on the lake shore, which was about half a kilometer away.

Bruce's mental problems were intensified by the severe stress he was experiencing. As he followed Debbie he began to hallucinate. He had left the house in only his sock feet. The hard patches of snow that still lay on the ground underfoot caused him to think he was running through shards of broken glass. As he stumbled blindly after his sister he became obsessed with the idea that Debbie might throw herself into the lake and drown; even though it was not yet spring and the lake was still frozen solid.

Debbie could hear her brother howling like an animal in the darkness outside Rick's cabin. But in her emotional state, she did not want to talk to anyone in her family. Years later Bruce confessed that for several minutes he had lain full-length in a state of utter despair, upon the railroad tracks that paralleled the lakeshore.

When Bruce returned, he took his medication but once again he may have taken too much. Later that night Bruce walked to Cathy and Darwin's trailer and implored his brother-in-law to drive him to the medical clinic. Once there Bruce told Darwin that he was prepared to die. He walked behind the clinic and sat under a tree to await the approach of death–just as Chief Dan George had done in the movie *Little Big Man*. Instead, Bruce was taken by ambulance to Prince George Regional Hospital where he was re-assessed by a different psychiatrist. For the first time, it was now clinically confirmed that he suffered from schizophrenia, the most debilitating of all mental illnesses.

According to the dictionary that Bruce brought back home with him from Ontario, schizophrenia was: "any of a group of psychotic reactions characterized by withdrawal from reality with highly variable affective, behavioral and intellectual disturbances." I have since learned that it is a chemical imbalance in the brain, which affects one in every hundred young men and women worldwide–in all races, in all cultures and in all social classes. Its symptoms are varied but the following are significant:
- Marked change in personality
- A constant feeling of being watched.
- Difficulty controlling one's thoughts
- Hearing voices or sounds others don't hear
- Increasing withdrawal from social contacts

- Seeing people or things that others don't see
- Difficulties with language–words do not make sense
- Sudden excesses, such as extreme religiosity
- Irrational, angry, or fearful responses to loved ones
- Sleeplessness and agitation

These symptoms, even in combination, may not be evidence of schizophrenia. They could be the result of injury, drug use, or extreme emotional distress. The crucial factor is whether the patient has the ability to turn off the imagination.

I sobbed helplessly into the telephone when the psychiatrist informed me of the diagnosis. His demeanor toward me was cold and condescending: "It's the same as any other chronic illness such as diabetes," he stated loftily, "in that the patient must take regular medication." I mumbled something about marijuana. The psychiatrist explained patiently that Bruce only used the street drug to lessen the sounds of his auditory hallucinations.

Bruce told me later that the doctor was wrong. He smoked marijuana because he enjoyed it. He did not mind the voices at all; in fact, he rather liked having them.

When Bruce first moved into Teresa's house, he and his cousin were somewhat shy of one another and did not communicate much. Although of the same age and in the same grade throughout their school years, they had been out of touch ever since Bruce moved to Edmonton in grade eleven. But Teresa's children were not a bit shy of Bruce. My son was amazed that Adrien the oldest who was only four years old, seemed almost able to read his mind. The child may have recognized that Bruce was not well. The medication merely controlled his symptoms, it was not a cure. Adrien was always eager to offer assistance to his mother's new housemate.

Bruce confided that he enjoyed having Teresa's children around –except during those times when they sneaked into his room and destroyed his belongings.

Like so many other young adults, Teresa and her friends sometimes smoked marijuana. I became concerned because Bruce seemed to be smoking it too, on a regular basis. The odour of it drifted through the house almost every time I visited. His short-term memory appeared to be deteriorating and he had skipped several dosages of his medication. He assured me finally that he'd given up on his use of pot, mainly because it cost too much money.

Now that Bruce was in the hospital, I went over to Teresa's to pick up some of his clothing and other belongings. He had been concerned that the children might get into his things. At the back of his closet, I spotted a large, green plastic bag. It was half-filled with what seemed to be an assortment of clothing, books and loose papers. At the very bottom of the bag I could see a bulge, which when I felt it, had the texture of tobacco or a similar dried substance. Teresa was not at home while I was taking Bruce's belongings out to the car. At the last minute I decided to take the plastic bag with me as well. I carefully placed it in the trunk and locked it. I was certain that the lump at the bottom had to be marijuana. Bruce had some hidden in the belly of his guitar when he visited us a few weeks earlier. When Fern noticed it and commented on it, he had thrown his "wad" into the woodstove. I had thought that to be the end of his pot smoking.

I drove around town in a state of near panic. Marijuana was an illegal drug and I knew that if I was caught with it, I could be charged with possession of a narcotic. Finally, I took the bag back to Teresa's house and handed it to her. I stammered as I tried to explain: "There's something at the bottom of this bag that I hope you'll throw out in the garbage–or–whatever?" Teresa seemed confused but willing to help. Much later I learned from Bruce that the lump was ordinary tobacco.

Shortly after Bruce was released from the hospital, he found some library books in his room that were very much overdue. He had no money to pay the fine. I lightheartedly suggested that he had a good excuse for being tardy. "Why not tell Pat you didn't get them back on time because you're schizophrenic, your sister's depressed, and your mother's paranoid?"

When he saw her, he told Pat the librarian just that. She laughed wholeheartedly at Bruce's joke. Pat told me later, "One thing about Bruce, he's still got his sense of humour!"

CHAPTER FOUR

The Path With Heart

"The path with heart
Is hard to follow
It's hard to see
So dark and narrow
But I will find me peace of mind
And leave this sorrow behind me..."

From the song "The Path With Heart"
by Bruce Ray, 1985

Bruce played the guitar almost every day. Perhaps he used it as a tool to relieve tension and to exorcise, for the moment, the illusory demons that plague the minds of those who suffer from schizophrenia. He had purchased his own instrument shortly before moving into his cousin's house in Fraser Lake. Leon's old Yamaha was delegated back to its original owner who preferred more traditional style music, over the often repetitious strummings of Bob Dylan and Bruce Springsteen.

He began to combine his talent for writing poetry with his newfound ability to locate chords on the guitar. One of the first songs he wrote was titled *"The Path With Heart."* It was an upbeat tune, reminiscent of the haunting strains of an old Celtic melody.

Debbie's depressive state showed no signs of improvement and on

March 27, she was admitted into the psychiatric wing of the Prince George Hospital. There she found a degree of satisfaction in participating in group and other forms of therapy. She learned a great deal about mental illnesses and made new friendships. She continued to participate as an outpatient, in the therapy sessions for several months after being discharged from the hospital.

Sunday April 9th was Debbie's birthday. That weekend was when I had promised Fern we would have a mini-holiday together in Prince George. My ten-year-old daughter had been looking forward to it for some time. I don't like to drive in the city, so we planned to take the bus. We would do some shopping, take in a movie and stay overnight at a motel. Since Debbie was still in the hospital, we decided to celebrate her birthday with her there on Sunday.

The evening before we were to leave I picked Bruce up at Teresa's house and took him uptown for a coffee. He had been out of the hospital for about a month, and I assumed he was taking his new medication, an anti-psychotic called Stelazine. Bruce was behaving strangely, as if he was intoxicated. I asked him if he was using marijuana which he denied emphatically, stating that he'd not had any pot for over a month. The oddest thing was, he appeared to sober up between puffs of his cigarette which I knew to contain only tobacco. Whenever he inhaled his eyes would narrow and he would begin to giggle for no apparent reason.

Darwin's brother Jim stopped at our table and commented on the fact that Bruce appeared to be stoned. Jim said he had read about THC, the active ingredient in marijuana. It could be stored in the fatty tissues of the human body, including the brain, for long periods of time. My son did did not appear to be interested.

When I was ready to leave, I mentioned to Bruce that Fern and I were travelling to Prince George on the early morning bus. Bruce stated that he wanted to come along so that he too could visit with Debbie on her birthday. Reluctantly, I took him home to our house to spend the night. My youngest daughter was not impressed when I informed her that Bruce would accompany us on our holiday. But as I explained to her, there really was no alternative. Fern could see plainly that her brother was not well. He should not be left alone.

Bruce was up and continued to have the appearance of being stoned when his stepfather arrived home from work shortly after midnight. Leon and I did not sleep much that night, and as far as we knew, Bruce did not sleep at all. I fervently hoped that he would fall to sleep in his motel room after we arrived in Prince George. If that happened, Fern and I would be free to shop and browse at our leisure.

When our bus arrived at the Prince George depot I suggested that Bruce take his medication, not realizing that he had already taken some before leaving home. At the motel his fingers became cramped and rigid as he attempted to sign the registry. He was not able to make the pen in his hand move at all. And he seemed very confused and disoriented. I implored the girl at the desk to call for an ambulance. Bruce's room was further away, so I guided him into ours which was just around the corner.

As we waited for the ambulance, Bruce began to pray and mumble quietly to himself. He said he wanted to phone his dad–long distance–in Duncan on Vancouver Island. He wanted to tell his father that he loved him. When I displayed reluctance, he insisted it was important that he do so–right away. To appease him, I dialed Ed and Connie's number. Connie answered the phone, saying Ed was not at home. Bruce did not want to speak to Connie.

He lay curled up on the bed in a semi-fetal position with his head cradled in both arms. Suddenly he lifted his head and I could see that his eyes had rolled back into their sockets. Leaning toward me, he stated accusingly, "You're not a ghost." I was horrified but determined not to show my emotions. Fern was becoming upset. I was worried that her unhappy protests might cause her brother to turn around on the bed and focus his eerie white stare upon her.

The ambulance attendants finally arrived and Fern and I rode with Bruce to the hospital. There, he was immediately attended to by two paramedics who seemed to be well-acquainted with his symptoms. One tapped him on the feet while the other explained to Fern and me that Bruce was once again suffering from side-effects to the anti-psychotic. His hands and feet had stiffened up from the double dose of medication. Stelazine, the drug he was on now, was similar in its effects to the one he had been on before. Bruce was admitted to a room on the psychiatric floor of the hospital, where his sister Debbie was already a patient.

It was still early in the day when Fern and I left the hospital to visit Pine Centre, Prince George's largest shopping mall. My ten-year-old loved to shop but was indecisive about what to spend her money on. She strolled blissfully from store to store with her mother in tow, until I was almost exhausted.

In the afternoon we returned to the hospital to visit with Bruce and Debbie. Debbie was in good spirits. She took Fern in hand and introduced her to several of the other patients, while I sat with Bruce. He was despondent at finding himself once again confined to the hospital. He had to stay in for a few days, he told me. The doctor needed to determine a few changes in his medication dosage.

That evening I wearily accompanied my daughter to the theatre to see the movie *The Return of the Jedi*. I embarrassed her by nodding off to sleep every now and then. I awoke for the kissing scenes–between the human beings. Fern liked the puppets. I told her that I was only interested in real people.

Weeks later I asked Bruce if he recalled uttering the words, "You're not a ghost" to me, while we were at the motel waiting for an ambulance. Those words, Bruce explained, stemmed from a memory of an hallucination he had during his breakdown. A woman who resembled me had led him into a room where a large book lay open upon a desk. After examining its pages, the woman had sadly informed Bruce that many bad things were forecast in it. They were to happen to those that she loved.

If that was what was written in my personal "Book of Revelations" I hoped and prayed that the time period of the prophesy was now over.

Shortly after Bruce returned home from his latest stint in the hospital, he moved into a cabin just up the road from us. It belonged to his aunt Vi. Teresa's sister LeEtta, aunt Vi and several others used the building once or twice a week as an artist's studio. Vi assured Bruce that as a fellow artist, he should fit right in. He ate his meals with us and in return for free board, promised to help me paint the outside of our house, but his medication dosage had been increased from 20 mg to 30 mg a day; its sedating effects left him with little energy for physical exertion.

During the long summer days of 1985 Bruce joined his aunt Vi, uncle George and cousin LeEtta at their regular oil painting sessions inside his living room. His first painting, a Rocky Mountain landscape, was delightful, I thought. Bruce's use of colour was quite accurate, especially for one who had not painted in oils before. The next painting he did was also a scene from nature. But in this one he had combined a classically idyllic background with an oppressively bleak foreground. The bottom half of the picture featured a flock of charcoal-colored birds perched along a dark fence railing. They were in sharp silhouette above an expanse of flat olive green pasture. I wondered if it was just my imagination, but Vi said she too felt a sense of foreboding whenever she viewed the painting.

Bruce's real forté as an artist lay in his pen and ink drawings. In 1982, he and I had self-published a book of my humourous verses and his cartoons that we titled *The Pumpkin Eaters*. The poems were taken from a column I had composed for a local newspaper. But it was probably Bruce's hilarious illustrations that had made the book a bestseller for a little while, in Fraser Lake at least. He had gained a reputation both locally and throughout the northern Interior, as an accomplished artist.

Sandra, another cousin, had an older model Ford car for sale that Bruce wanted to buy. Leon and I agreed to loan him the money to purchase it. We decided that if it turned out he was unable to pay us back, we could always make use of a second vehicle.

For years Bruce had been reluctant to learn to drive–possibly with good reason. It was uncanny how many of his previous attempts had ended with him driving into the ditch. Over the course of several years he had ditched my brother's bush buggy, a friend's all-terrain vehicle and his stepbrother, Brian's motorcycle. Bruce's worst accident had occurred when he was about sixteen. Leon had encouraged him to drive our pickup truck along a bush road while the two of them were on a camping trip together. Bruce was in third gear and driving too fast as he was approaching a corner. Panic-stricken he had hit the accelerator instead of the brake pedal. The truck lurched off the road and slammed into a stump. Leon's head struck the windshield hard. Bruce was nearly in hysterics as the glass cracked and the blood began to flow quite profusely from his stepfather's temple. As it turned out, Leon was fine but the truck was a complete write-off.

Bruce was also involved in a number of minor car accidents where he was a passenger. It had been a family joke for awhile that he was a jinx. But in the summer of 1985 I began to seriously teach my son the rudiments of driving his own car. It was time, I decided, to dispel the notion that he was a jinx; that he was incapable of learning how to control an automobile.

Bruce was very nervous at first. But he soon developed a measure of confidence and even a touch of bravado. He practiced along the back road above our place and, after a few weeks, had become reasonably proficient. I thought his reflexes may have been a trifle slow, possibly because of the sedating effects of his medication. During those weeks, he enjoyed himself immensely, but I never did take him in to apply for his driver's license test.

Ian Kluge was writing a novel and asked Bruce to illustrate it with some comic-book-style drawings. My son began the project but never completed it. He did a prodigious amount of writing himself that summer. Ian encouraged his literary endeavors. The high school English teacher told Bruce he had the talent to become an excellent writer.

The long summer days gradually shortened into September and then more quickly into October. Ian was now busy teaching at the school. When the artists discontinued their weekly sessions at his house Bruce sank back into his familiar lethargy. Sometimes I would knock on his door as late as noontime and find him still in his bed.

Quite by accident I learned that there were group homes in Prince George for people suffering from schizophrenia. I overheard a mother talk about her teenage son who apparently suffered from the illness. She said he was now living in a group home, and it was such a relief for everyone in the family. I made several phone calls and eventually talked to a woman named Ann Simpson* who worked for Mental Health. Ann was very helpful and within a matter of weeks Bruce moved into Beth Connelly's* big split-level house on the outskirts of the city. It was Mrs. Connelly's responsibility to monitor her residents' medication dosages, supervise their daily routines, and provide them with room and board.

Over the course of my few, sporadic visits to Prince George that winter, Ann and I engaged in some interesting talks about schizophrenia. I told her that Dr. Gow and other health professionals do not believe that marijuana causes schizophrenia. Ann replied that there was no doubt many cases of the disease were triggered but not necessarily caused by the use of street drugs. I wondered if my son would have been struck down by the same debilitating symptoms if he had not been a user. "After all," I caustically remarked to Ann, "if a gun doesn't have a trigger, it does not go off."

Beth Connelly's group home for people with schizophrenia was purported to be a well-supervised learning environment with the emphasis on residents developing life skills, such as cooking meals and doing laundry. Bruce shared the basement bedrooms with four other men whose names were Bill, Rick, Herman and Dan.

Rick appeared to be spaced-out and Bruce told me that Bill was a bit dozey. Dan was more personable than the others; he smiled politely and seemed to be tuned-in to his surroundings. Dan was originally from Ontario, Bruce told me. He had a sister whom he was fond of, who resided six hundred kilometers away in Kitimat. Herman was an older man, in his fifties or sixties, who spoke with a Dutch accent. According to Ann, Herman may have been misdiagnosed when he was a young man. The anti-psychotic drugs he had been on for many years had inflicted him with a permanent side-effect known as tardive dyskinesia. The condition had caused the muscles in his body to twitch, sometimes incessantly. To counter that, Herman had taught himself to play the harmonica. When he was engrossed in playing his music, he was temporarily free of the awful side-effect.

I was surprised to learn later that this well-supervised group home was not the haven it seemed to be. People occasionally found their way into the building who were not supposed to be there. One night a man, whom Bruce said later was a dope pusher as well as a deviant homosexual, broke into the basement bedroom that he shared with Dan. The Connellys were not at home at the time. Bruce got out of his bed when the fellow began to terrorize his roommate. He managed to intimidate the intruder and chase him back out on the street.

Whenever I visited my son I noticed that his fellow residents were invariably lounging in their chairs, silently smoking their cigarettes. They did not seem to communicate. Bruce said they seldom watched television, even though there was one in the basement lounge and another upstairs in the Connelly living room. Bruce had his record player and his guitar with him; when one wasn't blaring away, the other was. Ann agreed with my joyous assessment: that Bruce was definitely more with it than any of his roommates. In the afternoons the residents were encouraged to visit the Mary Harper Center. The drop-in center was not exclusively for the benefit of the mentally ill. Ann explained that it was a place where anyone who was down on their luck could participate in organized programs or just visit. Bruce joined in on their weekly bowling expeditions and other social activities. He contributed essays, poetry and illustrations to the Mary Harper monthly newsletter and was given the job of editing the December 1985 issue.

Bruce wanted to enroll in some courses at the College of New Caledonia. Before leaving Fraser Lake, he applied to the Prince George Outreach Program of the Emily Carr School of Fine Arts. His application had been turned down, possibly because he had made of point of telling the director that he was schizophrenic.

The other courses that he was interested in, such as English Grammar and Creative Writing, were already filled. Bruce did enroll in English Literature but he soon lost interest and did not complete the course.

Although still a member of the Baha'i Faith, Bruce did not participate in any of the Baha'i activities in Prince George. He told me it was the opinion of those at the Mary Harper Center that religion can be dangerous for people with schizophrenia. Because of their symptoms they are much too open to suggestion.

Bruce was at our place over the Christmas holidays. On New Year's Day after the big dinner was over and everyone had left for home, he picked up Leon's guitar and began to strum. I requested a song that he had composed himself and titled "The Path With Heart." I found it a pleasing alternative to the Bob Dylan tunes that he was so fond of.

That afternoon Bruce became a veritable songwriting machine, composing lyrics and tunes in what seemed to be merely a matter of minutes. One that I particularly liked was "Lazy Old Town," an uncomplicated melody with words that described the quiet, job-oriented way of life in a small community. It was based on Bruce's memories of when he had worked at the sawmill.

Shortly after New Year's, Bruce's medication dosage was reduced from twenty milligrams, to ten milligrams a day, which he explained happily was a maintenance dose. He was deemed well enough to move from Beth Connelly's monitored group home into more independent living quarters. The process, Bruce told me, was part of a mental health initiative called New Directions. He liked that terminology a lot.

But Bruce had little in common with the two men he ended up living with in the New Directions group home. One was an admitted drug dealer; both were only interested in smoking the marijuana that the dealer procured. The dealer was extremely weird, Bruce said. The other man appeared to be on the verge of a nervous breakdown. Bruce did the shopping and cooked most of the house meals. The rest of his time was spent holed up in his room, writing lyrics and composing tunes.

When Bruce visited us at home he played and sang almost constantly. I liked many of his songs, and one weekend recorded my favorites on tape. An especially pleasing rendition for me was one I referred to as his "Baha'i" song. He had titled it, "My Soul is a Rainbow."

At Beth Connelly's the medications had been dished out at specified times and Bruce could not miss taking them. Now, as spring approached he began skipping even his maintenance doses of Stelazine. Bruce told me he had decided to take the pills only when he needed them. He insisted that he was always aware of when that was.

On Easter weekend Bruce did not bring his medication with him when he visited. He said he had not taken any for several weeks and felt fine without it. But on Saturday afternoon he admitted worriedly that he was in need of some. In Fraser Lake the pharmacy and the medical clinic are closed Saturdays. There were very few stores anywhere that would remain open over the long weekend. I aimed Bruce's old Ford in the direction of the closest drug dispensary which was in Vanderhoof. "Just to be on safe side," I explained to Bruce.

But I had forgotten that the renewal for Bruce's prescription was only available through our local pharmacy. And it was fast approaching closing time at the Vanderhoof store. The very accommodating pharmacist and I took turns burning up the long distance telephone lines until we finally located George, the Fraser Lake druggist, who okayed the prescription.

Later that month, Ian Kluge suggested that Bruce sing some of his songs at a coffeehouse in Endako, twelve kilometers west of Fraser Lake. I took Bruce to the community hall on a Saturday night. He was able to overcome his initial nervousness and sang quite well to an enthusiastic audience.

Bruce's mental health seemed to improve daily despite the fact that he took little or no medication. On one of his weekend visits he assured me that he finally had this schizophrenia thing beat. I must have appeared somewhat skeptical because he added hastily, "But just in case, I'll make sure that my medication is always close at hand."

His optimism was contagious. "Bruce," I replied, "I am a firm believer in positive thinking. You can do anything that you set your mind to, just as long as you are able to stay in control of your symptoms. You are intelligent, talented, and you've certainly learned a lot since your breakdown in Toronto."

"That's right," Bruce agreed happily, "And I've got two other things going for me now. I am a Baha'i. And I know how to get into a group home situation again, no matter where I happen to be."

With that enthusiastic exchange ringing in his memory Bruce returned home to Prince George. Within a few days time he had convinced himself that he should travel to Toronto and move into a group home in that distant city. He had telephoned his old friend Dave, who agreed that Bruce could stay with him and his family for a period of one week. After that, Bruce was sure he could find alternative living arrangements through Ontario Mental Health.

Everyone in the family shared the opinion that it was not a good idea for Bruce to move back to Toronto. We could not understand his compulsion to return to the city where he had suffered such a horrendous experience. I phoned Ed and Connie and they agreed that it would be good for Bruce to visit with them in Duncan for a while. I then talked to Debbie, who now lived on nearby Saltspring Island. Debbie said if her brother visited that part of the province, he would likely be inspired by the beautiful surroundings and the warm climate to want to move down to the Vancouver Island region. He would forget all about wanting to move to Ontario.

Bruce spent a couple of weeks with his dad and stepmother in

Duncan and on Saltspring Island visiting his sister. He, Debbie and Debbie's newfound friend Terry had a great time together. My oldest daughter said later Bruce was so energetic and so much fun that she had enjoyed his company immensely. Terry who was a musician, was impressed by Bruce's singing and his songs. He told Debbie he thought Bruce could be another Springsteen.

When Bruce asked his sister if he could move in with her, she unequivocally said yes. He returned home, packed up his suitcases and took the bus back to Prince George to say good-bye to his roommates, before heading south to Saltspring Island. The day before he left home, Bruce and Fern made friendly bets as to whether his photograph would ever appear on the cover of *Rolling Stone* magazine. Fern bet him a dime that it would not. She bet him fifty cents that it would never appear on the cover of *Teen* magazine. That to her would have been the ultimate honour.

He took all of his writings with him when he left Fraser Lake: his poems, his songs and the essays that he had mulled over during the convalescent period after his psychotic breakdown. Bruce confessed that he was no longer interested in philosophy and religion. "That stuff" he said, "is all in the past."

Bruce stayed with Debbie on Saltspring Island for a little more than a month. Then—sometime in June—he called to tell me that he was now living with his dad and stepmother in Duncan. Bruce said he'd had a bit of a bad time just before leaving Saltspring. He could not remember why, but he had thrown the beautiful new leather coat that he had purchased in Prince George into the Pacific Ocean. The coat had floated out to sea with the tide and with it, his wallet and identification papers. "The problem now," he explained, "is that I can't get my medication without any ID. Will you ask Dr. Gow if he can help?"

I explained the situation to Dr. Gow and gave him Bruce's telephone number. The doctor assured me that he would advise my son how to renew the prescription for his medication. I was relieved. I thought, "At least Bruce has the presence of mind to know when he is in need of medication."

Debbie had moved to Saltspring Island eight months earlier, in the fall of 1985. The benevolent weather and the laid-back attitude of the islanders had agreed with her. As she explained to me on the phone, "Everyone down here is an eccentric. I fit right in." The severe depression she had experienced a year earlier was a nightmare that she never wanted to repeat. She had learned that long northern winters are devastating to those who are susceptible to bouts of depression. I was happy for her. Through our phone calls and letters, we had developed a closeness we had never achieved before.

Debbie now recalls that strange period of time on Saltspring Island after her brother came to stay: "I was happy to see him. He looked great, vibrant and alive, with a light in his eyes. I'd never before seen that poetic metaphor 'a light in his eyes' so graphically illustrated. He seemed happier than he had in ages, and he was great company, lucid and entertaining. Saltspring Island is the largest of BC's Gulf Islands but still relatively small, only six miles by twenty. Bruce was uneasy about being surrounded by so much water. It was his biggest complaint about living there, right from the start.

"It was fun having Bruce around again. It had only been a year or so since his diagnosis. I hadn't seen him for awhile and his illness didn't seem real to me. I had learned through my own experiences with psychiatrists to have little faith in their pronouncements. They had told me I'd have to take antidepressants for many years, and could look forward to repeated bouts of hospitalization like most of the other depressed women on the ward. Yet I discovered that working through my feelings and moving to a more welcoming climate and community had done wonders for me. I doubted that I would ever need to take antidepressant pills again, and in fact I have not. I had been told that my emotional and related problems were caused by a chemical disorder in my brain. If an alternative could be found for me, I reasoned, why could one not also be found for my brother? I felt sure that a change of climate and congenial company would work for him. I believed that the generic label mental illness was used as an excuse to eliminate through medication inconvenient or strange behavior and that little effort was being made to treat and understand the person or to explore alternate causes and cures.

"During this time his voices communicated with him almost constantly. It became a game for Bruce and I to ask them questions and watch the answers emerge from the tip of his pen. I had read about automatic writing and this was obviously what Bruce was doing. He watched the words form with the same breathless anticipation I felt, and had no more idea than I what was being said until we read it together.

"I cared for Bruce and wanted very much to understand him and his experiences from his own point of view. I felt we were breaking new ground, learning about psychic/spiritual dimensions of life communicated through his perceptions just as native shamans brought information back to their villages via their dreams and visions.

"He wrote reams of channeled information this way and I still feel that he was tapped into some kind of source material. What he wrote was often brilliant and quite original. I felt deeply touched in that part of me that hungered for greater awareness, spiritual meaning beyond cause-and-effect, cosmology broader and deeper than the clockwork universe that I had been taught. The time I spent with my crazy brother woke me to a larger context. For the first time I felt the presence of a higher power.

"After a while I began to experience a series of waking dreams or visions that I was very excited about and eager to share with Bruce. When I told him about them he seemed uncomfortable and began to withdraw from me. At first I was not concerned since he just seemed quiet and aloof, but over the space of a few days he changed from being open, communicative and intimate with me to dark, brooding and hostile. He destroyed all of his automatic writings, convinced that they were evil. He destroyed song lyrics and poems he'd written during this period, and threw away books and tapes he had loved, including those by Van Morrison, who had been a kind of spiritual mentor of his. He took to wandering the island at all hours of the night, talking out loud to himself and sometimes arguing. I began to hear stories from acquaintances about the weird guy on the loose.

"Before this his voices had been female; they'd called themselves lesbian witches. They were pacifist and loving and taught skills for embodying love and becoming spiritually independent. They were not passive, however; these voices counselled passionate aliveness and existential courage. I had loved them as though they were my friends, and when they were gone I felt bereft.

"When the turnaround came, so did the gender of his voices. Now they were what he called male Christians. They were very angry with him for listening to those bitches. He was caught up in an internal gender war, with the aggressors being male. They were trying to teach him to be a man and a warrior.

"During this time he began to refer to himself–when he spoke at all–as a lone wolf. He did a beautiful drawing of a wolf's head, very realistic and glowering rendered with forceful strokes. These two halves of himself, the gentle poet/troubadour and the wild wolf/warrior, were struggling for possession of his soul.

"Typically of many schizophrenics, he did not see the voices as representing archetypal parts of his own psyche, but called them spirits and believed the war was actually taking place in the spirit world. Over time, Bruce withdrew so far into brooding darkness that it felt difficult for me to even breathe in the atmosphere at home.

"Years later, he confided that his new voices had blamed me for drawing him into crippling feminine softness. They claimed it was my fault for imprisoning him on an island surrounded by water, and for being a woman and smothering him with my influence.

"During one of his nightly wanderings he lost his jacket in the ocean. He never explained how this had happened, but I had the impression that he felt the water had lured him into it with intent to drown him. He seemed to be at war with everything around him now. His wallet, with all his ID in it, was in the jacket pocket. Shortly after he lost it, he called Dad and arranged to stay with him and Connie in Duncan."

Expo came to Vancouver in the summer of 1986. I had budgeted all year so that Fern and I, like a great many other BC residents, could attend the first World Fair to be held in our province. Early in July we travelled south to take in the sights and sounds of the long-awaited event. We stayed in Vancouver for two exciting but tiring days, then took the ferry to Saltspring to visit with Debbie and her children. I phoned Bruce in Duncan and asked him if he would like to come over and visit with us there.

Saltspring Island had a bad effect on his mental health Bruce told me; for that reason he was very reluctant to come over. But the following afternoon he showed up on Debbie's doorstep. He had taken the ferry the short distance over from Vancouver Island. When I saw my son I was shocked and dismayed. He was like a zombie, seemingly out of touch and uninterested in anything that the rest of us said or did. He appeared to exist in his own little world. He perched on the sofa in the living room of Debbie's house, chain-smoking cigarettes and singing and strumming his guitar. Periodically I would try to initiate a conversation with him. Occasionally he would respond, then immediately pick up the guitar to go through his repertoire once again.

Bruce did express some animation when he described how he had made money as a street musician during a three-day stint outside a Duncan liquor store. He had picked up twenty dollars one day, he told me. But on the third day the manager asked him to leave. Bruce didn't feel too badly about the dismissal, though. An elderly woman had objected, saying she liked the young man's music.

His voice and style of singing had changed dramatically. I found his slower, deeper-toned renditions depressing. Debbie and Fern assured me that they did not mind Bruce's music. My daughters thought the changes indicated he was merely evolving.

I noticed Bruce now signed his songs "Misty Eyed Dreamer" with "Muse: Dale Olson." I recalled that Dale Olson had been the name of the stripper Bruce had known in Toronto. Later I asked Debbie what she thought about his strange new signature. My daughter explained that a muse symbolized a poet's spirit of inspiration. The signing of a muse was often used by poets as a kind of talisman, she said. Debbie thought I worried too much about Bruce. She compared his behavior to that of the Native Indian shamans who were revered by their people and protected because of their psychic abilities and magical powers. I told her that may have been fine for the shamans, but Bruce did not have a tribe to look after him.

Bruce told us he planned to travel to Toronto soon to earn some money as a street musician. He said he had already talked to the mental health people in Duncan about his plans. I did not know what to say to that. It had to be simply a far-fetched dream, I decided. Bruce did not have the finances for such a long trip. And in his present state of mind, it was a wonder that he had found his way to Saltspring–let alone eight thousand kilometers across the country.

That night I was sure he did not sleep at all. I crept out of bed several times, and noticed him standing, fully dressed in the living room. The couch that had been made up for him to sleep remained unrumpled. In the dimmed light I could see him staring straight ahead at the wall. I had the impression that he was listening very intently.

I wondered if Bruce had been taking any of his medication. He had not brought any pills with him, although I knew he'd had at least one prescription filled after talking to Dr. Gow on the phone. The next morning I felt badly about cutting Bruce's visit short, but he did not argue with my assessment that he needed to return to Duncan and take medication. I phoned Connie to let her know what time to pick him up from the ferry. After we said our good-byes, I embraced my son. He felt wooden—as if my arms encircled a mannequin. The real Bruce it seemed was someplace else.

While Fern and I were on the train travelling home, I wrote Bruce a letter expressing a fear that I was unable to suppress. I begged him to stay in BC and not to travel to Toronto at this time. When I arrived home I rejected a strong impulse to speak with my son on the phone. I had already spent enough money at Expo, I rationalized, without adding another long-distance charge to this month's bill. I mailed the letter instead. By the time it arrived in Duncan, he was gone.

CHAPTER FIVE

Children of the Damned

"I speak of a world
oh brethren
where we are exiles
Fallen angels
branded by our sadness
set apart from the
sweet face of grace
and condemned by our mistrust..."

From "Children of the Damned" 1990
The poem described Bruce's perceptions
while living on the streets of Toronto

The first phone call I received from Bruce was from a hospital in Sudbury, Ontario, which was approximately five hundred kilometers from his destination. He said he had boarded a Greyhound bus in Duncan several days earlier, but had miscalculated the amount of money he would need for food and cigarettes (years later I learned that he had only five dollars in his pocket when he boarded the bus).

Early in the trip he lost his on-bus bag that contained his music tapes, tape player and his medication. As they were crossing the

Prairies–after a day or two of no food or cigarettes–Bruce began to hallucinate: he found himself visualizing the lush rolling farmland as viewed from his bus window, even while he turned away from it. When he closed his eyes, the images persisted. It was like a slide show that was flashing continuously through his mind's eye.

The day before he called me from the hospital, Bruce had gotten off the bus in a small Ontario town and the bus left without him. He had no choice but to hitchhike the rest of the way to Toronto. As he walked, thumbing whenever cars approached him, he continued to hallucinate. No one stopped to give him a ride and he gradually became weaker and weaker until he could walk no further. At that point he implored a fellow pedestrian to please call the local police. He explained that he was mentally ill and desperately needed a ride to the nearest hospital. Eventually a police car arrived and transported him to the hospital in Sudbury. Bruce informed me that he was being treated with Haldol, and was now feeling much better. In a day or so, he said, he would be released from hospital with a supply of medication. But he needed some money so that he could board another bus for Toronto and catch up to his suitcase and guitar.

I had no idea, at first, about how I could send him the money. After several phone calls, I finally learned that I could transfer funds from our local Bank of Commerce to a CIBC in Sudbury. Bruce had assured me that when he reached Toronto, he would go directly to his friend Dave's house. From there he would contact a mental health agency about finding a permanent place to live.

I did not hear from Bruce for about a month. When he did call, it was to say that things had not been going well for him. Dave had moved away and Bruce had no other friends in Toronto. Despite taking the pills that were supposed to counter side-effects, he had experienced several bad reactions to his Haldol medication. His eyes had rolled back upwards in their sockets until he was unable to see. When this occurred he usually ended up in the hospital.

Bruce said he was tired of reacting to the anti-psychotic medications. He had decided to throw the word schizophrenia right out of his vocabulary. He felt fine without drugs, Bruce informed me, and had decided to stop taking them even though it meant he was not eligible to live in a group home, or obtain assistance from Mental Health. He was determined to stay in Toronto, he stated emphatically, even though he was a street person. As I listened to my son I realized with despair that my hope for him to find a safe haven within the Ontario mental health system was no more.

The weather in Toronto was warm and beautiful, Bruce assured me. He had been sleeping on park benches–during the daytime. That way, he said, there was less chance of his possessions being stolen while he slept. So far his efforts at making money as a street musician had not worked out. The police were strict about not allowing itinerant performers in shopping malls and other public places. They had chased him away almost every time he opened his guitar case.

But Bruce was optimistic about the future. Social Services had provided him with some finances, he said. He planned to sleep on a park bench for a few days until he could find a reasonably priced place to live. A few days later Bruce called back to assure me that things had now taken a turn for the better. A new friend whose name was Mike had invited him to move in and share his apartment. Bruce said he'd signed his welfare cheque over to Mike to cover a month's room and board. He and Mike were sipping on hot rums, he confided. A hot rum or two at night relaxed him so that he was able to fall asleep.

"You don't have to worry about me anymore," Bruce stated happily. Mike had told him about a number of locations in Toronto where he could legally work as a street musician. He gave me Mike's telephone number before closing our conversation with a cheerful and confident good-bye.

It occurred to me that Bruce's new friend could be a con artist. But almost any situation, I decided, had to be preferable to sleeping on the park benches of Canada's largest city. It was possible, I surmised, that Mike was one of those nice, friendly people we meet from time to time–even in the big city.

A few weeks later I dialed the number that Bruce had given me, and a male voice answered. When I asked to speak to Bruce Ray, the man sounded confused. There was no one there by that name, he said, and Mike was not at home. When I finally got through to Mike, he told me Bruce had decided to move out–into a boarding home. I took that to mean Bruce had finally contacted Mental Health and was likely living in a group home. He would be receiving medical help whenever he was in need of it.

It would be many years before I finally learned the full story of what had happened to Bruce at Mike's apartment in Toronto. Mike and his friends had sexually molested my son as he lay intoxicated and, most likely, psychotic in his bed. Later when he refused to accept their sexual advances, they had become increasingly hostile toward him. Mike accused Bruce of making loud noises during the night which, he said, disturbed everyone else's slumber. He told Bruce to leave the apartment but would not return any of the money Bruce had given him.

Eventually there was a forceful confrontation and Bruce was thrown out onto the street with nothing but his guitar and the clothes on his back. His suitcases were still inside but he was too frightened to go back and retrieve them. Bruce never did return to Mike's to pick up his luggage. He said later he had no place to keep it while he was on the streets anyway.

For weeks Bruce roamed the streets all day and slept in crowded hostels at night. He pawned his guitar in order to have a safe place to store it. The pawn shop owner gave him forty dollars and assured him that he could buy it back anytime within the next year.

When Bruce finally called me it was from a pay telephone outside of the hostel where he had spent the night. His voice was oddly flat as he related a few details about his experiences, before and after leaving Mike's apartment. I felt as if a cold wind whistled through the telephone line. I had been in a fool's paradise believing what Mike had told me–that Bruce had moved to a boarding home.

Bruce spoke matter-of-factly about life on the streets but said it was preferable to accepting help from Mental Health, or even the advocacy group I had heard about called The Friends of Schizophrenics. "Those people," he stated, "would insist I go back on medication." He refused to do that. The reason he had phoned me, Bruce explained, was to ask for two hundred dollars to make a deposit on a place to rent. He was fed up with hostels. As he was talking to me I could hear a woman's voice in the background. She was inquiring, "Will you get the money?"

I was suddenly angry. I told Bruce firmly that if I were to send him any more money, it would be for his transportation home. If he wanted to stay in Toronto, he should call his dad and, perhaps, get some money from him or Connie. I gave him Ed and Connie's telephone number.

When I talked to Connie a week or so later she answered, yes, she had sent Bruce some money, the two hundred dollars he had requested. The day after he received it, he had phoned back to ask for more because he had lost the original amount. Connie thought Bruce needed to make it on his own, if he insisted on staying in Toronto. I agreed with her that we would just have to wait for him to hit bottom and bounce.

It must have been about mid-October when Bruce next phoned. He had decided to come home, he said, because the weather was turning cold and he had no winter coat. His mental health was fine, Bruce declared. It was his physical health that was deteriorating. There was something wrong with his feet, probably caused by the miles of walking he did every day. The hostels where he slept at night chased everyone out at eight-thirty in the morning, after breakfast. He had to spend the rest of the day on the street.

Hostel residents did not receive any money from welfare, Bruce told me. If they wanted to supplement the free room and board, it was required that they participate in a job program. He had worked in a bar a few times, at a chemical factory and several other temporary jobs. The pay was slave-labour wages, Bruce said. Lately he had been too tired and his feet hurt too much, to do anything other than wander aimlessly along the city streets until the hostels reopened in time for the evening meal.

The hostels were awful places, Bruce stated. Many were infested with lice and the food was terrible. Worse, some of the men who frequented these places were the crud of the earth. They were criminals who laughed as they boasted to one another about past crimes like rape and murder. Bruce said he was in mortal fear of one such group who seemed to be following him from hostel to hostel.

One night he had overheard these men conspiring to get him when they believed he was asleep. They had circled his bed like a pack of wolves. But Bruce managed to throw himself from his bed to safety. He had struck one of his attackers before making good his escape. They would kill him–he was certain of that–if they ever caught up to him.

Bruce had barely slept at all since that night. My son sounded despondent. He said he was broke and could not even afford the forty dollars he needed to get his guitar out of hock. He asked me if I would phone a man named Tony who worked for an organization called Youth Services of Toronto. Tony would tell me how I could send the money out for his transportation home. Bruce ended our conversation by reiterating that his mental health was fine, he was just tired of living on the street.

A few years after his sojourn on the streets of Toronto, Bruce wrote a poem about his perceptions during that time. He titled it "Children of the Damned." In it he wrote:

> We live in the dark world.
> Set apart from the world
> of light where children
> laugh and mothers smile.
> Our only mother is the city
> and she has disinherited her children...

When I talked to Tony at Youth Services of Toronto he told me the truth about the state of Bruce's mental health. In Tony's opinion, Bruce needed to see a psychiatrist soon because he was in desperate need of medication for his schizophrenia. Tony thought Bruce was approaching a crisis, although he was still managing to cope, despite the stress of living on the streets.

Tony informed me that there were people in Toronto who had been concerned about Bruce. Although he did not recognize these people as being his friends, they had referred him to the Youth Services Organization. Tony said Bruce had an appointment in a few days' time to see a doctor about his sore feet. The doctor would then suggest to him that he see a psychiatrist.

Youth Services would pay for Bruce's bus ticket home, including his meals. They would monitor him throughout the entire trip, to ensure that he reached home safely. The organization could only do this, Tony stressed, if Bruce agreed to go on medication.

Tony seemed very concerned about Bruce's welfare and I was immensely grateful. I told him I had promised Bruce I would forward the money for him to retrieve his guitar. I wanted to include enough so that he could purchase cigarettes and magazines for the long trip. Tony said I should send the money directly to Youth Services. That way Bruce would get it—but only after agreeing to take medication.

I mailed the money with a note, recalling how well he had been when he was living in Prince George on a weak maintenance dose of Stelazine. I reminded Bruce that he'd suffered no side-effects, whatsoever. The note was cheerful and friendly and I took it for granted that after reading its message, Bruce would have no qualms about taking anti-psychotic medication.

But when Bruce called, his voice was as cold as ice. He asked if it was true that he could only have the money I had sent if he took medication. If that was so, he stated, he would rather die on the streets of Toronto. I was flabbergasted at Bruce's flat, grim refusal to take the drugs which, despite their side-effects, were therapeutic. I found myself backing down from the commitment I had made to Tony. It was not really an ultimatum after all, I told my son. In that case, he replied, he would be leaving Toronto tomorrow after taking his guitar out of hock.

He had enough money for the bus ticket, Bruce informed me, with some left over for food and cigarettes. I wondered about his suitcases. I had given Tony the phone number of Mike's apartment and requested that he try to retrieve them. But Bruce was not concerned about his belongings. The only possession he cherished, he told me, was his guitar.

I hung up the phone realizing that I had been easy to manipulate. But at least my son would be coming home. "If Bruce is as determined and as in control as he sounds," I decided, "he cannot be as ill as Tony claims."

But Bruce had a harrowing bus trip. He telephoned home from almost every stop—whether it was daytime or the middle of the night. After a few days of this, I could hear bells ringing when there weren't any. He had run out of money by the time the bus reached Winnipeg. "If I don't eat," Bruce said worriedly, "I could end up in the hospital." I told him I had no idea how to get money to him, especially in the middle of the night. We had no friends or relatives anywhere in Manitoba.

Bruce had no choice but to sell his beloved guitar for the sum of forty dollars to a bystander at the Winnipeg bus depot. It must have been heartbreaking for him to give up the beautiful instrument. My dad had given him the money to buy it shortly after Bruce's psychotic breakdown in 1984.

At that time, Dad was distressed by the changes he saw in his grandson's personality. The problem, he decided, stemmed from the fact that Bruce had no job and no car. "Every young fellow needs to have a car," Dad had declared, before handing my son six hundred dollars toward the purchase of one. But Bruce had no use for an automobile. He had purchased the guitar instead. It had been a beautiful instrument, well made with a pleasing resonance.

Bruce phoned several times complaining that the cross-country buses he was riding were all non-smoking coaches. He had been getting bad vibrations from some of the other passengers, he confided. Whenever that occurred, he'd been forced to change his seat. I was beginning to understand what Tony had been telling me. I was not looking forward to having my son back home.

But when the bus arrived in Fraser Lake I was surprised to see that Bruce looked very well; much better than after his breakdown two years earlier. His clothing was somewhat shabby but, otherwise, he appeared to have survived his ordeal with no ill effects. I did my shopping while Cathy visited with her brother at her usual coffee hangout. She said later that Bruce appeared to be just fine—mentally and physically.

My first mistake at home was in insisting that Bruce smoke his cigarettes outdoors. Both Leon and I were off the nicotine habit now and we were used to smoke-free air. I had hoped that Bruce would also give up the habit. "After all," I reminded him, "You did not smoke much when you lived on the street and you could not smoke on the bus." I assumed that the nicotine was pretty well out of his system. "It would be a good time for you to quit," I suggested.

My well-intentioned remarks succeeded only in inflicting a huge guilt-trip upon my son. Some days Bruce would roll up a supply of cigarettes on his machine; then throw them outside in the darkness of night. He was becoming increasingly nocturnal in his habits. During these periods of self-imposed restraint, he would become overwhelmed by the need for a cigarette before morning. Once, after throwing his makings outside in the pouring rain, Bruce trekked sixteen kilometers to town and back for tobacco and papers.

Late one night Bruce woke me up to say he was in need of some medication. Hesitantly I dialed Dr. Gow's home phone number. I knew the poor man would probably be sleeping after having worked at least a full day at the medical clinic. But I wanted his opinion on the therapeutic value of an old Stelazine tablet that I had found in a discarded prescription vial. I could not find any Cogentin in the house at all. Dr. Gow advised me to give the pill to Bruce, anyway. After swallowing it, he promptly fell asleep.

From that point on the situation would repeat itself. Bruce decided that a five mg tablet of Stelazine, plus one or two Cogentin pills, was the extent of what he would take. As soon as he felt better he took none at all. After not sleeping for several nights, his mental health would, once again, deteriorate. Bruce had a disconcerting habit of staring vacantly into space. His lips would move from time to time. When I questioned him about the lip movements, he said he was merely communicating with an inner voice; it was nothing to worry about at all.

Leon and I decided that it was best to allow Bruce to smoke indoors. He seemed to be more comfortable with that. Very often he sat at the kitchen table the entire night: writing, smoking cigarettes and drinking cup after cup of Ovaltine. He had given up drinking coffee at night, although he still drank plenty of that during the day. There were nights when Bruce would impulsively throw away certain books, music records and even some of his poetry. In the morning I would find these formerly-favored possessions crammed into the garbage can under the sink. He tried to be quiet, but there were times when Leon and I could hear him. We were not able to sleep much either.

Leon's big concern was Bruce's careless disposal of his cigarette butts. By morning his ashtray had often overflown onto the table surface. And my husband had spotted him smoking in bed–a no-no even when the two of us had the habit. Leon was constantly worried. The walls of Bruce's room were paneled in a thin varathaned veneer that was considered volatile. A similarly finished trailer-home in Prince George had recently been demolished by fire in less than eight minutes.

Bruce's symptoms seemed to be aggravated by his insomnia. The 5 mg of Stelazine that he would take only when he was desperate for sleep was not always effective. I gave him a mild sedative, from time to time, that was leftover from a prescription I'd once had filled. It was not very effective, either. Bruce mentioned that alcoholic drinks relaxed him. In desperation one evening I took him to the Endako Pub where he downed several hot rums. He was quite happy for an hour or so but still unable to sleep.

His habit of talking to himself, and even answering, became more pronounced. One night Leon overheard him telling himself a joke. My husband said Bruce had responded by nearly rolling off the bed with laughter. I was becoming concerned about our youngest child's reaction to this. Fern was understandably uneasy about her brother's strange behavior. In the past Bruce had been loving and attentive toward his little sister. But nowadays he ignored her completely. Fern was twelve years old; a typical child of the eighties who enjoyed watching the animated images of ugly-looking creatures that were shown on TV and in the movies. But when it came to real life, she was fearful of what she could not comprehend. When Fern heard her brother speaking to someone who was obviously not there, she had trouble equating it with an illness. She was especially afraid when the symptom occurred late at night, after she was in her bed. Despite my faltering explanation that Bruce was pretending, my daughter was becoming pale and withdrawn.

She was happiest when she stayed overnight at a friend's, or at her sister Cathy's, where she had the companionship of Jennel, who was two years younger.

Leon and I discussed where else Bruce could move to, so that the rest of us could relax and get on with our lives. The stress was particularly hard on my husband whose job at the mill was extremely strenuous. The constant lack of sleep would soon endanger his health as well as his efficiency.

The group home situation that Bruce had been in before in Prince George was now out of the question because he adamantly refused to take regular medication. There were no vacant and affordable apartments for rent within the village of Fraser Lake. Leon suggested the Northgate Motel, twenty kilometers away in Fort Fraser. It was managed by a fellow who, until recently, had worked with him at the sawmill. Fort Fraser was smaller than Fraser Lake but it had all the necessary amenities. Bruce thought he'd like to live in Fort Fraser. It was a friendly little town, he said. His pal Kevin used to live there with his family.

But Christmas was less than a month away. We decided to hold off Bruce's move until after the holidays. Our family always enjoyed celebrating this joyous, festive time of year. I usually prepared the turkey dinner with carrot pudding for dessert. Even during our poorest times, each child received at least one nice present. As the kids grew older, the situation reversed itself. Our children often presented us with the nicer, more expensive gifts. Back when Bruce had the finances, he invariably purchased tasteful, as well as useful, gifts for family members at Christmas and other occasions. I still have—and treasure—many of the gifts he gave me.

Bruce kept himself busy, writing and re-writing his growing collection of poems and songs. He managed to recall the words to a long, satirical poem he had composed and later lost while traversing the streets of Toronto. The poem, titled "Striptease With Violins" was an interesting contrast in styles, featuring short folksy narratives interwoven with tersely worded parables. I was amazed that he had been able to keep his creative mind active and efficient in the midst of what must have been pretty dismal surroundings.

I did not enjoy Bruce's new musical compositions which he now sang in a voice that would never need amplification even in a large hall. In our small house the walls vibrated. I tried to be tactful by suggesting that he sounded better when he restrained himself from singing and strumming Leon's old guitar so enthusiastically. But Bruce seemed incapable of lowering the volume. I was irritated by his unwillingness to please me—his audience. I understand now that he probably played his music as a therapy for his illness, rather than as entertainment for those around him.

Shortly after Bruce arrived home from Toronto, Ian and Kirsti Kluge invited us to join them at a coffeehouse session in Endako. Ian would be reciting some poetry, accompanied by Kirsti on the piano. I worried about whether Bruce would be well enough to perform, but he was eagerly looking forward to the opportunity. As it turned out, Ian and Kirsti were unable to attend and there was a shortage of performers.

My son did not hesitate at all when he was asked to play his songs. But I noticed that his music was not going over as well as when he had been on-stage the first time. The audience was becoming restless after listening to three or four of his songs. The coffeehouse organizers chatted in the kitchen, seemingly oblivious of what was going on. I was concerned that they were allowing Bruce to sing too long.

Finally I made my way into the kitchen where the other musicians clustered around the coffee pot. I asked one of the men, whose name was Peter, to relieve Bruce. "He's just had a nervous breakdown," I explained, "I'm concerned about the stress." Peter asked me if Bruce was nervous in front of a crowd; I answered, "No, he'd probably sing all night if you let him." I'm sure he suspected that I was the crazy one, and perhaps I was. I desperately wanted everyone to like my son and to appreciate his talent–if not his songs.

Bruce and I sat at a table by ourselves while we awaited the appearance of Ian and Kirsti. As we listened to the performers, he gradually drifted off into his own little world. I was horrified when his lips moved and then, he began laughing quietly to himself. Karen Harder had come over from another table to talk to Bruce. "What's so funny?" she inquired. Grinning sheepishly he replied, "It's a private joke."

Leon was becoming more and more concerned about Bruce's nighttime habits and, especially, his smoking in bed. I had reminded Bruce about the house rules for cigarettes, but to no avail. One night I implored Leon to have a man to man talk with him; to ask him to cut down on his late night activities, so that we could get some sleep, and to not smoke in bed. Leon said later he'd had a good talk with Bruce who had been copacetic about everything. But it was not long before Bruce forgot all about his promises to his stepdad. Much to Leon's dismay, he resumed his careless habits.

He talked periodically about finding employment, but it was obvious to everyone that Bruce would not be able to handle a job. When I took him to the Social Services office to apply for financial assistance, he had difficulty concentrating long enough to fill the forms out correctly. I confided to one of the workers about Bruce's problems and she suggested that I speak to Dr. Gow about signing a reference slip indicating that in his medical opinion Bruce was officially unemployable.

That way, costs of his medication would be covered by Pharamacare. He would also receive increased welfare benefits to cover the cost of his board at home or groceries in the event that he moved out on his own. When I asked Dr. Gow to sign the reference slip, he agreed that Bruce was indeed unemployable for as long as he refused to take regular medication.

Bruce developed strange twitches in his wrists and hands. When these occurred he would appear to be startled. One day I asked him about the convulsive movements and he became defensive, saying it was nothing for me to worry about. He sounded angry, and I thought he may have been a bit frightened. Several times I noticed him attempting to control the movements of one of his hands by grasping it firmly with the other. I wondered if Bruce might be developing tardive dyskinesia, the chronic disability that sometimes occurs after taking anti-psychotic drugs. But he had been on very little or no medication for almost a year. The erratic movements had to be caused by something else.

CHAPTER SIX

The Divided Self

"The divided self cannot endure..."

from "Berlin - The Divided Self"
a poem by Bruce Ray, 1990

One day Bruce decided that he wanted Dr. Gow to issue him a prescription for sleeping pills. He hoped they would help him to fall sleep at night; that way, he reasoned, he would have no need of any other medication. Dr. Gow advised him on the telephone that sleeping pills were not the answer for his chronic insomnia. But Bruce made an appointment to see him anyway.

On the afternoon of his appointment, I was with Fern during her regular figure skating practice at the arena. Bruce was to meet us at the shopping center across the highway from the medical clinic following his session with the doctor.

When Fern's lesson was over, she waited in the car while I searched the mall for her brother. I finally spotted him sitting at a table in the Fraser Lake Inn restaurant. I was relieved to observe him drinking coffee and looking calm and relaxed, while chatting animatedly to someone else. But when I looked more closely, I was horrified to see that he was all alone. He was talking and gesturing to no one but himself.

Bruce had led me to believe that his newly acquired habit of talking to himself was something he could curtail at will. I surmised that we were merely humoring him whenever he indulged in it at home. "But don't do it in public," I advised him. "Others may not understand." My son had explained away the solitary conversations as originating from loneliness; his inner voice was similar to the imaginary playmates that children sometimes have, he told me. He insisted that other people likely had inner voices who were not necessarily schizophrenic.

I had assumed that Bruce recognized his inner voice as being a part of himself, not a separate entity. A few weeks earlier during an emotional debate with Leon and myself, Bruce had cried out that he realized his problems existed mostly in his imagination, they stemmed from the trauma he had experienced on the streets of Toronto.

But now as I peered at him through the restaurant doors, I could see that he was oblivious to all the other patrons. It was obvious that his imagination, if that was really the problem, was out of control. I decided that I had to talk with Dr. Gow in order to understand what was going on inside Bruce's mind. I dropped Fern off at Cathy's trailer and sped off to the medical clinic before it closed at five o'clock. I told Elaine, the receptionist, that it was imperative I speak with Dr. Gow before he left for home.

I noticed immediately that the usually unruffled doctor was upset. He said Bruce had tried his best to manipulate him into writing a prescription for sleeping pills. When that failed, he had tried intimidation tactics, something my easy-going son had never done before, with Dr. Gow or with anyone else. The doctor had concluded Bruce's visit by giving him a few tablets of a sleeping potion. He was terribly frustrated by Bruce's continuing refusal to take his prescribed medication.

Dr. Gow said Bruce's personality changes were due to his deteriorating mental health which, he indicated, was approaching a crisis stage where he would need to be hospitalized. No one can legally be forced into hospitalization Dr. Gow emphasized, unless he exhibits clear signs of being a danger to himself or others. If Bruce showed signs of increasingly aggressive behavior, he may, conceivably, become dangerous. At that point he should be admitted to hospital against his will, if necessary.

This was a Friday, Dr. Gow noted. If a crisis was to happen, it would happen soon; most likely during the weekend. But I should remember, the doctor concluded, that Bruce was my son. I should continue to let him know that he was loved.

But back at home Bruce's behavior did not indicate any further deterioration. He continued to mull over his writings at night. In the mornings I often found some of them in the garbage as well as certain books and musical recordings. Though Leon and I watched him closely, he exhibited no aggressive or dangerous behavior. We made sure he was never alone with Fern although I could not imagine him hurting his little sister. I was certain that if there was anyone in the world he loved dearly, it was her.

One day while visiting with my friend Gina Dougan, who now managed the Fraser Lake Crisis Line and Drop-In Centre, I noticed a small flyer that advertised an Holistic Healing Centre in Vanderhoof. Bruce had mentioned that high potency vitamins had helped him for awhile when he was psychotic on the streets of Toronto. I encouraged him to take vitamins and zinc tablets at home; they were available for him, but he only took them once in a while. That evening I encouraged Bruce to call the telephone number listed on the flyer, if he was interested. He ended up having a long conversation with the woman who ran the centre. Although he informed her that he had been diagnosed with schizophrenia, she had sounded obliging. She said she charged thirty dollars for each of her relaxation sessions. She did not sell vitamins, she admitted, but she could help him obtain what he needed.

Dr. Gow was not impressed when I told him about the treatments Bruce was interested in. He said he wondered about the woman's knowledge of mental illnesses if she would still accept Bruce as a client knowing he was schizophrenic. The doctor admitted that some holistic programs are effective for alleviating simple stress. He used hypnosis himself in his practice, and hypnotherapy is a form of holistic treatment. But he would never use hypnosis on Bruce or on any other schizophrenic patient.

Ever since Bruce's initial breakdown in September 1984 I had devoured every book and magazine article I could find on the subject of mental illnesses, their causes and treatments. I had read that schizophrenia could be caused or aggravated by an allergy to wheat or by a lack of zinc or B vitamins in the diet. The theory that the illness was psychological in origin had been pretty well discarded. The disease resulted from an imbalance of chemicals in the central nervous system.

Symptoms could usually only be alleviated by introducing other chemical compounds into the body.

I had also read that multi-vitamin therapy combined with exercise and proper diet may be effective in reducing and alleviating symptoms of schizophrenia in some patients. The therapy must be followed religiously in order to maintain a proper balance of natural chemicals in the central nervous system of the body.

I asked Bruce whether, if I made an appointment for him to see a naturopathic physician, he would be willing to follow the strict regimen of multi-vitamin therapy. Bruce wholeheartedly agreed to that, and I made an appointment with Dr. Pontious in Quesnel for Tuesday, December 15. In 1986, Dr. Pontius was the only naturopathic physician in the northern interior of BC. Leon agreed with me that even if the treatment turned out to be hocus-pocus, it was definitely worth a try.

It was on the morning of December 13, two days before Bruce's appointment with Dr. Pontious in Quesnel, that I first learned of what I later came to call the Dale Phenomenon. Bruce had been telling me about his inner voice, or spirit as he sometimes referred to it. He now confided that it occupied the feminine side of his nature, and that she was very wise. He said there were certain aspects of the spirit's existence that must be kept secret. If I promised not to reveal them to anyone, he would tell me. When I agreed to that, Bruce confided that the spirit was actually that of a living person: she was Dale Olson, the nightclub dancer who had performed for him on his birthday in May 1984. According to her spirit, who was now acting as his personal guide, Dale no longer lived in the Toronto area but had moved to New York City.

I must have appeared skeptical because my son's eyes flashed with indignation, "If it hadn't been for her guidance," he stated fervently, "I probably would have died like a dog on the streets of Toronto." Dale had always given him good advice, he told me, and so far he had not gone wrong by following it. While Bruce did concede the possibility that the whole thing was his imagination, he did not believe it was. The concept fit in with some of the books he had been studying about ancient religions, such as that of the druids, who it was said had tapped into the wisdom of the universe. What they had learned could be of great benefit to modern-day theologians, doctors and scientists.

The story did seem incredible but the more Bruce talked, the more it seemed to make sense to me. The guiding spirit concept was intriguing. It fit in with the information I had once devoured on the topic of channelling; also with the enigma of walk-in personalities that had recently been documented in a book called *Strangers Among Us* by Ruth Montgomery.

The whole idea was an exciting one for me. I was still very quick to grasp on to any shred of evidence indicating that Bruce was not schizophrenic in the medical sense of the word. I would rather believe that he was being possessed by a good spirit. Another possibility I had in mind was that Bruce could actually be afflicted with a psychological condition known as multiple personality disorder. I had heard that with proper counseling, multiple personality disorder can be curable.

Bruce had said Dale wanted to talk to me. But that morning she wrote me a note instead. The handwriting, I immediately noticed, was in Bruce's slightly disjointed scrawl. It had changed since the days when he composed school essays in a cramped, angular style. In recent years his handwriting had become more rounded; similar to his sister Debbie's neat feminine script.

I had mixed emotions about reading the note from Dale. On the one hand, I was somewhat squeamish; but I was also tremendously excited. I felt as if I was on the verge of learning something new, something almost as important as the secret of creation.

It was on the morning of Cathy and Darwin's baptismal ceremony at the Lakeview Bible Chapel that I received the note from Dale. I was in good spirits that morning because I had been invited to attend the ritual that would confirm my daughter and son-in-law's commitment to the Christian Faith. Although I had recently joined the Baha'i Faith, my commitment as a Baha'i did not in any way conflict with my appreciation of their happiness at becoming Christians.

In the note Dale introduced herself to me as a spirit who was inside Bruce's head. The words were oddly stilted and their meaning obscure, but I decided that was of no real import. I placed the note in my purse and revelled in the excitement of Bruce's having confided his secret to me, which, I thought, could explain a great many mysteries.

A strange thing happened to me while I was in the church watching the baptismal ceremonies of Cathy and Darwin, Karen and Jim, and another couple. It was chilly when I drove the truck into town to pick up Cathy's Aunt Beth, who was also invited to the ceremony. I had left home without wearing gloves or mittens and my hands were cold by the time we reached the church. Inside, I sat down in a pew between Beth, and Cathy's daughter Jennel. Very soon I became immersed in the spiritual mood of the occasion. I enjoyed the testimonials, especially Darwin's; he is a most entertaining speaker. But at the close of the ceremony, while he and Cathy were being dunked fully-clothed into the water bath, I became acutely depressed. For me, the ritual also symbolized the differences between my religious philosophy and that of my daughter and her husband.

Shortly after I sat down in the church pew I noticed some small indentations on the back side of my left hand. There were about six or eight of these odd markings which followed, in an elongated "V" shape, my thumb-line and forefinger. They appeared to have been caused by something pressing against the skin; something with a series of hard round protrusions such as very small buttons or nail heads. I checked my clothing for projections that might have caused the indentations but found nothing. I was mystified although not really concerned. From time to time during the ceremony, I found myself glancing at my hand to see if the marks were still there. I thought they might be simply shadows projected from the ceiling lights. But when I moved my hand, the configuration remained the same. My numbed hands finally thawed out and I tried running my right forefinger gently over the apparent depressions. I could detect no breaks at all in the skin surface. I decided not to concern myself unduly about the marks. They faded slowly but were clearly visible for well over an hour. By the time I got up to leave, they had almost disappeared.

A few days later when I thought to mention the mysterious marks to Bruce, he looked startled. "Oh that was just an hallucination," he replied hastily. I wondered if it was him or if it was the Dale personality who had answered.

At the time of my hallucination I had never heard of stigmata, which my dictionary defines as "signifying the wounds suffered by Christ." Similar indentations to mine have been documented as having appeared, as a kind of visionary experience, to a significant number of people over the years. If the markings on my hand were, indeed, authentic stigmata, I am convinced that they came from a deeply concerned and infinitely loving source.

Bruce and I did not discuss the Dale phenomenon (as I now thought of it) until two days later while we awaited his appointment with Dr. Pontious in the north Cariboo town of Quesnel. We had stayed overnight in a motel after having arrived on the bus the previous evening.

I slept very little that night and Bruce probably never slept at all. In the semi-darkness of our shared accommodation he had smoked cigarette after cigarette, mumbling and at times even arguing with himself. He did not want the television set turned on although it would have provided me with some distraction. I found myself becoming more and more distressed. As much as I preferred not to believe it, I realized that my son was not well. And from what I could hear from their muffled disagreements, the good spirit Dale was really not that wise either.

At breakfast I was dazed and lethargic until after Bruce and I had finished our second or third cup of cafeteria coffee. I asked, mostly as a way of initiating idle conversation, when he had first encountered the voice that he now referred to as Dale.

"The first time I heard Dale," Bruce replied, "was while I was living with Debbie on Saltspring Island." He had adopted her name as a muse to inspire him with his poetry and his songwriting. Before long he realized she had become a distinctive presence inside himself, a wise and loving spirit who had mastered the science of soul travel. Dale was actually a white witch, Bruce continued, of the type referred to in books about ancient nature-worshipping religions. They should not be confused with the black witches associated with satanic cults. But the stigma attached to witchcraft, Bruce warned, was so great that even a white witch might be in danger even in our modern day society. It was not that long ago when suspected witches were tortured and burned alive at the stake.

It was while Bruce was in Toronto the second time that Dale once again joined him. She was with him during the time of his traumatic encounters with Mike and his friends. Later when he was living on the street, Bruce had been turned away from the hostels that were run by various churches groups because he refused to take medication. He had been forced to stay in fleabag joints that were frequented by drug addicts and criminals. The night a group of thugs encircled his bed was one that my son would never forget.

"I was very lucky to escape," Bruce said grimly. "After that, I didn't sleep for three nights in a row. I was afraid they would find me and kill me."

The Dale voice inside his head had finally suggested that he sleep at her uncle's house. But when he arrived at the address of the man she identified as being her uncle, there was no one at home. Dale assured Bruce that it would be all right if he entered the residence in order to have a good night's sleep.

The following morning when Bruce left the house, a patrol car pulled up and two policemen stepped out. Bruce recalled how they had jumped him and forced him to lie face-down on the cement sidewalk. The officers had laughed as they ground his face into the concrete surface. He had spent a few days inside a jail cell before being released back onto the street.

Bruce said Dale had been his sole source of comfort throughout the ordeal. She proved herself to be a wise and beautiful spirit, and there was no doubt that she cared deeply for him. My son likened the relationship to a soul marriage. It was an enjoyable liaison, he confided, and very important to him.

Dr. Pontious' office was located across the street from our motel. As we waited I chatted with the receptionist while Bruce retreated into his inner world. I could see the barely-perceptible movement of his lips from time to time. The naturopathic doctor was a friendly, muscular-looking individual who also doubled as a chiropractor. He led us into a room that was filled with packing cases and an older-style orthopedic table. From somewhere in a back room he brought us chairs sit on.

Dr. Pontious spoke directly to my son and I did not interrupt the initial discussion at all. He took Bruce's pulse which was fast–well over 80. He then encouraged him to describe his symptoms: the chronic insomnia, what had occurred during his nervous breakdown, etc. The doctor appeared to be puzzled. "Is there anything else you want to tell me?" he inquired. I hoped Bruce would say something about his inner voice, or anything else that was going on inside his mind. But he did not. His hands which were folded, twitched periodically but his lips did not move at all. The relaxed expression on Bruce's face suggested genuine sincerity and openness.

When I inquired about multi-vitamin therapy for diagnosed schizophrenics, Dr. Pontious related the case history of a former patient, a young man from Saskatchewan who had been acutely psychotic. He lived with a relative in Quesnel who had carefully monitored his vitamins, diet and exercise treatments. The patient's response, Dr. Pontious told us, had been dramatic. The young man held a job for the first time in his life, before returning to his former home in Saskatchewan. There, his treatments were neglected and he regressed to his former state.

I fervently hoped that Dr. Pontious could come up with a magic formula to work a similar miracle for Bruce to strengthen his nervous system and blend the normal with the abnormal so that he too would be able to hold a job again. The magic formula consisted of eight to ten boxes of natural vitamins plus a small vial of liquid with a dropper, all of which had to be taken at regular intervals throughout the day and at bedtime. Dr. Pontious stressed that it was also important Bruce's pulse rate be taken and recorded every morning before breakfast and again later in the day to provide a comparison. I should also itemize what he had eaten before the pulse rates were taken. He advised me to phone his office in one week's time and relay the information to him. It would help him to complete his diagnosis.

Since Bruce's pulse rate was now quite high, Dr. Pontius indicated that an allergy of some sort might be part of his problem. He said many schizophrenias were caused by allergies. In order to track down exactly what substance was the allergen, the heart rate must be carefully monitored throughout the day. An excessively high pulse rate would indicate when the allergen was in the bloodstream.

The receptionist bagged up the numerous bottles and vials of vitamins that Dr. Pontious prescribed. I thought the cost of ninety-eight dollars was a small price to pay if they did Bruce some good. Back in the same cafeteria for lunch, I relaxed while Bruce smoked a cigarette. His hands twitched and his lips began to move in silent conversation.

Once or twice he laughed out loud to himself. I was becoming embarrassed because I thought people were watching.

More to distract him than anything else, I asked, "Can I talk to Dale?"

Bruce's eyes lit up. "Yes," he said, "do you mind if she talks to you right now?"

I tried to observe Dale as she began to speak through Bruce. Her facial expressions and hand movements, even the way she crossed her legs, were very different from Bruce's usual mannerisms. They seemed to express her own particular personality. Bruce's hand movements, erratic and uncontrolled earlier, were now expressive gestures in ordinary conversation.

Dale's voice was the same as Bruce's, but her choice of words and phrasings was not. She spoke as a woman of the world might, I thought, not so much wise, but as someone who wanted to appear sophisticated. Dale used phrases like "as you would say…" and "in my country, I am known as…" She was twenty-eight years old, she said. Bruce was now twenty-three. Dale confided that she loved my son and that she knew he loved her. Her home was now in America, she said, although she had lived in a total of five different countries during her lifetime.

An alarm bell began to ring in my mind when Dale referred to herself as a stripper. Most women in her line of work would prefer to call themselves exotic dancers or something like that, I thought. Stripper was the word that Bruce had used.

As she continued to speak I began to fall under the spell of what she had to say. It all made so much sense to me. Dale discussed philosophy and religion and I was amazed at how much of what I believed in–and also a few of the things I wanted to believe in–were endorsed by this woman who appeared to be informed about so many things. Bruce was quite correct, I thought, Dale was definitely a wise person.

She certainly had the gift of the gab. Once in a while she would pause to ask Bruce a question or get him to verify a point that she wished to make. Bruce would grin sheepishly as he answered. It was obvious that he deferred to her, the feminine personality.

Dale did not have a high opinion of the Christian religion. She lumped all the denominations together and included them as one, in her anti-fundamentalist point of view. She didn't know much about the Baha'i Faith, she admitted, but when I described a few of the Baha'i principles, she seemed to approve. I told Dale about an ad I'd seen in a local paper advertising a religion or philosophy referred to as Eckankar, the science of soul travel. She said she'd never heard of Eckankar, but the science of soul travel was something she did know about. Soul travel was the method she used to join Bruce in the BC Northern Interior from her home in New York City.

She was not fond of Fraser Lake, Dale admitted. She missed the busy, bustling life in the big city. But right now Bruce needed her to help him with his poetry and songwriting. She was also available to help him out with everyday situations, when he was in need of her advice and assistance.

On the way home that evening I found out just how helpful Dale could be. Bruce had complained about the lack of smoking privileges on the bus we'd taken from Quesnel to Prince George. At that time Greyhound bus regulations were in a period of transition: some buses permitted smoking while others did not. For some reason I expected we would have a choice between several buses going west from Prince George. But there was only one westbound and it was another non-smoking coach. The driver was a big loudmouthed type who proclaimed this to one and all as he took our tickets. Bruce inquired politely if there would be another bus, one that permitted smoking. The fellow sneeringly replied that if Bruce could not do without a cigarette for a hundred miles, he was in a pretty sorry state.

I turned around when I realized Bruce was no longer behind me. He was admonishing the driver for his "fucking patronizing attitude." I held my breath, fearing he'd be barred from boarding the bus. But the driver, who was twice his size, seemed cowed by Bruce's tirade.

Once we were on board, I asked Bruce why he had collared the driver that way. "We could have been stuck in Prince George until the next bus came along at seven-thirty tomorrow morning." I remonstrated.

Dale was quick to reply. I could tell it was her because she addressed me as Doris, rather than Mom. Bruce had handled the situation correctly, she retorted, the bus driver had no right to be rude to his passengers. "Part of Bruce's problem is that he allows people to push him around," she stated. "He must learn to stand up to others."

I had no answer to that. Secretly I found myself agreeing with her. People who work with the public ought to be courteous to those who make their jobs possible, I decided. We should not have to put up with insulting behavior.

As the bus rolled along through the night Dale and I resumed the conversation we had begun in Quesnel. I was fascinated by the concept of soul travel. The way Dale explained it, she was able to return to her New York apartment almost instantaneously anytime she wished. At our Vanderhoof stop Bruce moved to the newly-vacated seat behind me, and I dozed back in mine. The Dale/Bruce personalities quickly became engrossed in themselves. Sheepish giggles and silly remarks indicated when Bruce was speaking, but the cool, calm Dale personality was definitely in charge.

Perhaps it was a lack of sleep the previous night; to this day I cannot explain it. But that evening as I relaxed on the bus between Prince George and Fraser Lake, I was absolutely convinced of the authenticity of Dale and her story. She seemed to be aware of certain things that I was sure Bruce knew nothing about. For instance I had read a book entitled *Secrets of the Atomic Age* by Pearl Adler. When I mentioned the book to Dale I mistakenly referred to it as Secrets of the Atom and she had corrected me. I was positive Bruce had no idea the book existed. It was not a library book; I had borrowed it from a friend. During the time that I was reading it, Bruce had been in his abstracted, unaware state of mind. I was sure he had noticed nothing that did not pertain directly to himself.

As I dozed in my seat I wondered what I could do to ensure that Dale's identity remain protected. "There must be others in the same situation," I speculated. If Dale was for real, Bruce was probably not the only person on the planet to be blessed by the loving assistance of a good witch. Nagging at the back of my mind, however, was the memory of my normally good-natured son's verbal attack upon the bus driver. It was not so much what Bruce had said that had intimidated the larger man, I decided. It was the look of intense fury that blazed in his eyes.

CHAPTER SEVEN

Animal Presences

*"Beneath the deaf flesh of reason
there lives the animal presences
pouring out their essence
into the shape
of seasons..."*

from "Animal Presences"
by Bruce Ray, 1991

A person who suffers from a disorder of the central nervous system such as schizophrenia can manifest some strange symptoms. Reality perceptions are sometimes distorted because of impairments to the sense of sight, hearing, touch, smell or taste. As well the person can appear to be "possessed" by a being or beings other than that which is perceived as "self." This last is to me the most confusing symptom of all.

My religion does not recognize the existence of an entity referred to as the devil. The devil, to Baha'is, is simply a word that symbolizes man's base, or animal nature. Similarly the word evil is defined as lacking in good spiritual health, much the way that darkness is merely a lack of light.

The central nervous system controls the many levels of consciousness that make up what we are as human beings. When that system becomes impaired, we may begin to switch back and forth involuntarily between varying levels of consciousness, or personalities. When good-natured, gentle people express odd or frightening behavior, I believe it indicates their level of consciousness has reverted to their lower or animal nature; to one of the animal presences that Bruce referred to in his poem.

The morning after we arrived home from Quesnel was day one of Bruce's new multi-vitamin therapy. I counted out all the vitamins he was to take throughout the day and placed each dose into a labelled plastic bag. That morning when he got up he insisted on having a cigarette and coffee first, before letting me take his pulse. It was very high, even higher than it had been in Dr. Pontious' office.

For about three days with an occasional prompting from me, Bruce followed the naturopathic routines. He expressed neither enthusiasm nor reluctance. His pulse rate remained high and he showed no interest whatever in exercising, as Dr. Pontious had suggested. On the morning of the fourth day I observed that Bruce did not take any of his vitamins. He was surly and appeared to be harboring some resentment toward me. When I reminded him about the vitamins (I may have mentioned how much they cost) he became hostile.

From now on, Bruce proclaimed, he would no longer permit me to tell him what to do. He was an adult. I was not to advise him when to take vitamins, when to take his pulse or anything else. Bruce wondered accusingly if I might be the cause of many of his problems. For that reason, he declared, I would no longer be Mom to him; he would call me by my given name, Doris. I was nonplused and made no reply. Soon after this furious outburst, he retreated into his own private world and took no vitamins at all for the rest of the day.

Over the next few days my husband and I saw more bizarre changes in Bruce's personality. He began to complain about evil spirits inside his room. Because of them, he decided not to sleep in his usual bed at night, but dozed fitfully on the living room couch. The curtains in the room had to be pulled well apart. Why, he did not say and I did not ask.

Bruce seemed to regard the appearance of these evil spirits not so much as being dangerous, but merely startling–and at times irritating. One afternoon after he had been lying down quietly in Fern's bedroom,

Bruce suddenly erupted out of her door and rushed blindly into the living room. There he peered intently about, then began muttering to himself, obviously annoyed.

One day Leon noticed Bruce ostensibly chasing after something inside the house. He stopped abruptly to peer at a spot on the living room ceiling. When Leon asked him what he was looking at, Bruce mumbled something about a bug. But there was no bug on the ceiling at all.

Once in a while Bruce played the guitar. He would launch enthusiastically into singing and playing and then stop suddenly, almost as though a plug had been pulled. At times during the night I thought I could hear him moan, a strange haunting cry that brought to my mind the phrase a soul in torment. This sound would be cut off shortly, leaving me wondering whether I had heard it at all. Fern later recalled hearing the moaning sounds in the middle of the night.

It was obvious to us all that Bruce was not improving. After the first few days, he no longer took vitamins and I did not attempt to take his pulse. Our trip to Quesnel had been a complete waste of time and money.

By this time, I had lost faith in the Dale phenomenon. If she were really a wise and loving spirit, I said to myself, then why was Bruce deteriorating like he was. I speculated that my taking Dale seriously may even have worsened his condition. Undoubtedly she had been created by his own lonely imagination. But now she had become an integral part of himself. Most of the time my son appeared to be inordinately tired and withdrawn. But when he was forced to respond to any one of us, his mood would suddenly become strained and intense. It was as if he was living on the raw jagged edge of his emotions, a complete change of personality in a young man who had always been easygoing and good-humoured.

I was terribly frustrated and so was Leon. Fern was unhappy. She confided that she could not talk to her brother anymore; he became angry about the least little thing. I decided that it was time for me to be honest with him. "I was wrong to talk to Dale that day in Quesnel," I told Bruce, "because I no longer believe that she is real."

He looked oddly blank as if in a trance. For several seconds he did not respond at all. Finally, I told him that if Dale wished to communicate with me, she should do so by note. I preferred that she not speak to me anymore. Bruce picked up a pen, wrote something on a piece of paper, and handed it to me. What I read was, "I must survive."

Later that same day I spoke the words that caused all hell to break loose. I asked Bruce if he had tried to call Dale on the telephone at her New York apartment. His face contorted in rage as he confronted me. "How did you know about that?" he growled. I reminded him that it had been part of our conversation on the bus ride home from Quesnel. "You lie!" he shouted. "I never would have told you that!" I was furious. I told Leon that Bruce had accused me of lying.

"That is something I just cannot take," I fumed.

My husband confronted Bruce and inquired what the argument had been about. As I started to explain, Bruce turned around in his chair and glared at me. I could tell he thought I was about to divulge his secret. His lips curled back from his teeth and he hissed at me. My son's face was that of a stranger and the intensity of his rage was frightening.

Later Leon and I talked in private. I said I thought Bruce had reached the stage Dr. Gow had predicted was imminent a few weeks earlier. He had warned me that, as Bruce's condition approached a crisis, he could become dangerous to members of his own family. Perhaps, I suggested worriedly, we should alert Dr. Gow and the RCMP, so that Bruce could be hospitalized and forcibly given the medication he so desperately needed.

Leon agreed that the situation was indeed critical. But it was a Sunday and our family doctor was not on call that particular weekend. We decided that, for starters, I should drive Fern over to Cathy and Darwin's trailer. Leon would keep an eye on Bruce.

I decided to drop in on the Kluges and ask Ian for advice. As a young student Ian had worked for awhile in a mental institution. And in university he had taken courses in psychology. He was Bruce's friend as well as my own. I soon learned to my overwhelming relief that Bruce had already confided the secret of Dale to Ian, weeks before he had told me. I would not be betraying my son's confidence if I discussed the situation with Ian.

Ian said he had been very concerned about Bruce's mental health for some time and had recently discussed those concerns with his own family physician. The split personality syndrome that Bruce now exhibited was indicative of acute schizophrenia. He was probably on the brink of a crisis, any kind of stress could precipitate one.

Bruce had been expecting Dale to telephone him since the first Sunday in December, Ian recalled. As each successive Sunday went by without a phone call, he had likely become more frustrated and despondent. Whether my conversing with the Dale personality had worsened Bruce's condition was a matter of conjecture.

Bruce had scribbled a New York telephone number on several scraps of paper he'd left around the house. I had checked under Information in the phone book and the Brooklyn, New York exchange was correct. For the sake of my curiosity, Ian suggested I try dialing the number. The Dale story, as Bruce first told it, had intrigued him too. But the next time they discussed it, Ian noticed discrepancies in Bruce's story that clearly indicated he was delusional.

Ian thought a male authority figure was needed to control the situation. It should not be me, he advised, because my son no longer respected what I had to say. Leon would have to be the one to give Bruce the ultimatum: to go on medication or else leave home. Bruce would likely be furious with his stepfather, Ian warned. But it was better that he handle the situation than I. If Bruce became violent, that would be Leon's cue to call the RCMP.

I phoned my husband and relayed Ian's suggestions to him. Leon agreed to the plan. If my son opted to leave, Leon assured me he would transport Bruce to a motel room in Fort Fraser.

By the time I left Kluge's, I was in an emotional turmoil. Ian and Kirsty urged me not to worry. "Whatever happens," they said, "Bruce will be safe and in the hospital tonight, or at the very latest, tomorrow." They reassured me that despite his adamant stand against taking medication, Bruce would one day thank Leon and I for doing what we had to do.

As usual when I desperately needed a sisterly shoulder to cry on, I turned to my former sister-in-law, Leon's cousin Hazel. As I was about to leave town, I was drawn to her home and fireside like a moth to a bright light. Before I realized it, I had divulged the entire story to her, even the part I had promised Bruce I would not tell a soul–that Dale was a white witch.

Hazel promised that she would keep the secret. She warned me though, that it was possible Bruce had come in contact with members of a satanic cult and somehow been deceived into believing it was a good thing. She had recently read a book about satanism called *Michelle Remembers* whose author, a Victoria psychiatrist, claimed that the cult was flourishing in the Vancouver Island area.

Hazel recalled that the book had documented a series of hypnotherapy sessions with a troubled young woman. The psychiatrist had regressed her memory back to her childhood. The treatments revealed that as a small child she had been forced to participate in horrific satanic rituals involving witchcraft.

I explained to Hazel what Bruce had told me; that the witches or wicca of ancient religions had nothing to do with Satanism. Devil worship actually originated in more recent times as a kind of backlash to Christianity.

Leon arrived while I was still at Hazel's. He informed us that Bruce had been entirely agreeable about leaving the house and moving into the motel in Fort Fraser. He adamantly refused to take medication, but did not express any hostility when Leon presented him with the ultimatum.

Hazel telephoned Dr. Kelly, whose turn it was to be on call over the weekend. The doctor admitted that he had been frustrated in his practice by a law that made it virtually impossible to hospitalize mentally ill patients against their will. These people were often in desperate need of medication, Dr. Kelly stated, but it had to be proven that they were a danger to themselves or others before anything could be done.

I admitted to Dr. Kelly that Bruce had not, as yet, proven himself to be a danger to himself or others. The fact that I had been afraid of him when he was angry was in no way proof that he would harm me. Anger, in itself, is a normal human emotion as long as it is under control. Dr. Kelly advised that Leon or I should visit Bruce every few days to monitor how he was coping. We should call the RCMP if his condition approached a crisis, hopefully, before he harmed himself. It was far less likely, Dr. Kelly assured me, that Bruce would harm anyone else as he had not previously been a violent person.

On his way to work the following morning Leon stopped in to check on Bruce. He reported that all was well. A day or so later I bundled up my son's record albums, our old record player, his cigarette rolling machine, plus other essentials. With some trepidation on my part, Cathy and I drove to Fort Fraser to visit Bruce.

Bruce was coolly polite toward both of us. I noted that his suite appeared clean and comfortable. There was even a kitchette for him to prepare his meals. Cathy stayed with her brother while I shopped at the combination store and restaurant for a few items that he was in need of. I picked up coffees and hamburgers for the three of us for lunch. After lunch, Cathy cheerfully reminded Bruce that Christmas Day was approaching. She invited him to her house for a turkey dinner. Bruce was quiet and reserved. He made no reply whatsoever to the invitation.

A few days before Christmas, both Cathy and Darwin went with me to visit Bruce at the motel. Darwin accompanied us to the door, then changed his mind and said he would wait for us out in the car. Once again Cathy invited Bruce to her home for Christmas dinner. This time he politely declined. Later Darwin explained why he had not entered Bruce's suite. He had not felt that he was welcome, he said. As Darwin approached the open doorway, Bruce had looked directly at his brother-in-law with an expression of undisguised hatred upon his face.

I could not understand why Bruce would be so hostile toward Darwin. Perhaps, I surmised, it was because his brother-in-law exemplified so many things that were missing in Bruce's own life. He was both a husband and a father, and he also had a job. But Darwin suggested there might be a more sinister reason behind Bruce's hostility; something less personal. The church that my daughter and son-in-law belonged to subscribed to a belief in demonic possession. Darwin stated hesitantly it was possible that Bruce was in a state of being possessed.

By his own choice, Bruce spent Christmas Day alone. On Boxing Day, his Aunt Beth accompanied me on my trek to Fort Fraser. I brought along some Christmas goodies and a basket containing a yellow plastic floral arrangement which, as I elucidated to my son, would brighten up his new home. Bruce said he had been trying unsuccessfully to talk to his dad and Connie on the telephone. Following that comment, he became distant and preoccupied. I was grateful that Beth initiated the remainder of our conversation.

A few nights later Bruce phoned. His voice was high and thin and he sounded frightened. "Please, let me come home," he begged, "Something weird is going on at this motel. I promise I'll take medication if you'll let me stay the night."

I asked Leon to please maneuver our old truck down the icy highway to pick up Bruce. Approximately forty-five minutes later my son walked through the door. I crossed the room to embrace him, but he held himself stiffly erect, not acknowledging the overture in any way. He then sauntered into the kitchen toward the refrigerator and proceeded to eat as though he were starving to death.

When he had finished eating I mentioned the promise he'd made to take medication. Bruce stated loftily that he would only take five milligrams of Stelazine, no more. My temper flared. Five milligrams was a ridiculously low dose, I declared. He could stay the night, but only if he took ten milligrams of Stelazine, plus three milligrams of Cogentin. That he flatly refused to do.

I took Leon aside. I said I felt I was once again being manipulated by my son. The arrogant young man in my kitchen did not in any way resemble the frightened voice I'd heard on the telephone. My husband had worked all day and was tired. But he knew I was afraid to drive the wintry roads after dark. Leon assured me that he would take Bruce back to his motel room. "That way," he said, "we can all get some sleep."

When Bruce learned that he was going back to Fort Fraser he became angry and belligerent. "I hope I never see any of your fucking faces again," he snarled. Later after Leon returned, he said Bruce had berated him all the way to Fort Fraser. He had tried to ignore the abusive tirade, so uncharacteristic of Bruce's normal behavior. Finally, he turned up the volume full blast on the truck radio.

The next day I called Dr. Gow to tell him about my most recent confrontation with my son. When the doctor had heard my story, he mildly suggested that it might have been better in the long run if Bruce had taken the five milligrams of medication and stayed the night. Dr. Gow probably suspected what I refused to admit even to myself: I did not want Bruce back in our house.

I was overwhelmed by feelings of guilt and a helpless sense of duty. If the severity of Bruce's illness had been physical rather than mental, I knew that leaving him on his own would have been unconscionable, akin to allowing him to bleed from an open, untended wound. We were letting him down, I realized, but I had no idea what to do.

I began reaching out desperately for any straw to cling to. Recently I had accepted a job as the Fraser Lake correspondent for a Vanderhoof-based newspaper. A few days before Christmas I had interviewed a young man who attended a naturopathic college in Oregon. Bob, whose parents resided in Endako, was in his sixth year of a seven-year course to obtain his certification as a naturopathic physician. He'd had first-hand experience, he told me, as to the effects of drugs, alcohol and poor nutrition on the human nervous system. He'd also stressed something I'd never heard from a medical professional: that maintaining one's spiritual health was an important component of being well.

For months Bruce had flatly refused to see Dr. Gow or any other practitioner of conventional medicine. Bob was an affable young man and a firm believer in the health benefits of multi-vitamin therapy. When I'd interviewed him, I thought he would be an ideal person to speak with my son and possibly establish a rapport with him. Perhaps Bruce would, at least, take the vitamins that Dr. Pontious had prescribed.

When I suggested it to him, Bruce said he wouldn't mind talking to someone who was into holistic medicine. Bob had already agreed to visit my son over the holiday season if he had time. I called his parents' home and learned that he and his friend planned to leave for Edmonton the following day, on the early morning Greyhound bus. But Bob suggested I could drive them to Vanderhoof instead, stopping off to visit Bruce in Fort Fraser along the way. From Vanderhoof, they could catch the Fort St. James stage to Prince George, and from there connect with the bus to Edmonton.

The stage would be leaving Vanderhoof at ten-thirty a.m. which meant Bob had about half an hour to become acquainted with my son. His friend and I drank coffee at the cafe while he attempted to establish a connection. When we picked him up, Bob reported that Bruce did not appear to be that bad. Bruce had told him about our differences, and stated that the move to Fort Fraser had been good for everyone. On the way home from Vanderhoof, I stopped in to see Bruce. He told me that Bob seemed like a nice guy, but he hadn't wanted to confide in someone he had just met and probably would never see again.

Bob had suggested that he begin exercising regularly. Bruce told me he might be interested in taking up jogging, if he had the appropriate footwear. I took him into Fraser Lake to buy some shoes. He also purchased a small bottle of wine because it was New Year's Eve.

The next time I visited Bruce I was amazed and pleased to find him appearing like his old self. I showed him a copy of our recently published history book called *Deeper Roots and Greener Valleys*. It had been put together by the local historical society of which I was a member. Bruce's contribution had been a silhouette drawing of Simon Fraser, featured as a part of the introduction.

"Say, that looks all right!" Bruce exclaimed. His voice was warm and enthusiastic as he leafed through the pages. I noticed that the bottles and vials of vitamin preparations were on the kitchen counter and that the bag containing his most recent prescription for anti-psychotic drugs was open.

Bruce's recovery, if it was that, did not last long. Two days later he was once again impassive and withdrawn. He retrieved the copy of our history book from where he had placed it behind a kitchen cupboard, and handed it to me. I noticed that several pieces of black vinyl plastic were in the garbage container. They were record albums that had been broken and discarded. While still at home, Bruce had confided that he no longer liked listening to the Beatles' music. He had learned that the late John Lennon was a witch.

One morning my neighbour Joan Bruns telephoned. She said hesitantly that she wanted to talk to me about Bruce. Her son-in-law, George, who was the assistant manager of the Shoppers Food Mart store and coffee shop in Fort Fraser, was concerned about him. George wondered, Joan said, if I realized just how bad Bruce's mental condition had become.

I called Cathy and she drove me to Fort Fraser to converse with George. Once there we drank several cups of coffee with him in the cafe. George told us that Manuel, who owned the motel where Bruce stayed, also wanted to talk to me. Bruce was definitely not dangerous to the public, George emphasized. But he was embarrassed for my son because he was becoming an oddity and a laughingstock to those who frequented the premises. Bruce often came into the cafe to order a fairly expensive meal. He would pay for it; but after talking and arguing with himself, he would sometimes leave without eating a bite. One evening he had chased back and forth between two opposite chairs at the table, apparently having a serious argument with someone who wasn't there.

After our discussion with George, we walked across the parking lot to the Country Kitchen Cafe, which was managed by Manuel and his wife in conjunction with their motel business. When I explained that I was Bruce's mother they both appeared to be upset. Manuel said quietly that he wanted my son to leave the motel. He was embarrassed to tell me this, he admitted, because he knew Leon and considered him to be a friend.

Manuel's wife was not embarrassed. She told me Bruce had been given the nicest room in the motel, and did not keep it neat and clean. The biggest problem was that he made too much noise in the middle of the night. "He talks loudly," she said, "and then he cries."

I promised Manuel and his wife that Bruce would be out of the motel before the coming weekend when his next month's rent was due.

Later that day I thought about what Manuel's wife had said. Cathy had recently referred to her brother's new, aggressive persona as the macho Bruce. When last I had talked with Ian, I asked him if it was possible that Bruce had personality splits other than the Dale phenomenon. Ian had answered yes; there were at least four distinct personalities that he had noticed.

I usually do my best thinking with a pencil and paper. That evening I scribbled down some character traits I thought might be associated with each of the four personalities. The Silly Bruce giggled and laughed hysterically at Dale's jokes. Sometimes he danced and sang little songs during his conversations with her. Dale was the female personality I had met in Quesnel. Macho Bruce was arrogant and said "fuck" a lot. The Old Bruce was my beloved son, who was mature, intelligent and had a good sense of humour. I had only observed him once in recent weeks, on the day that I showed him the copy of our history book.

Now I wondered if there might be a fifth personality, one that was lonely and unhappy and cried at night. I recalled the frightened high-pitched voice on the telephone when Bruce had pleaded with me to let him come home. Earlier there had been the muffled moaning sounds that Fern and I thought we heard at night.

I recalled how Bruce had been an adventuresome toddler who often tried to sneak away from the play area near our home, to explore forbidden and dangerous territory near the river and in the bush. I now wondered if that little boy might have become trapped behind the stronger personalities inside Bruce's adult psyche. That little boy personality, if he existed, must be desperately unhappy.

But the big problem at the moment was finding a place for my son to live. Lately whenever I found myself having to confront a situation head on and make a decision about what to do about it, I experienced alarming symptoms of stress overload, notably chest pains. Although the pains were mild, I was concerned because I had watched my mother die of a massive heart attack in 1983. During a recent checkup the ECG had not indicated any evidence of heart problems. But I'd heard of people who had dropped dead of a heart attack, despite having passed their ECG with flying colours. I did not want to be one of them.

I talked to Dr. Gow about my dilemma: my personal health concerns and the problem of what to do with my son when he left Manuel's motel. I suggested to the doctor that Bruce's strange behaviour in the Fort Fraser coffee shop could lead to a dangerous situation. If a drunken or aggressive person confronted him, the Macho Bruce would likely surface and he was quite unpredictable. Dr. Gow agreed that the bizarre development should be sufficient evidence to have Bruce committed. He gave me a prescription for nerve pills to relieve my stress symptoms.

When I talked to Hazel, she said the chest pains were probably a signal for me to call for help. Hazel pointed out that I would be of no use to anyone if I dropped dead of a heart attack. It might be a good idea, she suggested, if I called Ed and Connie and filled them in on what was happening.

While I was talking to Ed on the phone I found myself losing control of my emotions, nearly reaching the point of hysteria. I managed to let him know that I could no longer cope with Bruce's situation. Ed consulted with Connie and they decided that Bruce could live with them in Duncan where he had stayed for several weeks during the previous summer. There were facilities available, Ed stated, both in Duncan and in nearby Victoria where Bruce could move to a group home situation when he was ready.

I felt as if a very heavy load had been lifted from me, and Leon said he felt the same way. Dr. Gow expressed relief when I said that if Bruce was agreeable, he would soon be flying south to live with his dad and stepmother. They would do their utmost to persuade him to enter hospital and receive treatments.

Dr. Gow said he was concerned about the lack of long-term care facilities, such as adequately supervised group homes, here in the northern part of the province. The Victoria facility sounded like a great place for Bruce to convalesce.

But first I had to persuade Bruce to move back to Duncan. He hadn't enjoyed being there during the summer; he had described the sprawling Island Highway town as being too dull. But its appeal to him should have grown by now, I decided, after having resided for months in relative isolation in the frozen north.

Friday evening was the deadline for me to inform Bruce about his situation. My daughter Cathy whom I'd come to rely upon so often, accompanied me to the motel. Bruce did not even blink an eye when I told him that he was being evicted. But when I stated that we, Leon and I, felt that he was in desperate need of medication, a flush of anger colored his face and he growled, "I smell fucking hospital." I said yes, we would call the RCMP and have him hospitalized against his will, if it became necessary. But I pointed out that he had an alternative, "Your dad and Connie want you to come down there to live," I said. "If you like you can phone them right now." Bruce was silent for a minute or so. Then he put on his coat and boots, and proceeded toward the motel office to make the call.

By the following afternoon Bruce was packed and ready to go. Leon's cousin Rosemarie had volunteered to drive us from Fraser Lake to the Prince George airport. I had spent the morning helping Bruce sort through his belongings. He had expressed no emotion at all during that time–except once. As I was transporting him from Fort Fraser to meet with Cathy and Rosemarie, he had grinned and mumbled under his breath as we approached Fraser Lake. I noticed him thumb his nose at Mouse Mountain, a favourite local landmark, as we passed by. I took that to mean he was not unhappy to be leaving.

CHAPTER EIGHT

Truth and Madness

"Oh, divine madness
give me the fruit of your sorrows.
Madness is the other side
of truth but so close
to wisdom as to be mistaken for it..."

from "I am the Poor Fisherman"
by Bruce Ray

One evening shortly after Bruce had been safely ensconced at his dad and stepmother's home in Duncan, I decided to dial the telephone number that he had left behind scrawled upon a piece of paper. I felt somewhat embarrassed as I picked up the phone, even though I was the only person in the house. Leon was at work on the afternoon shift at the sawmill, and Fern was staying overnight with a friend. Nobody was watching me except for one of our two cats.

The operator put me through to a New York exchange and somewhere in Brooklyn a telephone rang several times. A woman's voice answered. When I blurted out that I wished to speak to a Miss Dale Olson, she drawled back, "Sorry honey. Ain't nobody 'round here by that name," and hung up the phone.

In February, I began working full-time for the Village of Fraser Lake on a project to research the history of the area and help set up displays in a building that was to house a community museum. I had always been interested in BC history and as a member of the Historical Society, had helped publish *Deeper Roots and Greener Valleys*. Sometimes I found myself more interested in the distant past than I was in present day life. Perhaps it was a way of escaping from the nebulous glimmerings of guilt I still experienced, because I had been unable to cope with Bruce's mental illness.

One day I noticed several brightly coloured posters in town, which advertised an impending visit from a psychic named Isabelle. She would be setting up her business in a room at the Cataline Hotel in Fraser Lake. I had heard of Isabelle's uncanny ability to unearth the past and predict the future, from a neighbour who had consulted with the psychic the year before. For thirty dollars, my neighbour had received a tape of the interview, that she confided was beyond belief.

The posters extolled Isabelle's psychic powers and stated that she was also proficient in the science of handwriting analysis. I remembered the note Bruce had given to me from his alter ego, Dale, on the morning of Cathy and Darwin's baptismal ceremony. Although I realized Bruce had been acutely delusional at the time I was still inordinately intrigued by the Dale Phenomenon. I decided to take the wrinkled slip of paper to Isabelle for a handwriting analysis.

After work I stopped off at the Cataline and proceeded hesitantly toward the room where Isabelle had set up her office. Several young woman were clustered in the hallway outside the door. I gathered they had been in to see the psychic the year before and were going back for the sequel to last year's story. Thirty dollars was a bit expensive, I thought, for what I understood had been mostly bad news. I sat down with the others on the carpet to await my turn.

I was the last of Isabelle's clients for the day. The slightly overweight, motherly woman was not at all like I had pictured a psychic to be. I unfolded the note and explained that the handwriting was that of my son. Isabelle swiftly scanned the writing style and concluded: "He never finishes anything he starts." She said that was evident to her because of the way he compressed his sentences into the central part of the page. Bruce, she added, was also unpredictable. He had changed the way he capitalized his letter Bs, almost every time he wrote them.

She studied the message contained in the cramped barely decipherable prose. The first line read, "I am one of the voices in Bruce's head."

"Was your son on drugs when he wrote this?" she asked. I explained that Bruce suffered from a mental illness called schizophrenia, and that one of his voices, who was a female, had written the note. She took that piece of information in stride. "In that case," she declared, "for the rest of this analysis, I will refer to the writer as 'she'."

Isabelle clarified her philosophy by stating that she was not into the occult. "I am into reality," she said. "But the person who wrote this note is not a good person. She has no substance, like a child who thinks she knows everything but does not."

The psychic looked thoughtful. There was something in the note, she stated hesitantly, which reminded her of a well publicized murder cases: "The one where all those movie stars were killed." She pondered for a moment. "You probably remember," she said finally, "The Charles Manson case."

I was confused. What on earth would Bruce's situation have to do with the Charles Manson case? Manson had somehow managed to convince a number of young people that they should go out and murder a lovely young movie actress named Sharon Tate, as well as several others. There was no way I could take a comparison like that seriously.

"Do you believe the person who wrote this note could be dangerous?" I asked.

Isabelle answered, "Yes, I think she could be." She added, "I hope you can get your son away from her, but I don't think so. I think he's hooked on her."

I noticed that Isabelle was looking at me with an incomprehensible expression on her face. "That person is not good for you either, Mama," she said softly. She would only accept five dollars from me because, as she put it, "I could not help you that much."

Isabelle's warning was unnecessary. For me, the nightmare had ended when Bruce left the motel in Fort Fraser early in January. But for Bruce's stepmother Connie it had just begun. A few days after Bruce arrived at the small motel she managed in Duncan, her husband Ed learned he was to be transferred to work on a construction project in Kenora, Ontario. Ed was a millwright, and the company he worked for was to fly him into the jobsite for approximately one week's work. As it turned out, the job lasted six months and Connie was stuck with the sole responsibility of looking after a very sick young man.

Connie recalls that at first she did not realize how sick he really was. She had picked up a prescription for his anti-psychotic medication from her doctor, and assumed that Bruce was taking it. He was lucid and appeared to be mentally stable. He spent most of his time in his room, while she worked in the downstairs office.

The motel was located along the busy Island Highway. Soon Bruce began to complain about the loud traffic noises at night. Sometimes he would dart outside, ostensibly to escape the sounds. An hour or so later he would return to the motel and go back upstairs to his room. One morning Connie became concerned when she realized that Bruce had not come back inside after his usual nocturnal wanderings. She finally located him, sleeping under a tree at a nearby elementary schoolyard.

Bruce's actions appeared to be influenced by characters he unwittingly created in his own mind. But the actors and actresses on stage gradually assumed more adversarial roles. His nighttime jaunts became more frequent and were often preceded by arguments that he seemed to be having with himself. One night Connie overheard Bruce speaking loudly. He was ordering someone whom he referred to as 'The Bitch' to go away. Other times he exhibited a timid, even frightened demeanor toward an invisible adversary.

Connie had been Bruce's stepmother since he was a small child, and was well acquainted with his lifelong aversion toward taking a bath. I used to wonder if my young son's fear of the bathtub could be traced back to the doctor's attempts to induce labour before Bruce was born. The procedure had released a torrent of amniotic fluid, but it was a full twenty-fours before the baby arrived. As Bruce grew older he had always preferred a shower over a bath. In recent years because of his mental illness, he usually put off all personal hygiene routines for as long as possible. Now Connie observed that Bruce was bathing several times a week. Long, luxurious baths using Connie's expensive soap that contained cold cream. She told him specifically not to use her soap in the bathtub. Bruce had said he liked it because it smelled nice.

Connie waited impatiently one morning outside the bathroom door. Bruce was soaking in the bathtub and her urgings to hurry up and get out of the tub, seemed to be falling on deaf ears. The door had not been properly latched. It swung open and she could see Bruce lathering up, once again, with her bar of soap. The fatuous expression on his face was completely alien to the young man she had known for so many years.

Ed recalls a very odd scene he observed when he accidentally barged in on Bruce in the bathroom. His son lay stark naked on the floor, and appeared to be in serious communication with nothing other than the toilet bowl. Years later Bruce talked about his attempts to expel, orally, certain devils or demons that he believed were inside of his body. This may have been one of those instances.

But there were times when Bruce appeared to be in control of his mental illness. Ed was home from Ontario for a week's holiday when his son announced that he was packing his belongings and moving to America. He said he would catch the bus into Victoria and from there, walk onto a ferry bound for Washington State. Bruce assured his dad that he had enough money for transportation and meals. He said he planned to find a job, and eventually work his way across the United States to New York City.

Bruce was gone for a total of two days. Ed and Connie later agreed that the misadventures he described could not possibly have occurred in that short of a time period. Bruce admitted that he had some memory gaps but insisted he had, indeed, made it to Washington State where, for some inexplicable reason, he had found himself being chased through the thick underbrush by a number of armed border guards. During the course of the pursuit he had, once again, lost all of his belongings.

Ed and Connie noted that Bruce's running shoes were caked with mud. But they remained unconvinced that Bruce's brief journey had taken him away from Vancouver Island.

Despite Connie's persistent urging, Bruce would seldom take antipsychotic medication. When he did, he sometimes took too much or else forgot to take Cogentin to counter side-effects. As a result he experienced mental confusion, muscle rigidity and worst of all, the disconcerting phenomenon where his eyeballs would roll upwards into their sockets. When this occurred, Connie would frantically phone for an ambulance to take him to Emergency at Cowichan District Hospital.

On April 26 Bruce was admitted into the hospital for consultation with resident psychiatrist, Dr. Robin Routledge. According to Dr. Routledge's consultation notes, Bruce had been taken to hospital via ambulance following a call from Connie:

> "Bruce has been deteriorating for some weeks. He's been refusing to take his Stelazine. He has begun hearing critical voices commenting on his "values" and speaking critically to him... His mother is concerned because he's been sleeping outside ("voices won't let me sleep inside") and also wandering away...

> "Examination: Unkempt, but looks as though he is normally tidy. Alert but preoccupied, not really compliant. Eyes staring laterally, odd posture. Seems frightened. Seems more responsive to hallucinations than medical staff.

> "Diagnosis: schizophrenia (provisional)"

Bruce was given medication in the hospital but following his discharge, refused to take any. His nocturnal wanderings continued. More than once, he was picked up by the RCMP for being drunk in a public place. Connie would receive the phone call from police headquarters and have to explain that her stepson was sick, not drunk. He belonged in the hospital–not in jail.

Connie was at her wit's end. While she was occupied with her duties downstairs in the motel office, she constantly worried that Bruce might forget about pots or pans that he sometimes left unattended on the burners of the kitchen stove. He was also becoming careless with lit cigarettes and with the disposal of cigarette butts. One day to her horror she discovered that he had been emptying his ashtray into a dresser drawer. Connie was terrified that Bruce might burn down the motel, and kill himself in the process.

One of her tenants, a fellow named Jim, was quite supportive. Connie found herself relying on Jim to keep an eye on Bruce whenever she needed to run errands that took her away from the motel. On one occasion Connie's tenant likely saved Bruce's life. Jim, who was a bit of an eccentric himself, was also in the habit of taking long solitary walks at night. During one of his excursions he spotted his landlady's son wandering aimlessly in the middle of a street. Jim managed to catch up to Bruce in time to pull him away from the path of an oncoming truck.

Years later Bruce admitted he had been a danger to himself during the time that he resided with his stepmother in the city of Duncan. He had been off medication for almost a year. Living with the hallucinations and delusions that were symptomatic of his illness had become an addiction:

> "When I was in Duncan, I heard voices and I could see spirits...In the sense of my not working, not having children, not having a family; in that sense, I was in this other world and this other world appealed to me. The attraction toward that lifestyle was, at times, quite strong...It was like having a bad relationship with someone. It's very hard to break it off because its something you've lived with for a while. You accept the bad things as well as the good...you need them both."

Connie was determined that somehow she would persuade Bruce to take medication on a regular basis. Her doctor suggested that she initiate a program to monitor each and every one of his prescribed dosages. Twice a day she would go upstairs to his room with a glass of water. She watched Bruce place the tiny tablets into his mouth and wash them down. Before she left she would carefully count the number of pills that still remained in the bottle.

A week went by and there was no noticeable change in the state of Bruce's mental health. The mystery was solved when Connie emptied the wastepaper basket in his room. At the bottom of the plastic container she noticed a number of small white pills. Bruce had somehow managed to fake swallowing the pills. After Connie had left the room, he would spit them into the basket.

But the routine had not been totally ineffective. Bruce finally recognized that he needed medical treatment. One day without being prompted, he checked himself into the Cowichan District Hospital. In the psychiatric ward, he met others who suffered from symptoms similar to his own. One was a young woman named Kara* whom Bruce later came to know quite well.

Kara was an attractive girl with short brown hair and small features. She told Bruce that when she was twelve she had been raped by an older brother. Now in her early twenties, she constantly battled the debilitating symptoms of chronic schizophrenia.

Kara told Bruce a very disturbing story. She had first become overwhelmed by voices that seemed to be coming from inside of her head when she was about sixteen. Late one night these voices had compelled her to enter her brother's bedroom armed with a sharp knife, and sever his penis. Bruce did not know whether to believe her story or not.

Soon after, Kara was released from hospital into a group home on the outskirts of Duncan which was called Wisteria House.

Bruce had been admitted into hospital on June 5th. At that time he confided to Dr. Routlege that he wanted treatment for voices that were harassing him. He said he had been spitting everywhere he went because he had a bad taste in his mouth.

Dr. Routledge was concerned that in response to his auditory hallucinations, Bruce could become a suicide risk. In his notes he suggested: "I think Bruce will remain recurrently ill until he agrees to [taking] injectable long-acting medication."

During his stint in the psyche ward Bruce developed a strong rapport with Connie's doctor, Dr. D.M. Smith. Bruce told me later that Dr. Smith supported my long-held theory that his 1984 mental breakdown had been caused by the high quality marijuana that he'd been indulging in. My son confided that having a mental illness was less painful to him when he perceived it as being caused by a street drug, rather than a precondition he was born with.

Drs. Smith and Routledge, at Bruce's request, made all the arrangements for him to be discharged into the care of the management at Wisteria House. Bruce had admitted he needed to be in a monitored environment. But his thoughts and feelings were still polarized. Late one night he slipped away from his hospital bed and returned to Connie's motel dressed only in his pajamas. The next morning when Connie approached him, he refused to take any medication.

Eventually the doctors were able to persuade Bruce that he should try a medication called Modecate, which would be administrated every three weeks through an intermusclar injection. They explained to him that Modecate's anti-psychotic ingredients would be released slowly into his bloodstream and he would no longer need to take daily medication.

Early in July, Bruce moved into a room at Wisteria House and a few days later, phoned to let me know of his new address and telephone number. He was back writing poetry again, he told me; and for the first time in years he had a job, working part-time at a local greenhouse. The greenhouse was part of a giant horticultural project that had been specifically developed to employ people who suffer from mental illnesses. Bruce said he enjoyed working in the soil and watching plants grow. I told him he probably took after his grandfather, my dad, who was now in a nursing home at 100 Mile House. Feeble as Dad was he still found joy in helping to cultivate a small vegetable garden outside on the grounds.

It was wonderful to hear Bruce's warm, friendly tone of voice again. His voice had always been a barometer of his mental health and to me, it was as if he had risen from the dead.

Bruce described the sprawling municipality of Duncan as a highway town with very little happening in the way of culture or entertainment. But Victoria, a much larger city, was only a short bus ride away. The group home attendants were lenient with residents who wished to visit out of town. Bruce had recently been invited to stay overnight in Victoria with a friend from Saltspring Island. He had accompanied the fellow on a day trip to a secluded beach. Bruce later confided that he had been embarrassed because he was the only one on the beach who wore clothes. Eventually he doffed his garments, and felt less conspicuous.

Kara was Bruce's constant companion. Their friendship soon developed into a fragile, mutually affectionate relationship. Both had been diagnosed with schizophrenia but their symptoms differed. Kara was often paranoid and easily frightened. She firmly believed that certain people were able to tune in to her thoughts and read her mind. Although Bruce's condition had improved immensely, there were times when the voices in his head were loud and bothersome. Kara would attempt to dispel these voices by stamping her feet and yelling, urging the voices to go away. Bruce found her efforts appealing. They seemed to help and he was grateful that she cared.

But schizophrenia is a lonely disease. Bruce found it difficult to cope with his own symptoms and maintain a relationship with a woman who was even more mentally unstable than he was. His sister Debbie recalls that the romance was not as fulfilling as it might have been:

"I met Kara once when I was camped on Saltspring with the kids. Bruce brought her to visit us there. She seemed very nervous, and her responses had little to do with what was said. The day was sunny and beautiful. We sat around on the grass and talked. She and Bruce didn't talk together the way a couple would, or touch. They each seemed very alone, though at times she seemed to feel threatened and leaned toward him for protection. I thought she seemed frightened.

I tried to reassure her by being open and friendly but her fears didn't seem to have anything to do with my behavior, or with anything outside herself that I could see."

I was ecstatic when Bruce told me about Kara. "Now that he has a real flesh-and-blood girlfriend, that should be the end of Dale," I predicted to Leon and Fern. I had recently told them about my conversation with the voice that had occupied the feminine side of Bruce's psyche. Fern, now thirteen, was intrigued by the story. Leon was less impressed.

My job at the museum ended in August, just in time for my husband's annual vacation from the sawmill. We had recently purchased a small travel trailer and decided to take it out to Leon's parents' farm in Alberta for its inaugural journey. Most summers we just holidayed at home, and his parents visited us here. The elderly couple usually arrived early in July, his dad all set to troll the lakes for char and fly-fish the rivers for rainbow trout. Brian, Leon's son from a former marriage, his wife Jackie and two daughters also enjoyed camping and fishing in the Fraser Lake area. Sometimes Leon's older son Gene would make it out as well.

We usually timed Leon's vacation to coincide with everyone else's visits. But this year his dad was not well. The family farm was about to be sold, and for the first time in their lives, Leon's parents would be moving into a house in town. It was a bittersweet time for his mother especially because she loved the farm, but it was also an occasion for a big family get-together. All but one of Leon's five older children, with their spouses and children, arrived for a visit. Fern became reacquainted with her nieces and nephews, many of whom were her age and older. Everyone asked me how Bruce was, and I was happy to finally be able to tell them that he was fine.

But Bruce was having difficulty adjusting to his new medication. Although Modecate is a long lasting injectable drug, its properties are similar to Stelazine; especially in regards to side-effects. On November 30, Dr. Routledge made the following observations after having admitted Bruce into the hospital:

> "Past History: When we first gave Ray neurolptics, he had severe torticollis and spasm of the muscles of mastication (throat and mouth cramp). These resolved with Cogentin.
>
> "History of Present Illness: Bruce notices sudden cramps in his eyes that roll his eyes up. Once these start, they keep happening. Once they start, he hears voices that don't make any sense and attributes the eye cramps to the voices.
>
> "Examination: Well dressed and groomed. Compliant to exam. Alert. Well oriented, good access to all memories. Thought is self referential and a little illogical. . . Mood is embarrassment. No suicide thought. Cogwheel rigidity is present.
>
> "Conclusion: This is a break-through side-effect of long acting neurolptic. The stress of these cramps (which ARE easier to have once you've had one) activates sub-verbal hallucinations and delusional perceptions of made movements, primary symptoms of schizophrenia.
>
> "Suggest: Increase Cogentin."

I was finally able to visit my son in the spring of 1988. This time I travelled by myself on the bus. Ed was out of town on a construction project at Tahsis on northern Vancouver Island, and Connie had invited me to stay with her at the motel. Debbie planned to join us the following day from her new home on Hornby Island.

Debbie's move to Hornby from Saltspring Island represented a positive transition in her self-image, she had told me. To commemorate her new life, she was changing her name from Debbie to Phoenix. I was not pleased, although I tried not to express my feelings to her on the telephone. It had been me who had named her back in 1957. I had been a big Debbie Reynolds fan, along with every second mother-to-be at the time. My poor daughter had been only one of numerous Debbies in almost every class she attended at school. I understood why she wanted to change it, but it was going to be difficult for me to get used to her new name.

It was a beautiful spring day when Connie and I drove to Wisteria House to visit Bruce. The group home was located several kilometers from downtown Duncan, in a semi-rural neighbourhood carpeted with dense brush and trees. Because of all the foliage, the houses appeared to be more isolated from one another than they really were.

The residence was a large rambling building with plenty of varnished wood and country charm. Connie was acquainted with almost everyone. She introduced me to a tall gangly man named Fred who seemed to be in charge–of the kitchen, anyway. Fred announced that square pizzas were on the menu for supper that night and he would be the one to cook them. At that, everyone within earshot cheered enthusiastically. Bruce came up from his basement room and appeared to be cheerful too although quiet. It was an awkward time for the two of us. We had not seen each other since our unsettling farewell at the Prince George airport in December 1986.

I returned with Bruce to his room to peruse his recent artwork and writings, while Connie visited with Fred and the others in the kitchen. Later Bruce led Connie and I down a long narrow corridor to a front room that was blue with cigarette smoke. A number of people sat stiffly upon sofas and chairs in almost complete silence. Each puffed diligently on a cigarette and stared at the blank screen of an inoperative television set or out the open window. Bruce brought out his own makings and proceeded to roll a cigarette. Soon he too puffed in silence.

Connie introduced me to Kara who appeared to be in a world of her own. She barely acknowledged our introduction. Bruce told me later he was still fond of her even though he had not been able to handle the stress of sustaining the relationship.

When Fred came into the room, the atmosphere lightened considerably. He was so full of vitality and enthusiasm that I assumed he was a member of the staff. Connie told me later that he was a resident. He too suffered from schizophrenia.

Connie drove Bruce and I to a downtown shopping center where I purchased a pair of blue jeans and other clothes for Bruce. He had gained a considerable amount of weight since going on the new medication and none of his old clothes fit. Later we picked Debbie –now Phoenix–up at the bus depot and returned to Connie's motel for a visit.

Bruce told us that he planned to move about 50 kilometers up-island to the city of Nanaimo. He wanted to attend classes at Malaspino College, perhaps enrolling in jazz guitar and creative writing courses. Connie and Ed were thinking of moving up there too; to the community of Ladysmith, just south of Nanaimo. They would be near enough to provide him with a home base, if he should be in need of one.

As I took photographs of my son and daughter beside the daffodils that grew in brilliant yellow clumps outside the motel, I reflected on the snow and ice that still permeated the landscape back home. There was no doubt in my mind that Bruce and Phoenix were both much better off down here in southern part of the province.

Bruce's psychiatrist and his assistants were supportive of him, offering counseling services as well as monitoring his medication needs. According to Dr. Routledge's progress reports, Bruce was a very reasonable, gentle and caring person who was gradually coming to terms with feelings of guilt, anger and helplessness toward various family members. On June 9, 1988, the doctor wrote:

> "I met Bruce alone in my clinic at Shawnigan. He tells me he is moving to Columbian House in Nanaimo to go into a music course at Malaspino College, majoring in voice. This seems a wise idea for Bruce. I had him sing a recent song he has composed and he does indeed have a powerful and original voice.

> "Bruce and I spoke more of bridges, and of him being a bridge within his family...He spoke with his father about not needing him as a father, but as a friend, and father agreed with this. He also raised this topic with his mother, but she reacted badly: perhaps she took his idea as a condemnation of his mothering..."

In July, Bruce left Duncan for Nanaimo. Ed and Connie helped him pack his belongings and moved him into a group home called Columbian House. That fall he applied for a student loan to cover expenses for a full year of studies in jazz guitar and music at Malaspino College. When he phoned to tell me that his loan application had been accepted, he was ecstatic. Bruce was especially pleased because the funding would include money for him to purchase a guitar.

With Christmas approaching, I invited Bruce to come home to Fraser Lake for the holidays. He assured me that he was now mentally stable and able to handle the long bus ride. It was to be our last Christmas at the old place. We had purchased a log house about eight kilometres down the road and planned to move in as soon the building was warmed. It had been unoccupied for some time and log houses take forever to heat during a typically cold northern winter. When the logs have warmed, however, a comfortable inside temperature is easy to maintain.

I suggested to Bruce that he come up early in time to attend one of our newly-formed writers' group meetings. Ian Kluge was a member as were a few other published writers. Our meetings were usually constructive and a lot of fun.

Bruce arrived on what turned out to be the coldest day of the winter. It was thirty-seven degrees below zero and he was not dressed for the weather. When the poorly heated bus finally stopped in front of the Fraser Lake Inn, he was almost comatose with the cold.

Our first stop was at Cathy and Darwin's house trailer. I was pleased to note that Bruce's animosity of two years ago toward Darwin seemed to have dissipated completely. The familiar comments about NHL players and games that once again dominated my son and son-in-law's conversation, were like music to my ears.

I was grateful that Cathy had invited us to her home for the annual Christmas dinner. Fern and I had been packing seldom-used household items into cardboard boxes and stacking them in every available space throughout the house. We could barely walk around. The last snowstorm before the recent cold spell had blocked the driveway to our new home. Until Leon found time to do some plowing, the boxes could not be moved. It was a good thing, I thought, that this year's

Charlie Brown Christmas tree did not take up much room.

Bruce brought with him the guitar that he had purchased with a portion of the money from his student loan. He was registered to begin college courses early in the new year. He now had a repertoire of new songs, including one that he and a friend named Louis Devoin had collaborated on. Bruce wrote the lyrics and Louis, an accomplished jazz guitarist, had improvised the tune. They had added some musical accompaniment and recorded it professionally in a studio. I listened to the song and found it to be quite pleasing.

The office of the Canadian Mental Health Association in Nanaimo was equipped with electronic typewriters and copiers that Bruce had received permission to use. He had typed and photocopied many of his poems and compiled them into two volume sets, which he planned to give out as Christmas presents.

I particularly liked the title poem from one volume which he called "Tracks."

> When I write I scratch images
> in the sand of imagination.
> The wind blows and fills these scratches
> causing them to disappear.
> Such is the transientness
> of my thoughts
> they vanish as if
> they were never perceived...

Bruce was disappointed because Ian Kluge was unable to attend our writers' group meeting. We did have a good turnout of other members, though, despite the fresh snow that came with the warming temperatures. Following introductions Bruce read aloud from his latest composition, a poem he had titled "The Laughter of the Gods." The poem was well written but I had trouble discerning its message. It seemed to be a somewhat vitriolic diatribe directed against those who practice religious hypocrisy.

Bruce received an enthusiastic response from his audience. One fellow, a budding playwright who also wrote contemporary poetry, was particularly impressed. He insisted that Bruce's poem was publishable.

He stated that in his estimation, "The Laughter of the Gods" was one of the best pieces of poetry ever written.

I was less enthusiastic. Bruce's poem contained a number of biblical references. I was terrified that Cathy and Darwin might one day read "The Laughter of the Gods" and be offended by his clever use of words and phrasings. I mentioned later that I thought he had come down a little heavy on the church-goers. Bruce replied that the intent of the poem was to be farcical. He had not meant it to be a put-down of those who lived by honest Christian principles.

Years later I realized the poem "The Laughter of the Gods" was missing from Bruce's collection of writings. I wondered guiltily if he had thrown the piece away during one of his depressive moments; perhaps because of my timid, self-serving criticism.

Ian Kluge did manage a visit with Bruce on the very day that we were moving into our new home. Ian was overjoyed at finding Bruce to be mentally stable again. The two of them chatted animatedly while Leon and I removed boxes and small pieces of furniture from around the couch where they sat.

After Bruce left Fraser Lake for Nanaimo I experienced an intense feeling of well-being. "The nightmare is over," I announced happily to everyone who was interested, including Dr. Gow. "Thanks to the injectable medication, Bruce's schizophrenia is under control. He is now able to take college courses and carry on with his life as he had intended to do back in 1984."

A few months earlier I had begun the self-imposed task of compiling bits and pieces of information concerning the history of my son's schizophrenia. I have since learned that family members sometimes need to assimilate thoughts and feelings relating to a loved one's illness. Writing Bruce's story was probably my way of coping. I began to neglect my housework and most of the indulgences I normally extended to husband and daughter. I became obsessed with an overwhelming compulsion to document each of the bizarre events that had caused us consternation over the past four years. By the time Bruce arrived for his holiday visit, I had almost completed the narrative, titled *A Journey Through the World of Schizophrenia*.

Now that he was gone, I decided to culminate my *Journey* with a happy ending: "My son is now mentally stable," I wrote. "He lives comfortably and contentedly in the Vancouver Island city of Nanaimo."

CHAPTER NINE

Impressions
(Nanaimo, BC)

"Maybe in some far-off romantic place
where lilies grow
and doves rustle their feathers
by the pinions of the sea
I will taste the coconut milk
of summer and think of love..."

From "Impressions"
by Bruce Ray, 1991

N anaimo has been affectionately described by those who live there as an ugly old town with a sense of community. It is a people-oriented city where those who have homes and a job are usually not too proud to assist those who do not. For many years it was the home of the late Tommy Douglas, founder of the New Democratic Party of Canada. Mr. Douglas, known as the voice of the common people, is fondly remembered in Nanaimo.

The downtown area of the city, population about sixty thousand, is dominated by several old mortar and brick-faced buildings trimmed with ornamental latticework. These enduring structures loom loftily above less imposing wood-frame shops and businesses. Narrow streets and avenues wind helter-skelter across the hilly landscape. At times the stink from a nearby pulp mill combines unpleasantly with the odor of salt spray and fish that permeates the harbour. But the view from almost everywhere is spectacular.

During the summer months a large banner is strung from the rooftop of the Tally-Ho Motel and Restaurant, proclaiming Nanaimo to be the Belly-Flop Capital of the World. A bungee-jumping enterprise and the well-publicized annual bathtub races to Vancouver are other claims to fame.

But Nanaimo has a strong cultural core. Over the years it has been home to many artists, writers and musicians. Malaspina College is well-known throughout the province for its commitment to offering quality courses in the performing arts and music.

Bruce was confident that he was now mentally stable and he looked forward to the challenge of attending classes. But he was dismayed to learn that the group home where he now lived, located on the north side of the city, was many kilometers away from the college.

Columbian House was a tightly monitored facility with rules that controlled almost every aspect of everyday living. Bruce particularly had trouble conforming to the rules about where and when he could smoke his cigarettes. His fellow residents were far less mentally stable than he was. Despite his complaints, the people at Mental Health Services seemed reluctant to move him into a less-structured environment.

The friendly and relaxed atmosphere Bruce had become accustomed to at Wisteria House in Duncan was now just a fond memory. At times he bitterly regretted having broken off the romance he had shared with the troubled but very-often-charming Kara.

Bruce developed a strategy that would persuade Mental Health to transfer him to a different residence, preferably one closer to the college. Later he told his dad that he had deliberately broken the house rules limiting cigarette smoking. The strategy worked, but he did not endear himself to the staff at Columbian House or to the people who worked at Mental Health Services. He was moved first to a semi-independent living residence on Stewart Avenue and later to a boarding home only a few blocks away from Malaspina College.

Semi-independent living residences are ideal for many people with schizophrenia. The mentally ill are often able to perform everyday chores as well as anyone when their symptoms are under control. They can cook meals, clean, and do their own laundry with only a little help from a house parent or supervisor from time to time. Bruce was too well for the structured environment at Columbian House, but he was not able to cope entirely on his own. Even when his mental condition was stable the voices were always there, mumbling and muttering at the back of his mind. Most of the time he could ignore them, but sometimes they were a distraction.

It was during his Christmas visits to Fraser Lake in 1988 and 1989 that Fern heard the almost imperceptible droning sound of Bruce's voice in the middle of the night. The disconcerting noises emanated from his bedroom, directly below her own. It was during those visits, in particular, that I had rejoiced in what appeared to be the excellent state of Bruce's mental health. He visited with friends and attended family get-togethers just like in old times. Fern did not want to burst my bubble. But one time I recall her telling me, "I don't think Bruce is as well as you think he is, Mom."

But Bruce had no problem making new friends and maintaining relationships. Fern's unthinking remark, "If you didn't know he was schizophrenic, you'd think he was normal" seemed to be very apt. Most of the time, anyway.

One of Bruce's new friends in Nanaimo was a part-time musician named Louis Devoin whom Bruce met in the fall of 1988:

"I met Bruce at The Inside Passage drop-in center. A friend of mine, Peder Long, ran this tiny place which was almost like a hole in the wall. It was in the basement of the Bank of Montreal building. Peder didn't make any money from it; it's just that he likes to support music and all other creative endeavors. Sometimes there were lots of people there and sometimes there were none.

"He opened it for people who liked to practice their music, recite a bit of poetry or hang their artwork on the walls. It didn't cost them any money. Peder was usually there between nine and eleven every night. People just dropped by to work on their stuff and have a coffee.

"Some of these people just drifted in off the street. Lots of unusual characters. But Peder had a way of making everyone feel comfortable–with no real formalities and as much as possible, unconditional acceptance of everyone who came in the door.

"Peder and I played jazz music together. He played the saxophone and I play guitar. Sometimes I worked at music with the people who came to Peder's place. It was sort of a project for me. I would play melody or backup for them.

"Bruce started coming in quite a lot. I first met him when he was living on Stewart Avenue. I had worked with another schizophrenic before, on my own. But Bruce was easier to work with. His work was pretty good. I liked the imagery he put into his songs. He had very little musical sophistication which really isn't a necessity. You can get other musicians to do that. Bruce and I set up one song together and put it on tape. It was called "When You're in a Dream."

"I didn't know much about the disease of schizophrenia, but I liked Bruce as a person. He had a sense of humour and was an interesting character to be with. He told me about his voices. It was kind of eerie. It was like he had a relationship with them and they had a life of their own. But most of the time I had a hard time believing that Bruce was even sick. He was a gentle man, a poet, who never displayed any violence. If anything, he went out of his way to avoid trouble...The only really disturbing interpersonal trait about Bruce that I noticed was that he would drift off and laugh to himself sometimes.

"When Bruce was on-stage he appeared calm. But I sometimes wondered if he really knew where he was. He didn't make the connection with his audience that he needed to do. Sometimes he would go off into his own world and people would sort of look at him...He never worked on his stage presence, which you have to do if you want to be a musician."

When he was up for Christmas, Bruce had mentioned his dream, which was to become a trained musician like his friend and mentor Louis Devoin. Later after he had moved his belongings into a house only a few blocks from the college, Bruce felt he was one step closer toward realizing that dream. He told me on the phone that he was looking forward to attending classes soon.

Bruce's new home was located at the top of a long steeply-sloped hill. The three-storey house was managed by a pleasant energetic woman named Gail, who cooked, cleaned and did laundry for her residents. Bruce told me he was happy to be living there. From his upstairs bedroom window he had an excellent view of the Nanaimo harbour. And in the evenings he could see the far-off lights of North Vancouver.

As it turned out Bruce was not able to handle the stress of carrying a full-course college load. He told me later that some of his courses were extremely complex with little in the way of explanation from the instructors. He found himself falling further and further behind in his studies. After two stressful confusing months he decided to give up.

My heart ached for my son when he phoned to tell me he had given up on his dream to attain a college degree in music. His voice was strained as he expressed another concern: the bank was after him to repay his student loan. "I just can't do it," Bruce stated. "I don't have that kind of money."

My dad had passed away in November leaving me a small inheritance. I assured Bruce that Grampa would have wanted me to pay off the loan. That way he could keep the guitar with a clear conscience. To be fair to Grampa's other grandchildren, I decided that they too should receive a few dollars.

It was in the summer of 1989 that my husband and I exchanged roles. For years Leon had suffered from the chronic pain of arthritis. That summer he took early retirement from his increasingly arduous job at the sawmill, and I found myself a real job. For the past year I had been working off and on at a local hardware store. I was also the Watkins products salesperson for Fraser Lake. One of my customers suggested that I apply for a job as a home support worker. She said the agency where she worked preferred to hire middle-aged women rather than younger ones, because they were better able to relate to the needs and preferences of incapacitated seniors. The job would be mostly housework, she warned, but it was rewarding because the clients were usually very appreciative.

I got the job, and it did turn out to be rewarding. My first clients were a nice man who was a paraplegic and his frail but determined wife. She was looking after his needs despite the fact that she was not well either.

The love they shared was inspirational. One of my fondest memories is of the two of them sitting side-by-side on a swing that she had set up in the living room. They smiled and held hands as the swing rocked gently back and forth. He was a heavy man, and it was a job transferring him from his bed, even with the help of a hydraulic lift. But it was worth it. The job had an added bonus for me, for when I was concerned with the needs of others I was not worrying about Bruce.

But my son is a resilient and optimistic individual. Bruce and I share the philosophy that if an endeavor is not successful, it was probably not meant to be; one should pursue other interests and goals. He continued to visit Peder Long's drop-in center in the evenings to sing and play guitar. Louis Devoin and his wife had loaned him a drafting table. They assured Bruce that the slanted desk would make it easier for him to fulfill his drawing aspirations. He immersed himself in writing poetry and began to connect with other Nanaimo writers. Fellow writer Mildred Trembley recalls that Bruce often attended the Nanaimo Writers' Group meetings:

> "I remember when he first began to attend and bring some of his poems to workshop them. (In that group, we critique each other's work.) I remember feeling very moved by some of Bruce's work; I recognized the soul of a true poet. The love of words, rhythm, beauty was very apparent. At that time, he was very attracted to the work of William Blake. (I am too!) But we encouraged him to move into more modern stuff, which he did. He also shared a story or two with us that he had written; I think one was the schizophrenic experience. They were quite good also; Bruce is a born writer...
>
> "I talked to Bruce at length once, after a meeting, about his illness. He seemed to have a remarkably good grasp of it. He described the schizophrenic world to me, and as I write a lot of surrealistic sort of thing, it didn't seem too alien to me...
>
> "Another time, I did a poetry reading with Bruce and three other poets. We read in a small bookstore on Commercial Street in Nanaimo and all enjoyed ourselves."

Members of the Fraser Lake Writers Group also liked Bruce's poetry. All four of his poems, which I had submitted, were selected by the editorial committee to be published in an upcoming anthology entitled *Seasonings*. The book was published in the spring of 1990.

One year after I began my new job I became eligible for that wonderful entitlement: summer vacation. Instead of using the money I had accumulated on an actual holiday, I decided I would send it to my oldest daughter. Phoenix could use the money to transport herself, her children and her brother to Fraser Lake for a visit. She had recently purchased an ancient Toyota which, she assured me, was in good enough shape to make it up from Hornby Island.

Phoenix had not seen her brother since he moved to Nanaimo two years earlier. She stopped at his residence for a short while, before proceeding on with him to Fraser Lake:

> "With my younger boy Cory, I drove up the hill to the house on Selkirk Drive. It was high on a hillside with a gorgeous view of the city and the water.

> "The house was tall. Three storeys, I think. Very imposing. The yard was well-kept and the whole place gave an impression of affluence. Once inside, Cory and I went upstairs to the kitchen where I was offered a cup of coffee by the lady who ran the place. I sipped while Bruce got ready. The place was beautiful, with sundecks and lush, new-looking furnishings in every room. Nothing looked old or uncared for. The lady, whose name I can't remember, was friendly and seemed to care for Bruce and the other residents. I was glad to see him in such a good situation.

> "The trip to Fraser Lake was fun. Bruce and I talked comfortably and I sang songs to keep myself alert while driving. I sang every country and western song I had ever learned, and Bruce didn't seem to mind. The car ran well and Cory especially liked having his uncle along with us. Krys (as Crystal now preferred to be called) and Travis were in Edmonton that summer. They caught the bus out and joined us for our two week's stay in Fraser Lake."

A few days after Bruce arrived at our place with Phoenix and her children, I visited with him out in the camper trailer where he slept. I had set up a television set, ghetto blaster and typewriter out there for his use. Bruce appeared to be despondent. He told me he felt isolated from everyone else in the family. I wondered if it was because I had set him up in the trailer, away from the house. "You're the only smoker in the crowd," I explained. "Out here, you are free to light up as many cigarettes as you wish without bothering anyone with second-hand smoke." I suggested that if he preferred, he could move his writing and smoking paraphernalia to the front porch; the weather was warm and a table was already set up out there. After that, Bruce spent much of his time out on the front porch.

But the next two weeks did little to elevate my son's inordinately depressed state of mind. Phoenix was enjoying the opportunity to spend time in Fraser Lake with her children. She buzzed over the backroads in her little car, transporting them to the beach, to town and to our old house. Fern was occupied with a summer job, but sometimes Cathy's children would accompany them home. My grandchildren were all in the early stages of adolescence. Bruce may have been somewhat overwhelmed by their noisy exuberance. I know I was.

Bruce did mention that he was looking forward to participating in a magazine publishing project. It would be sponsored by Canadian Mental Health in Nanaimo. He had already written the first installment of a darkly humourous tale entitled "The Return of the Piltdown Man" which was to appear in the first issue of the magazine. He planned to serialize the rest of the story in subsequent issues.

Later that summer Bruce and Phoenix were destined to meet once again, this time at a poetry festival on Galiano Island. Phoenix had been developing her talent for writing poetry in recent years. Both she and Bruce had been invited to participate at the outdoor event. Bruce told me later that he had read the first installment of "The Return of the Piltdown Man," in the pouring rain, to a very appreciative audience.

The CMHA magazine publishing project was tailor-made for Bruce's talents. He was equally proficient in writing and in the graphic arts. In the fall of 1990, a creative writing instructor named Cheryl Penner* was hired by the mental health agency to, as she would describe it, hone the literary abilities of a small but dedicated group of students. Cheryl had little knowledge of the disease of schizophrenia, although almost everyone in her class was designated as suffering from a mental illness.

In the introduction to the first issue of the magazine, appropriately entitled *Voices*, Cheryl wrote: "There has been an invigorating exchange of ideas throughout the classes and a great deal of learning has taken place on all sides. Through our discussions of fiction, poetry and non-fiction, we have explored our common passion for the written word. A special thank you to Bruce Ray for his striking graphics and comic strip pages. The drawings he has done expressly for this issue aptly capture the essence of the words expressed in this volume by his classmates…"

In January 1991, Bruce was once again enrolled at Malaspina College. This time the course was in desktop publishing, and the tuition was being paid for by CMHA. His creative writing instructor had enrolled in the course as well. She looked forward to producing issues of *Voices* magazines that would reflect desktop publishing polish.

Cheryl was an attractive young woman. She appeared to accept Bruce for what he was despite his schizophrenia. He basked in her encouragement and the praise she so often expressed of his multi-talents. Bruce very soon found himself becoming infatuated with his teacher. But when he boldly phoned her at home to inquire if she would go out with him, Cheryl was dismayed by the infringement upon her privacy. She replied that it would not be appropriate because of their teacher-student relationship.

Bruce did have a girlfriend, a fellow creative writing student named Lisa*, whom he visited quite often in her home. The two friends were not intimate and, possibly because she still resided with her parents, never got past the hand-holding stage. Lisa was nineteen years of age and a talented poet. She and Bruce had much in common. They conversed for hours on almost a daily basis.

Lisa did not have a mental illness or disorder, but she confided to Bruce that she suffered from the psychological pain of ongoing sexual abuse by a trusted family member. She had not disclosed her secret to anyone else, even to her mother. Bruce was concerned about Lisa. He told me later it was ironic that so many of his female friends had been sexually molested by family members.

On January 15, 1991, Bruce phoned to tell me about how his life was finally turning around. He was very happy, he said. The first issue of *Voices* was hot off the presses with the second issue right behind it. But the most important thing he wanted to tell me was that his mental health was now completely stable. It had been that way for some time.

Bruce sounded excited when he said his doctor Dr. Walker had some information about schizophrenia which suggested that the disease sometimes burns itself out. The only way to learn if this had indeed occurred would be to go on what was termed a drug holiday. Dr. Walker had agreed to monitor the withdrawal of his medication dosages. It had to be done gradually, Bruce stated. Otherwise it might be too much of a shock to the central nervous system.

Bruce had apparently blamed his medication, at least in part, for his inability to manage the stress of taking college courses the previous year. Dr. Walker later wrote the following in a Nanaimo Regional General Hospital report: "Patient had previously been well controlled on I.M. Modecate but gone off because he felt it would impair his enrolling in Malaspina College this fall..."

By the end of April, Bruce was completely weaned from all medication. During the final stage of this process the dosage had been decreased to the point where he no longer took the anti-psychotic by injection. On April 27, when he phoned me, he said he had swallowed the last of his pills.

On May 5th, Bruce's birthday, I called his residence on Selkirk Drive. The male voice on the telephone sounded sympathetic. He told me Bruce had gone into the hospital the previous evening. When I contacted Nanaimo Regional General Hospital, I learned that he had been transported almost a hundred and sixty kilometers up-island to a hospital in Comox.

Later I talked to Gail Asselin, Bruce's landlady, and learned that despite his optimism my son's mental health had seriously declined in recent weeks. Gail had been completely in the dark as to why this was so.

"Bruce was doing quite well when he came to my place," Gail told me. "He was capable of handling his own medication and able to remember when to take it...I did not know that he was being weaned off his medication. Perhaps his doctor should have gotten in touch with me and asked me if I could see any changes? I remember thinking, 'What's wrong with him? How come he's not well?'

"The people at my house usually did not get ill," Gail clarified. "They took their medication because they didn't want to go into the hospital. But weeks and weeks went by and Bruce wasn't getting any better…I guess he was just too ill to go back to the doctor on his own.

"Bruce always stayed up later at night than the others. He usually went to bed around one o'clock. The guys all had the run of the kitchen. I got up in the middle of the night and there was this mess. Bruce was wandering around. He didn't know what he was doing. He was rolling cigarettes and throwing the tubes around. I told him to get in the car and I took him to Emergency at the hospital.

"But trying to get him in there was like pulling teeth! They looked at me as if I didn't know anything at all. They just asked, 'What's wrong with him?' They seemed to think he shouldn't be there because he was not a danger to himself or anyone else."

I asked Gail if Bruce had put on the appearance of being well after they had reached the hospital. She answered, "No way, any ordinary person could have seen he was not well! But it was a Friday. They wanted him to wait and see his doctor on Monday. I told them he needed to see a doctor right away. They said there was no room in the hospital. I said, 'Take him someplace where there is room!' So they took him to Comox Hospital."

According to notes written on May 5, by Doctor Wayne Crowe of St. Joseph's Hospital in Comox, Bruce was suffering from paranoid delusions of being raped and needed treatment for his own safety. A few days later he was transferred back to Nanaimo. Bruce sounded despondent when he phoned me from Nanaimo Hospital on May 7. He said he had learned one thing from the experience: "It's quite obvious," he stated, "that I need to be on medication."

Bruce added that he would soon be moving away from Gail's boarding home where he had been living for the past two and a half years. He planned to move into a residence that was managed by the CMHA. Their office was located in the same building and he would be free to work on their computers.

"That way," Bruce explained, "I can be right there whenever I want to work on *Voices* magazine."

CHAPTER TEN

Witchsong

"I am a song
That whispers in the treetops
I am the wind
Caressing the grassy hills
I am a hawk
Soaring on the breeze
I am the antelope
Running wild and free
I am a driftwood
Circling in shallow waters
I am a feather
Falling gracefully on the air."

Bruce Ray 1986

In June 1991, my sixteen-year-old daughter Fern and I made plans to vacation together for a week in the vicinity of Vancouver Island. Phoenix had been invited to participate in the second annual Gulf Islands Poetry Festival on Galiano Island and I wanted to attend. Bruce too had been invited to the event which was scheduled for the weekend of July 20.

I remembered that when we had visited Phoenix on Saltspring in 1986, our ferry had stopped at all the loosely patch-worked islands between Tsawwassen on the mainland, south of Vancouver, and Swartz Bay near Victoria. Galiano Island had been the long narrow land mass just east and slightly north of Saltspring. At the time I had thought it would be great fun to go island hopping. Now I would have the opportunity to hop–a little bit.

On the first leg of our trip Fern and I planned to take a bus to Courtney, approximately one hundred and fifty kilometers north of Nanaimo. The ferry terminal that serviced the northern gulf islands of Denman and Hornby was located just thirty kilometers south of the city.

In Courtney we would pick up the automobile I had reserved at a rental agency. Fern had recently obtained her driver's licence, and was ecstatic at the prospect of driving a brand new car. "You can drive for short distances where traffic is lighter on the smaller islands," I promised Fern. Her sister would be our designated driver when we travelled south on the busy Island Highway toward Galiano.

Bruce phoned and expressed a strong desire to visit his home town of Fraser Lake. I told him of our vacation plans for July and that he'd see Fern and me at that time anyway. I suggested that he come up for Christmas instead. He insisted he wanted to come up and view the familiar countryside now while it was still green and beautiful, as opposed to in the winter. He had decided to sell his guitar, Bruce told me, and use part of the money to pay for the bus trip up. I agreed to advertise it on a local radio program called Tradeo and put up posters on the bulletin boards in town. Later I phoned him back to tell him that I would purchase the musical instrument myself, as a Father's Day gift to Leon from Fern and me.

It was on the July 1st long weekend that Bruce arrived in Fraser Lake with his bags and guitar in hand. I noted how well he appeared to be. He said he had just moved into his new residence, in the building that also housed the Nanaimo office of the Canadian Mental Health Association. The only problem was that he had to do his own cooking. Bruce grinned as he stated, "I still can't boil water without burning it." But he spent most of his time at the Dairy Queen next door anyway, he added. He had found that he did his best writing in restaurants.

His new residence was convenient to where he could work on the publication of *Voices* magazine. The first two issues of the attractive anthology were in the process of being distributed at two dollars a copy. Bruce presented me with a copy of each issue. I was pleased and proud when I realized how much work he had put into them. Besides doing the computer work, he had drawn most of the illustrations, including those on the covers.

That weekend an annual event known as Mouse Mountain Days was happening in Fraser Lake. In past years the Canada Day celebration had included a parade, canoe races, games and fireworks and had lasted for two full days. One year, a huge canvas tent had been set up to include food and beverage booths and games of chance. Now the festivities had been scaled down to a softball tournament followed by a community picnic on the grass alongside the bandstand. Local musicians and poets entertained while everyone feasted on cake and donated ice cream. The evening usually concluded with an outdoor dance.

Cathy, Darwin and family had already set up their lawn chairs by the time Bruce and I approached with ours. The entertainment at the bandstand was slow and the emcee was calling for more volunteers. Darwin suggested to Bruce that he get up there and even borrowed a guitar for him to play. Bruce was quite willing, but for some reason I was uncomfortable with the idea of him performing on that day. He sang a recent composition entitled "Black Butterfly." It seemed to me that his voice droned, and I did not find the dark melody pleasing. It reminded me of the songs he had sung at Phoenix's house on Saltspring island in 1986, a time he had not been at all well.

A few days after his arrival Bruce told me he'd like to climb Red Rock Mountain, an extinct forested volcano a few miles from where we had lived when he was growing up. The older children in the neighbourhood had sprinted up its steep slopes at least once or twice a year. Sometimes their mothers had followed along behind, content to proceed at a slower pace.

The day Bruce and I climbed Red Rock was a memorable one. He and I took photographs, but they failed to duplicate the iridescent beauty of the lake and the sky as viewed from the top of the mountain. An eagle flew just above our heads, and Bruce took its picture. After we ate our lunch, Bruce slid down over a precipice onto a narrow ledge in order to view some hidden caves. I have never had the courage to climb down and observe these interesting recesses in the rock face of the mountain.

Later Bruce and I meandered down the mountain away from the trail, following a rocky slope. He pointed out the charcoaled remains of a long-ago campfire, built the night he had camped out by himself when he was about fourteen. We sat down to reminisce in the warm sunshine. Bruce finally blurted out, "I wasn't going to tell you this, but I am not on medication." I was surprised, because as I told him, he seemed to be so well.

When I told Leon and Fern what Bruce had said, they were not surprised. They had been at home while I was at work and observed his increasingly odd behavior. He spent much of his time alone in our travel trailer where he was free to smoke cigarettes and use my typewriter to compose his songs and poetry. Lately for no apparent reason, he had begun a habit of running into the house and almost immediately darting outside again. It was as if he saw or heard something that neither Fern nor Leon could. This erratic behavior was not apparent at any time when I was around.

Apparently he had only wanted to hide his deteriorating mental health from me.

After his confession that he was not on medication, Bruce no longer troubled himself to don his mask of sanity around me. He withdrew into his own impenetrable existence and gave up even the pretense of interest in everyday happenings.

Before we prepared to leave on our trip, I asked Dr. Gow to make out a prescription for Stelazine and Cogentin tablets. "Just in case," I told Bruce placatingly, "you need some medication on the long bus ride home to Nanaimo."

Bruce appeared to be fine on the bus and slept most of the way between meals and cigarette stops. Fern and I kept an eye on him, and we did not sleep much at all.

We said good-bye to Bruce in Nanaimo and proceeded up the island toward Courtenay, where our new car awaited us at the rental agency.

As was usual when Fern and I traveled together, the weather was beautiful. When my mother was still alive and living in Vancouver, she would often comment on how the weather had improved when we arrived for our annual visit.

Hornby Island is an interesting cultural experience as well as being one of the most beautiful of the Gulf Islands. The architecture of some of its buildings reflect its back to nature, but with style creativity. In summer the island buzzes with activity as the residents set up displays of beautiful art objects, paintings and crafts for the benefit of crowds of tourists. In winter, Phoenix told us, the island settled back into being a quiet but vigorous community.

On July 18, Phoenix and my ten-year-old grandson Cory helped us load the car with sleeping bags, a tent for Fern and me, and clothing. As a performer, Phoenix would have sleeping accommodations provided. We piled in and headed south toward Galiano Island and the Poetry Festival. I wondered if Bruce would be well enough to travel with us. He had accepted the invitation to participate, and had mailed a list of the poems he would read to the festival organizers. I had given him the medication from Dr. Gow and hoped that by now he would be taking it.

When we reached Nanaimo, Phoenix phoned Bruce for directions to his new place of residence. He told her he was feeling well and was prepared to come along with us. The two-storey older building on Victoria Road was home to two other young men besides my son. We found Bruce in the kitchen eating Cup-o-Noodles soup from a throw-away carton. He said he ate most of his meals at the Dairy Queen restaurant next door, but he was broke now and could not even afford to buy cigarette makings. I told Bruce not to worry. I would pay for his meals and cigarettes for the next two days at least.

Bruce appeared to be extremely listless. He had not been sleeping well, he explained. The traffic noises kept him awake at night. He was not able to sleep in either. The CMHA office, which was quite busy in the mornings, was located across the hallway from his room. It was at the top of a narrow, creaking staircase. The sounds of people walking up and down the stairs was very distracting. When I asked Bruce about his medication, he handed me the two vials of pills. As far as I could tell, he had not taken any.

He sat in the front seat of the car with Phoenix, who was driving, while I joined Fern and Cory in the back. Bruce had changed into a blue sweater and a clean pair of jeans. I thought he looked quite handsome, despite the stubble of beard on his face. The Don Johnson look was "in," I remembered. Perhaps he had not shaven on purpose? We hoped to reach Galiano before dark so that Fern and I could see to set up our tent. The quickest route would be to leave Vancouver Island from the ferry terminal at Crofton, just north of Duncan. There we boarded a small ferry which took us to Vesuvius Bay on the west side of Saltspring. We raced eastward across that island to Long Harbour, in order to catch one of the huge BC Ferries on its regular passage between Swartz Bay and Tawwassen.

Bruce almost didn't get off the ferry when we reached Galiano Island. I ran around in a state of panic trying to find him before the ferry left for Tawwassen with both of us on it. I finally located him on the upper deck, staring off at the wide blue expanse of sea and sky. We were the last of the foot passengers to leave the ship, and finally catch up with Phoenix and the children who waited anxiously for us in the car.

Fern and I did not need to set up our tent after all. We were all invited to sleep in various places at Geoff Inverarity's lovely big home on Galiano Island. Geoff was one of the festival's organizers. A number of off-island poets were to share his home with him that weekend. Phoenix opted to sleep on my air mattress upstairs in the dining room with Fern. I shared her bed with Cory, and Bruce was assigned the other double bed in the basement bedroom.

For me, the weekend was a mixed bag of emotions. I enjoyed the literary performances which included readings by well-known poet Dorothy Livesay and novelist William Deverell. But I was constantly on edge because I was worried about Bruce. He did not sleep at all the first night in Geoff's house, and neither did I. The next day he wandered around the hall during the reading sessions. I kept one eye on him to ensure that he would be available when it was his turn to appear at the podium. When it was, he became instantly transformed. He was bright and alert.

His voice conveyed just the right touch of emotion as he enunciated the powerful words he had written. The poems he had selected were quite profound, and as Phoenix said later, they came alive as Bruce read them. The audience applauded, at first hesitantly, then with enthusiasm.

Phoenix's friend Ralph, a fellow poet from Hornby Island, appeared to be nothing short of awe-stricken. He shook his head and whispered, "Heavy, man!" as Bruce rejoined us in the audience. Bruce seemed pleased. He held his head up and listened to the other performers for a while. Soon his shoulders began to slump and his head drooped. That night he took two tablets of Stelazine and one of the Cogentin. He fell asleep instantly and later so did I.

On Saturday afternoon Phoenix enthralled her audience when she recited several poems and then sang an appealing rendition of a song she had written entitled "The Hall of Mirrors." The song's lyrics described the bitterly lonely perceptions that shape the thoughts and feelings of a victim of major depression. The crippling self-pity and self-blame totally encompass the sufferer. She is unable to find an exit from her hall of mirrors.

We left Galiano Island shortly after Phoenix's last session at the podium. Geoff had announced the festival was a complete success. It had achieved its goal, to raise money for a Galiano Island residents group to purchase land that was forested with old growth trees. The group wished to protect the trees from a company that had recently acquired MacMillan Bloedel's timber-cutting reserves on the island. Mac-Blo had been fairly conscientious about preserving the old growth. The residents were much more skeptical about the new company's logging practices.

The car had to be back in Courtenay by Tuesday and I wanted to spend one day at least with my stepdaughter Diane and her family who lived in Parksville. When we dropped Bruce off in Nanaimo, I gave him enough money to keep him in groceries and cigarettes until he received a cheque from Social Services. I also gave him the two vials of medication.

I did not hear from Bruce for the rest of the summer. I was very busy at work, filling in for other home support workers who were on vacation as well as satisfying my obligations to my own clients. It was a relief, though, when Bruce did phone on Labour Day weekend to inform me that he was back on Modecate injections and was now feeling much better.

Early in September, five other women from Fraser Lake and myself commenced a routine of driving to Vanderhoof three times a week to complete a course we had begun in January. The course was necessary in order to obtain our certification as home support workers. We enjoyed the classes and learned much about the diseases and conditions that can rob our fellow human beings of the freedom to enjoy life to the fullest. I noticed there was little in the course about mental illnesses, other than Alzheimer's disease. There was no mention in our text, whatsoever, about schizophrenia. I brought the subject up to the instructor and we did discuss the symptoms. None of us had ever been asked to work with a client who had the illness.

Later that month I noticed an advertisement in a local newspaper that promoted an upcoming meeting on the subject of schizophrenia. The meeting was to be held at the medical clinic in Fraser Lake. I experienced a sharp pang of emotion–a mingling of excitement and pain–at seeing the word "schizophrenia" printed in the notice. I was astounded that a meeting concerning the disease was to be held in our small community. It was to be on a Monday night, the night of our Home Support class. I informed my classmates that I was about to play hooky. There was no way I wanted to miss that meeting.

I learned that the meeting had been arranged by a long time acquaintance of mine named Jeanette. The father of her small grandchild had recently been diagnosed with schizophrenia. Jeanette had endured the childhood trauma of having a parent with the devastating illness. She well knew the social stigma attached to it because of the lack of understanding on the part of others. The odds of Jeanette's adorable grandson someday being stricken with schizophrenia were increased slightly over that of the general population because the disease had occurred on both sides of his family. Jeanette was determined that the world, beginning with Fraser Lake, would soon become a more informed and kindlier place for those afflicted with schizophrenia.

The meeting was well attended by people from the community and surrounding area. A few had loved ones or acquaintances afflicted with schizophrenia, but most were merely interested in learning about a disease they knew little or nothing about.

A group of women had driven up from Prince George. They were members of an organization called the BC Friends of Schizophrenics. They had with them several guests who had experienced symptoms of the illness, but were now on medication and appeared to be mentally stable. An attractive middle-aged woman spoke eloquently and with humour about her many adventures since being diagnosed with schizophrenia when she was a young girl. Lynne Turnbull, a representative of the Friends of Schizophrenics group, displayed a lamp in the shape of a lighthouse that gave off a rosy glow. This beacon, she explained, represented a symbol of hope for people with the illness. Lynne signed up eight people, including my daughter Cathy and me, which was enough to establish our own branch of the BCFOS.

As small communities go Fraser Lake was fairly accepting of those displaying eccentric or unusual behaviour. The initial reaction to Bruce's strange symptoms in September 1984 had been mostly sympathy, although hardly anyone knew anything about the disease. But small towns have a tendency to stereotype their citizens. Bruce had been an introverted teenager. He was just beginning to develop some social skills when he was afflicted with schizophrenia. Later, with the exception of close friends and relatives, his reclusive tendencies were perceived as being merely an extension of his previously shy nature. As time went by and his behaviour became more and more irrational, it seemed to me that most people just looked the other way.

Now, learning that there were others in the community who had experienced the same pain and frustration I had because of a loved one's schizophrenia was almost like a miracle for me. The guilt I felt because I believed I had failed as a mother began to dissolve. From now on, I resolved, I was up to any situation that involved Bruce's illness. I would be able to react as a home support worker should, in a practical and helpful way without the emotional turmoil that was so debilitating to both Bruce's health and my own.

My new resolution was put to the test in a matter of days. Bruce phoned to say he wanted to move back to Fraser Lake in order to write a book where it was peaceful and quiet. I assured him that I would find an apartment for him to rent in town. The entire family would assist in helping him to settle in, but only if he agreed to stay on medication.

When Bruce stepped off the Greyhound bus, I noted how his worldly possessions and the way he packaged them for travelling had changed throughout the years. At one time he possessed three large leather suitcases, several sports bags and even a steel trunk. The leather suitcases had been lost or stolen and had been replaced by cheap vinyl ones and later nylon bags. Now all of his belongings were encased in two small cardboard boxes. An ancient electric typewriter had somehow survived the trip without being packaged or covered.

The bachelor suite I had reserved for Bruce was on the second floor of what was locally referred to as the brown apartment complex in Fraser Lake. The three-storey building was a ten minute walk from the downtown area. It stood side-by-side with an equally large structure known as the black apartments. The buildings were located below a large pine-covered butte that loomed skyward at the east end of town. The butte, Mouse Mountain, provided a picturesque view through the patio door of what was to be Bruce's new home.

Cathy and I pooled our extra kitchen utensils and other essentials that Bruce would need for daily living. I brought over a table, two chairs, and a foam-filled mattress. There was an old chesterfield in the suite that the previous occupant had left behind. Cathy's friend Priscilla offered Bruce the use of a television set. She told him he could purchase it on very easy terms after he had the money ahead to pay for cable hookup.

As it turned out, there was very little left of his Social Assistance cheque after he had paid for rent, electricity and groceries. From time to time I helped him out financially. I decided to ask a friend who was a member of a Native Indian band, to purchase tobacco for me at a reduced price from the band store. I reasoned that, for Bruce tobacco was an essential drug. He had tried many times to give up smoking, and each time his mental health had worsened. The price of tobacco had risen to such an extent that it had become a case of buying tobacco or sufficient food. When he was on his own, I suspected it would be the food he would rather give up.

I had worried about whether Bruce would stick to his promise to take medication for his schizophrenia. At Cathy's suggestion, I typed out a contract which, I admitted to Bruce, would never stand up in a court of law. It stated: "I, Bruce Ray, agree to take medication for as long as I reside in the BC Central Interior. And I, Doris Ray, will refrain from worrying." We both signed it.

Bruce had received an injection of the drug Modecate the day before he left Nanaimo. He said the effects of the anti-psychotic should last for three weeks. But the first night he was alone, he phoned me from his landlady's suite. He stated hesitantly that he was not well, and perhaps needed an ambulance to take him to the hospital. I told him I would be right over.

When I arrived at Bruce's apartment, he told me he was feeling nauseous. He was also experiencing a frightening cacophony of voices in his head. He did not yet have a phone, and the landlady had retired for the night, so we drove downtown to where there was a pay telephone. I dialed Dr. Gow's home number, and Bruce explained his symptoms to the doctor. I had not thought that there might be side-effects to the injectable drug, but of course that was the problem. Bruce had a few Cogentin on hand which he took before going to bed. I lay on his lumpy couch for a few hours before going home to finish up the night in my own bed. Bruce was sick to his stomach and not entirely well for almost a week.

It seemed to me that the effects of the Modecate wore off before Bruce's next injection was due. The day I drove him to the medical clinic, he appeared to be in a daze, laughing quietly to himself from time to time. A day or two after his shot, he again experienced nausea and other side-effects. In the ensuing weeks, I surmised that Bruce had only one good week out of each three-week period between Modecate injections.

I began a routine of visiting Bruce's apartment almost every day after work. I realized he wanted to feel independent, so I assured him I was only there to help him with everyday cooking, cleaning and shopping activities in the same way that I helped my clients. For a while this worked quite well. He learned to cook the food that the two of us had budgeted for and purchased at the local grocery stores. I was an old hand at shopping for bargains, and Bruce seemed to be interested in learning.

On Sundays I picked him up and took him home to our place for family dinners. He borrowed back his old guitar from Leon and began to write songs again. He also wrote a lot of poetry, and as in Nanaimo, did his best writing at one of the local restaurants while drinking cup after cup of the cheapest coffee in town.

The book Bruce had planned to write seemed to be on hold. I thought Fraser Lake may have been a bit too quiet to inspire him for that. Ian and Kirsti Kluge had moved to Prince George and their absence put a damper on Baha'i activities. Our writers' group seemed to have slipped into a malaise as well. We had published our *Seasonings* anthology the previous year, and membership had dwindled after the glow of satisfaction from that endeavor wore off. Bruce made a list of Canadian literary magazines that might be interested in publishing his poetry. I composed a query letter for him and he bundled up his selections to send in the mail. His poetry was not accepted, but he did receive some encouraging replies.

It was Fern's graduation year. She was involved with the activities of a group called The Dry Grad For A Year Club. The group hoped to become role models for other students who very often indulged in alcoholic beverages. Members signed pledge forms promising to abstain from drinking alcohol until after graduation in June of 1992. They participated in fund-raising projects that would hopefully result in them traveling together to some as-yet-unknown destination at the end of the school year.

As it turned out, their finances were sufficient to take them to Disneyland in time to join in the annual Grad Nite festivities there.

Fern's group planned to hold a carnival at the recreation centre early in November. Bruce agreed to sit at a table and do sketch portraits in pencil and charcoal. He would also do caricatures for those who preferred a humourous drawing of themselves. The booth was quite popular for a while. Finally, Bruce confessed that he was finding it stressful and I agreed to take him home. He told me later that seeing all the young people, many of the boys with their arms wrapped around their girlfriends, had caused him to become depressed. He had not been much older then they were when he was struck down with schizophrenia.

One weekend when Bruce was feeling quite well, he and I attended a minor hockey league game in the same arena where he had played many years earlier. Cathy and Darwin's son Tyler was thirteen and on a team that played a very entertaining game. Bruce enjoyed watching it, as did most of the spectators. That same weekend, he was invited for dinner at his cousin Linda's home. She had invited several other friends and relatives with whom they had hung out when they were in school. Most of Bruce's former classmates were now married with jobs and children. After dinner they played games and rehashed old times. Bruce said later that he enjoyed the evening very much.

Toward the end of November the days grew shorter and darker. Most families in Fraser Lake began preparing for the Christmas holiday celebrations. Bruce became more and more quiet and reserved. When I stopped by his apartment in the afternoons, I often found him still in his bed. He was no longer interested in having me help with the cooking and cleaning and at times seemed to resent the intrusion.

Dr. Gow had given him a prescription for anti-ulcer medication because of his chronic stomach pain and nausea. I suggested to Bruce that coffee and cigarettes were probably upsetting his stomach. One afternoon I found him lying in his bed clutching a bag of mint candies. He explained haltingly that the candies were to help him stave off nicotine cravings. He had not had a cigarette for twelve hours, and his body was now almost in a comatose state. He could barely move. I rolled a cigarette for him, which he smoked before slowly emerging from his cocoon.

The telephone in Bruce's apartment was in my name because he could not afford the monthly charges or pay for any long distance calls. On December eighth when I picked him up for Sunday dinner, Bruce confessed that he had used the phone to make a long distance call to Ladysmith. He had asked his dad if he could move in with him and Connie for a while.

Bruce admitted that he was not well enough to manage living in one of the semi-independent residences in Nanaimo. But he was homesick for the friends and activities he had left behind in that city. He particularly missed Lisa, the girl with whom he had spent so much time during the previous winter.

Ed agreed that Bruce could stay with them until such time as there was an opening in the monitored group home in Nanaimo called Columbian House.

When Bruce left Fraser Lake in December of 1991 I experienced a deep sense of relief. I realized he still loved his childhood home. For him the area represented a refuge away from the real world where he really thought he should be. My son had often said he felt like a loser whenever he returned. I hoped he had reconciled childhood memories, hopes and dreams, and was now free to carry on with his adult life. But this was not to be. In October, 1992 Bruce phoned to implore me to help him move back to Fraser Lake.

I expressed my dismay by reminding him that it had not worked out the last time he was up. I did not mention that the vacancy rate for rental units had shrunk to zero. I had been very lucky to secure an apartment for Bruce the previous year.

He cried out that it was the cruelest cut of all–that I was deliberately exiling him from his own home town. Before I could explain, he hung up the telephone. I realized that what my son had accused me of was partly true. Whenever he was in Fraser Lake, he was my responsibility and I did not have the strength to deal with his schizophrenia. Bruce wrote me an angry letter. In it, he suggested that Leon and I were responsible for his illness. Soon after we received the letter, he phoned to apologize, saying it had just been a way of venting his frustration. He explained that some stressful things were happening to him at his Nanaimo group home.

I had been a good mother, Bruce assured me, and was in no way responsible for his mental illness. Later he phoned Leon to say he loved and respected him. He said he knew that Leon had always tried his best to be a good second father to him.

The letter from Bruce was the first correspondence we had received from him since the onset of his schizophrenia. It was written in a stilted, poetical style, but I recognized it as a communication from the heart. I wrote back, encouraging him to communicate his innermost thoughts and feelings to me. It was healthful, I wrote, to express anger and other so-called negative emotions.

A few weeks later the telephone rang and it was Bruce. His voice sounded high and frail. He told me he had just had a distinct memory of being raped when he was three years old. He said he could recall the man's face clearly; in fact, he could probably draw his portrait. His assailant had been in his late teens, had dark hair, a gaunt face and was wearing a plaid shirt. Bruce had been on one of his forbidden forays into the woods when the man had made him remove his clothing and had raped him.

Bruce admitted that the incident may have been a false memory, but the fact that he was still able to experience the fear associated with it had convinced him that it was for real. He described in detail the panoramic view that was superimposed in his mind of the landscape around where the attack must have occurred. As far as I could recall, it was an accurate description of an area close to where we had once lived.

My mind raced back to September 1966, when Leon and I had first lived together near my hometown of Forest Grove, BC. The children had spent the summer months with their dad and Connie, and Leon had recently moved in with me at my newly-rented home. The house was small but the neighbours were friendly. Not one matched the description of the man Bruce had elucidated as being his long-ago assailant. We had moved away from the area in May 1967.

Bruce had described an area near our house where some old cars and haying equipment were kept. Tall grasses and rose bushes grew in that corner of a neglected hayfield. He remembered Leon and me warning him not to play with the machinery, because it was dangerous. Almost the entire outdoors in that vicinity was a dangerous place for an inquisitive and impulsive youngster to play.

Above the field was a steep clay bank that led up to some dense woods. Below the field was a fast flowing creek where at least one child had drowned in past years. Leon and I had kept an eye on Bruce almost all the time he played outside. He was like a will-o-the-wisp and seemed able to disappear in seconds. Once he even left the house after dark while the rest of us were watching television. The girls and I knocked on every door in the neighbourhood where there were children he might be playing with. Leon raced for the creek with a flashlight in his hand. We finally found Bruce at an elderly neighbour's home, eating cookies and watching her television set.

I sometimes wondered if my small son was incapable of learning. The spankings he received for leaving our fenced-in yard only seemed to slow him down for a day or two. Leon insisted that Bruce did not have a learning disability. One day he pointed out the living room window to where my son was peering intently in every direction. When Bruce had determined that no adults were in sight, he darted full-speed ahead in the direction of the creek.

Now after listening to Bruce's startling revelation on the telephone, I began to speculate on whether it was possible my small son had been sexually assaulted during one of his forays away from home. At least once he had disappeared for what seemed like an inordinate period of time. But I was certain I would have noticed if he had sustained any cuts or bruises, or if there had been bloodstains on his underwear.

I wrote my former neighbour and my brother who still resided near the community of Forest Grove. I asked them to enquire around as to whether anyone had ever heard of a sexual predator prowling around in the bush during the time that we lived in the area. They both came up with nothing. I contacted the RCMP in 100 Mile House and was informed that any records regarding inquiries made that long ago were most likely destroyed because of a lack of storage space.

It was possible that the assault–if it had occurred–had been an isolated incident. What made me cringe in horror was the knowledge that if Bruce had been missing from home, he would most likely have received a spanking from Leon and a tongue lashing from me after he was found. That, on top of the horrific experience of being raped, would have been doubly traumatic.

CHAPTER ELEVEN

The Fields of Make-Believe

"I walked the footsteps of a little child
Through the fields of make-believe
With the crooked house and the bearded lady
Part of some strange dream
The seven wonders of the world
Hidden inside a dark tent..."

From "Lost America"
by Bruce Ray

Bruce left Fraser Lake early in December 1991. He spent a few days visiting with his old school chum Kevin who had moved from Fort Fraser to Vancouver. On December 19, he phoned to let us know he had arrived safely at his dad and Connie's home in Ladysmith.

Six weeks later, I picked up a letter in our mailbox that had originally been mailed to a Toronto address. A post office stamp neatly imprinted on the envelope stated: No Such Address. The postmark was from Ladysmith, BC, but the return address was ours. My heart sank when I saw that the name of the addressee, scrawled in heavy black ink above a Toronto address was "Miss Dale Olson."

I have always respected my children's privacy and am extremely reluctant to open a letter that is not my own. Leon suggested that I really had no choice. Bruce might well be on his way to Toronto if he were not already living on the streets of that city. I opened the envelope, and as we had suspected, a note written in that same heavy black ink stated that Bruce would be arriving at the Toronto bus depot on a date that had already passed by on the calendar.

I frantically dialed Ed and Connie's phone number and almost cried with relief when Connie said she had just moved Bruce into a group home in Nanaimo. He was in the monitored residence, Columbian House, and would be there until such time as his mental health became more stable. Bruce had been alone in their house trailer much of the time over the past few weeks, Connie confided. Both she and Ed had been working full-time. She realized Bruce must have missed his Modecate injection when she spied a mound of cigarette butts that he had carelessly emptied into a combustible wastepaper basket.

Bruce was supposed to have visited the medical clinic for his injection, but it was obvious that he had not done that. It was a miracle, Connie conjectured, that sparks from a hot cigarette ash had not ignited the paper in the basket and caused a serious house fire. A few days later, Bruce phoned to inform me of his new address and phone number. He sounded pleased that he would soon be seeing a psychiatrist.

My friend Jeanette, of the Fraser Lake branch of the Friends of Schizophrenics group, wanted me to help her with a slide presentation about the disease to be followed by a discussion forum at the local high school. Fern, who was now in the second semester of Grade 12, volunteered to help. She had a copy of *Sassy* magazine, a publication for teenagers, which contained an article written by a young girl whose brother had schizophrenia. Fern said she could relate, to some extent, to the thoughts and feelings expressed by the author. She thought she could use the story to help explain to our audience some of her own perceptions regarding Bruce's illness.

Our first presentation, which was to the Grade 11 Family Life class, went very well. Fern's insights regarding the *Sassy* magazine article were of special interest to the students. Sadly enough, one of the twenty-five or so students in attendance now has many of the symptoms of chronic schizophrenia. I still recall her fresh-faced lively interest when we discussed the symptoms of the disease. At the time, she was looking forward to taking college courses in psychology after she graduated from high school.

We were scheduled to repeat the presentation to Fern's Grade 12 Family Life class in the afternoon. As most teachers will attest, every class is different. The Fraser Lake graduating class of 1992 was considered to be one of the most intellectual of all time. As Fern sardonically put it, "They tend to analyze a problem, then decide how to make money out of it." Fern had to work very hard to achieve passing grades, especially in math and the sciences. At times she felt alienated from some of her more left-brained classmates.

After the slide presentation, my daughter began to speak clearly and eloquently about the magazine article on schizophrenia. Suddenly she put the magazine down and bolted from the room. She found refuge in the girl's washroom where she burst into tears. She felt better a few days later when one girl confided that she too had a brother who suffered from the illness. Until she had viewed our presentation, she told Fern, she had always thought her brother was just weird.

Soon after our school presentation, Jeanette and I arranged a community meeting with guest speakers Dr. Gow and a young RCMP officer with an unusual first hand knowledge about the disease of schizophrenia. Because his brother-in-law was afflicted with the illness, he was familiar with its sometimes socially disruptive symptoms. In the tiny rural community where the man resided, a mental health nurse made the rounds regularly to visit with the man and his family.

This routine worked well for everyone, and was similar to the way public health nurses used to interview mothers of newborns in their homes to provide advice and alleviate fears. A nurse had stopped by periodically when my son was a baby. Bruce and I would have appreciated her visits even more after he had been diagnosed with schizophrenia.

The RCMP officer confided that his training as a police officer did not include any specific procedures about how to deal with people suffering from mental illnesses. I could believe that. I had read a newspaper article which stated that a number of psychiatric outpatients in BC had recently been shot by police officers.

The name of our BCFOS organization had been changed to the BC Schizophrenia Society. Jeanette and I advertised our telephone numbers as contacts for the Fraser Lake branch.

One day a woman who was visiting Fraser Lake telephoned me. Ellen said she was from northern Ontario but had just arrived from the BC lower mainland after spending some time searching for her youngest daughter Kathleen. As a teenager, the girl had hitchhiked across Canada rather than take prescribed medication for her schizophrenia. Ellen's voice quivered with joy when she imparted the news to me that she had finally located her daughter in a dingy room of a seedy downtown Vancouver hotel room. Kathleen, who was now a young woman, was poorly nourished and extremely reclusive but she was alive. She continued to refuse any kind of medical intervention, but was in fairly good physical health. Some people from a nearby church were keeping an eye on her and making sure she had food. Ellen's hopes and prayers were finally answered and she could return home to Ontario with a peaceful heart. She concluded our conversation by confiding that three of her grown children had been diagnosed with the disease. The other two, she stated happily, were doing very well.

Mothers of schizophrenics, I have noticed, often have a good sense of humour. Very likely, it is a survival tool to cope with their loved one's illness. An outspoken down-to-earth matron on Hornby Island once discussed her mentally ill son's peculiar behaviour with me: "He would get into my closet and put on my clothes," she recalled. "Once he put everything on, including pantyhose and my high heeled pumps. He was going to go the mainland, he insisted. I phoned the cops because I could see he was not well.

"They caught up to him pretty easily, though. He was striding down the Island Highway all decked out in my good clothes and shoes. What gave him away was that at the time he was sporting a full beard!"

When I heard this story it reminded me of my son's tendency to revert to a different personality—particularly one of the feminine gender. I had read books on the subject of multiple personality disorder, and had often wondered if one of his most bizarre symptoms could possibly be defined as such.

According to the American Psychiatric Association's *Diagnostic and*

Statistical Manual of Mental Disorders, multiple personality disorder is: "the existence within the individual of two or more distinct personalities, each of which is dominant at a particular time. Each personality is a fully integrated and complex unit with unique memories, behaviour patterns, and social relationships that determine the nature of the individual's acts when that personality is dominant..." The Dale Olson persona which emerged from Bruce's psyche had appeared to fit that definition. But later Ian Kluge and I discussed the phenomenon and discovered discrepancies between what Bruce had previously told him, and the story that had been told to me. There was no doubt my son had unwittingly created the whole thing from his own runaway imagination.

For me, having a loved one with schizophrenia meant there was always something to worry about. After Bruce left Fraser Lake in December 1991 I began obsessing about why he had not responded well to the Modecate injections. I decided he needed a change of medication. But my son had described the injectible drug as a blessing because it released him from the responsibility of having to take pills every day.

Perusing through the reams of information I had received as a member of the BCSS organization, I learned that there were several long-lasting injectible drugs besides Modecate. Any change could only be for the better, I thought confidently. I outlined my observations about the side-effects and my concerns about the effectiveness of Modecate in a letter addressed to Bruce's doctor and mailed it to my son. He should read the letter himself, I suggested, and make the decision about whether a change was necessary. If so, he should present the letter to his doctor or psychiatrist.

In March of 1992, Bruce phoned to tell me that he was now on an injectible drug called Flauanxol. But a few months later he denied that there had ever been a change in his medication. Flauanxol, he insisted, was merely the generic name for Modecate.

Bruce sounded despondent when he told me he was about to be discharged from Columbian House and would soon be back living in the old semi-independent living quarters on Victoria Road. He did not think he was stable enough, he confided, to be living in an unmonitored environment. But he had no choice. A fellow who was worse off than himself was in need of a bed. This fellow had a habit of setting fires indiscriminately around town and was deemed to be a danger to himself and others. "They know I'm not going to cause any trouble," Bruce stated wryly. "That's why I was the one who had to go."

He phoned me in April and again in July to ask for small sums of money—twenty or thirty dollars—to tide him over until he received his next cheque from Social Services. As in past years, I mailed him the exact amount he had requested, no more and no less. Even when he was well had never been able to handle his finances. I disliked the idea of our hard-earned money being spent in a frivolous manner.

I had scheduled my holidays that summer to coincide with Fern's appointment to apply at Camosun College in Victoria for the courses she wanted to take in September. If the courses were available, we would also have to look for a place for her to live. Her sister Cathy suggested that Fern stay with a couple in Victoria who were interested in supplying room and board to a suitable college student. The couple—he was a church pastor—were holidaying in Parksville, but would meet us at three o'clock on August tenth at the Tally Ho Restaurant, near the bus depot in Nanaimo.

I had reserved a rental car from a Nanaimo agency, and we planned to drive up-island the following day to visit Phoenix and her children. If Bruce was well enough, I had thought I might invite him to come along. One of the waitresses at the Tally Ho overheard my remarks, as Fern and I discussed our holiday plans with the Victoria pastor and his wife. The waitress apologized for butting in, but said she had just learned that the Denman Island Ferry was out of commission.

The ferry which carried passengers and vehicles between Vancouver and Denman Island, the first lap of the two-ferry route to Hornby Island, had been anchored at the Denman Island terminal when a loaded logging truck slid off the ferry ramp and now lay partly submerged in the water.

Nobody was hurt, and the trucker had even managed to save his dog from drowning when the water began rushing into his cab, but the ferry was effectively pinned in place by the weight of the truck. It would be several days at least before a heavy-duty crane could be brought in from Vancouver Island to hoist the truck from where it hung in the murky water. There was no way we could get to Hornby Island.

In retrospect, Fern has frequently voiced the theory that the unavailability of the Denman Island Ferry at the very time we wanted to use it may have been part of a fickle finger of fate scenario that effectively detoured her from her preconceived path in life on Vancouver Island. Fern had not been able to achieve the high marks needed to register at the University of Victoria–her first choice–and the courses she wanted to take at Camosun College were not available by the time we arrived on her registration day. She ended up taking college courses in New Westminster, on the mainland, where two years later she met the man who would become the most important person in her life.

I sometimes wonder from the perspective of peering back through the passage of time whether or not there could have been any significance to the events that occurred on that date–August 10, 1992–when Fern and I were in Nanaimo. It would be one year later, to the day, when Bruce's schizophrenia would take a sudden and devastating turn for the worse.

We checked into the Tally Ho Hotel, then took a cab up Victoria Road to where Bruce sat waiting for us under a tree outside his residence. He greeted us with a cheerful smile, and the three of us sauntered up the street in search of a good restaurant. Detour signs were everywhere, and Bruce explained that construction projects were happening in order to upgrade the narrow streets. He said the city had an interesting history. Much of the residential area was built up over old mining tunnels that had been constructed before the turn of the century.

After dinner, we debated on the choice of movies that were being shown in the theatres. "Death Becomes Her," with Meryl Streep and Goldie Hawn, was one that none of us had previously seen. It was supposed to be a comedy.

At the theatre, Bruce said he did not want to sit in an aisle seat. It was characteristic of people with schizophrenia, he explained, to avoid places where they feel they are vulnerable to others. I recalled that when Bruce was first diagnosed, he had exhibited symptoms of claustrophobia–fear of enclosed places. At that time he would have preferred an aisle seat because it was closer to an exit.

The movie was hilarious, but it contained some gruesome scenes. In one, Meryl Streep's body parts tumble separately down a flight of stairs. Although Meryl was supposed to be dead, she was able to mouth indignant words and phrases from her lipsticked mouth, while her cranium was seen to bounce from step to step.

Bruce did not enjoy the movie. He said, because of his schizophrenia, he would have a hard time getting some of the more grotesque images out of his mind.

Before going home, we relaxed over milkshakes at the Dairy Queen which, because of its proximity to Bruce's residence, was his home away from home. Bruce sheepishly confessed that he had been barred from the premises for a while. One day, for some reason, he had begun to drool uncontrollably into his coffee cup. He had been asked to leave because he was grossing out the other customers.

Although Bruce spoke lightly of the incident, I felt a stab of sympathy for him. I noted that he had lost weight since leaving Fraser Lake eight months earlier. Over the years, when he was on the Modecate medication, he had been fairly heavy. Now he was almost too thin. An acne infection had caused one side of his face to become noticeably swollen. Bruce assured me that he was eating properly. He said he was happy to have lost weight. He had not enjoyed being fat. He admitted that he was out of bread at home, and asked me for ten dollars which, he said, would last him until payday. I gave him the ten dollars.

Fern and I perused the folder of recently composed manuscripts that Bruce pulled from his carryall bag. I noticed that the style and content of some of his essays had changed. Bruce explained that this was because he no longer was afraid to express anger in his literary endeavors.

Lately he had been writing about social issues such as the sexual abuse of children. One of his stories, which included a rape scene, had been published in the third issue of *Voices* magazine. The short piece of fiction had caused such a furor of controversy in Nanaimo that all funding to continue publication of the magazine had been cancelled.

While we conversed, I noticed a strange phenomenon. Bruce's eyes appeared to vary in their reflective qualities, as if they were fitted with interchangeable lenses. It also seemed to take a split second or so before his mind was able to assimilate what we had to tell him. Fern later likened this process to a computer that was receiving new data.

Bruce's mind was still quick when it came to a good comeback, though. Fern and I took turns embracing him when we said our good-byes. When it was her turn, she recognized that the difference in their height was less, now that she had grown taller. "My God!" she exclaimed, "You're short!"

"No, I'm not," Bruce retorted. "I've got ten dollars."

CHAPTER TWELVE

The Dweller on the Threshold

"There is a hell
I know because I have walked it
with my faith as my only light
and death walked by my side.
He smiled to see me
and paid the ferryman
as I didn't have any money…"

From "The Dweller on the Threshold"
by Bruce Ray 1989

Bruce told me he was not happy living in the house on Victoria Road. Some of his fellow residents were exhibiting extremely erratic behavior. The residence had recently become a shelter for people in crisis whom the police had taken off the street. Most of these people were mentally ill, and there was nowhere else for them to go.

One fellow had a habit of fashioning crosses out of pieces of wood and setting them out in strategic places throughout the house. Another stashed knives everywhere, including burying them in the grass outside on the lawn. Bruce also told me that some of the fellows who stayed at the house were abusers of the mental health system. I took that to mean they were not really mentally ill at all.

When Bruce learned I would not help him move back to Fraser Lake he became very upset. Later he told me he had spent several days visiting with his dad and Connie, and found himself better able to cope with all the stress when he returned to the residence.

On the first of December, Bruce phoned from his friend Kevin's apartment in Vancouver. He said he was considering a move to that city if Mental Health could find a place for him to live. Kevin told me later that he was shocked at how thin Bruce had become. He said Bruce had barely eaten anything at all. One night Kevin heard him cry out from his bed, most likely because of a bad dream. But otherwise my son had appeared to be mentally stable.

As the holiday season approached I decided that the best present I could wish for would be to have Bruce and Phoenix home for Christmas. Fern had already arrived home from college. I had enough money left to cover bus fare for the other two, and for Phoenix's son, Cory.

Bruce said he would come up shortly before Christmas when he expected to receive his monthly cheque. I could reimburse him the money for his ticket after he arrived. But when I next talked to him, he stated stiffly that he would prefer not to come up at this time. He said he would rather come up during the summer when the landscape had turned green. His voice sounded flat and the intensity of it varied erratically even as he spoke. I wondered if Bruce had been skipping his medication injections. I was reluctant to query his house parent, Jim Draper, because he might think of me as being a nosy mother who was attempting to undermine his authority. I finally telephoned his office. Jim assured me–a bit patronizingly I thought–that Bruce had indeed had his shot on the previous day.

It was wonderful having Phoenix and Cory home for Christmas. Cathy and Darwin and their teenagers, Jennel and Tyler, were over for dinner and it was a real celebration. But I was a little depressed because Bruce had not made it up. I assumed that he would be visiting Ed and Connie on Christmas Day, but as it turned out, they had prior commitments and were out of town. Bruce spent the day alone in his residence on Victoria Road.

Bruce told me later that Christmas was no big deal to him, anyway, because he was not a Christian. He said he no longer wanted to be a member of the Baha'i Faith either; he did not wish to be bound to any particular religious affiliation.

A few days after Christmas, I was invited to my friend Ruby's home, which was just down the road from our place. Ruby's son Donovan was up from Vernon with a videotape of the Baha'i World Congress celebration that had happened in New York City earlier in the year. Donovan's twelve-year-old son Tyler and some friends planned to go skating on the lake, so I suggested to Cory that he come along. The only skates I could find were a pair of Leon's size elevens.

Poor Cory had to struggle to remain upright on skates that were four sizes too large for him.

In many ways, Cory reminded me of Bruce when he was a boy. Like Bruce, Cory is good-natured with a terrific sense of humour. He is also tenacious when it comes to accomplishing what he really wants to do. I recalled that when Bruce first played minor hockey, he was the only kid on the team who did not know how to skate. He fell down before, after and during almost every play. Before the season was over, though, he had become one of the best skaters on the team. I still had the trophy that Bruce had received for being the most improved player in the Pee Wee Division of minor hockey.

Phoenix was enjoying herself immensely, visiting with relatives and friends whom she had not seen for years. She had studied astrology on Hornby Island and was now quite accomplished at calculating birth charts for her friends. Her cousin LeEtta in Fraser Lake had asked her to do a chart and Phoenix had finally completed it. She had purchased a secondhand computer and it was a tremendous asset to her in her newly acquired profession. Phoenix had also brought a set of tarot-like cards with her. She and her daughter Krys, who now lived in Edmonton, had designed them. Each card was unique. The coloured picture symbols were combined with associated words and short phrases. Phoenix emphasized that her job was only to make suggestions; she did not try to interpret a meaning behind the cards that were being dealt.

I decided to participate in a game that was played with these cards–together with Fern and Cory. My first question was predictable:

what could I do to be of help to Bruce in the future?

The drawing on my card was of a single vertical line which resembled the upright frame of a wall in a building construction project. The name on the card was The Wall. Phoenix suggested that this symbol might signify Bruce would have to build his own structure: perhaps there was nothing new I could do that would impact positively on his life. That thought fit in quite appropriately with what I was beginning to believe.

Lately whenever I tried to communicate with Bruce, I seemed to cause him more stress. I had mulled over the contents of Bruce's angry letter and—among other things—he had accused me of being afraid of the voices that were symptomatic of his illness. I realized that, in some respects, he was correct. When I thought of the voices as being separate from Bruce, they did frighten me. But when I recognized that they merely represented a dysfunction of his thought processes, I was no longer afraid.

One night I experienced an extremely vivid dream that I believed was in some way prophetic. I found myself inside a house with a woman whose son had recently been admitted into a psychiatric hospital. I began walking up a steep narrow flight of stairs when I found my way being blocked by two adolescent boys. The youngsters were tanned and appeared to be healthy, but I knew that they were ghosts. I was not the least bit afraid and enjoyed seeing them. Shortly after that I was downstairs conversing with the woman whose son had been hospitalized. She nonchalantly informed me that the staircase led into an attic where a very sick black dog lay slowly dying. The image of what she said frightened me terribly and I awoke screaming.

For days after I wondered what could be behind the ominous implications of that extremely vivid dream. I was positive its message pertained to Bruce's voices which he had so often said were a blessing. My subconscious mind had visualized them as being the adolescent ghosts upon the stairway. But the significance of the black dog alluded me.

I decided to write a letter to Bruce. He had always been interested in discerning the meaning behind our nightly adventures. Perhaps, I suggested, I had been disturbed upon learning about the existence of the black dog because it had represented the unknown. Was there anything about his voices that I did not know? I queried.

Bruce phoned shortly after receiving my letter. His voice sounded high and thin as he muttered something about the dog in the attic. He said he remembered a dog dying at our house when he was about nine. I reminded him that the dog had not been kept in the attic and it was not black. It had been his dog and it had died of distemper. I did not realize that, because of the deteriorating state of his mental health, Bruce was not able to comprehend the abstract qualities I had perceived in my dream. My letter had only succeeded in opening up old psychic wounds from the time when he had suffered the loss of his dog.

On January 9, 1993, I had an appointment with a Vancouver specialist to determine if I should undergo a minor medical procedure. I phoned my son and suggested he meet with Fern and me at a Vancouver restaurant for a belated Christmas dinner. I would bring along a carrot pudding which the three of us could enjoy later in the hotel room I would reserve for him and myself. Bruce sounded elated at the prospect of our reunion. I mailed him the money for a bus ticket to Vancouver and with it a note saying we would meet him at the depot in two day's time.

I stayed with Fern at her room in Surrey during the first night of my visit. Early the following morning she accompanied me on the long transit bus and Skytrain ride into Vancouver. Bruce was supposed to be on the bus that would arrive from Nanaimo at 1 p.m. He was not on it.

When I phoned his residence he told me he no longer had enough money to take the bus into Vancouver. He would try to borrow the money or perhaps earn some by shovelling snow from a neighbour's driveway, and then meet us later in the day. But Bruce failed to show up on any of the later buses. I ended up mailing the carrot pudding to him from a post office in Surrey. When I phoned from home two days later, Bruce said he was sharing it with some of the other guys. They all agreed that it was very good.

I was feeling quite complaisant when I talked to Bruce. I had finally convinced a dear friend whose son had schizophrenia to attend one of our BCSS meetings. My friend was concerned because her son had stopped taking his medication. The normally good natured young man was becoming high-strung and behaving strangely. Every night, she confided, he opened the curtains wide on all of the windows in the house. Sometimes he rubbed soap across the panes of glass and over all the mirrors. And lately he seemed to be consuming huge amounts of salt. She was worried that too much salt could be harmful to his health.

At the meeting we viewed the video *One in a Hundred*. It had been written and produced by the Victoria branch of the BC Schizophrenia Society. The video featured three young people who spoke candidly about how the disease had interrupted their schooling and disrupted their lives. All three were intelligent and well-spoken individuals. My friend and her daughter, who also attended the meeting, agreed that the video really tells it like it is.

Bruce phoned on January 23rd to inform me that his group home now had a new address. The residence had been moved to a building across the street from the new CMHA office on Bowen Road. Bruce said he had been spending much of his time at the office, accessing the computers that had been set up in the basement.

He stated laconically that he was recuperating from a beating he had suffered earlier in the month at the hands of a fellow resident. He had complained to Mental Health that the man was actually an abuser of the mental health system. The fellow had retaliated by punching him repeatedly in the face and had loosened several of his teeth. Bruce had been fearful of resisting his attacker who was a veteran of the streets and would have no compunction about coming back at him later with a weapon.

The incident was reported to the RCMP, and the fellow had been charged with common assault. Later Crown counsel entered a Stay of Proceedings, and all charges were dropped. A restraining order was issued and the man had been ordered to stay away from Bruce or risk further prosecution. But Bruce's attacker had inordinately altered my son's appearance. His formerly straight teeth now protruded unevenly whenever he smiled.

In February, I received another phone call from Bruce. His voice sounded thin and frail. He told me he had been taken once again to Emergency at the Nanaimo Regional General Hospital. Because he appeared to be in a passive state of mind and deemed not dangerous, they had refused to admit him. Bruce did not tell me what his symptoms were. I had no way of knowing that, despite medication, he was experiencing new, more frightening voices inside his head.

Bruce said he was unable to handle the stress of living in an often unsupervised residence. The other guys argued amongst themselves all the time. Right at that moment someone was screaming loudly that it was not his turn to make coffee. Bruce had talked to Ann Simpson at Mental Health Services, but she didn't seem interested in moving him back into Columbian House. "I don't think she takes me seriously," he said.

This was the same Ann Simpson who had been the Group Home Coordinator for Mental Health Services in Prince George when Bruce lived there in 1985. I assured Bruce that I would phone Ann and implore her to help him. I had found her to be an intelligent and caring woman when I had talked with her eight years earlier.

I asked Bruce about his medication, and he assured me he was taking Modecate injections regularly. I reminded him that a year earlier he had informed me he was on a new drug. Bruce became very upset. "Has it come to that," he cried, "that I don't even know what medication I'm on!"

On February 17, I called Ann Simpson at Nanaimo Mental Health. As we talked, I thought she seemed hesitant and perhaps a trifle harried. I reminded Ann that, in the past, when Bruce was mentally well he did not wish to reside in a monitored environment. The fact that he now wanted to move into Columbian House meant that he definitely needed to be there.

Columbian House was full, Ann replied, and there was a waiting list. She would try to get him in, she added, but Bruce seemed to have a problem with the rules against smoking in his room.

When I told Bruce what Ann had said, he was noncommittal. He planned to visit Ed and Connie for a while, anyway, he informed me. His dad and stepmother had been living on the west coast of Vancouver Island while Ed worked on a construction project. But for the time being they were back home in Ladysmith.

One day as I was driving home from work, I heard an announcement on the car radio that excited me so much I almost drove into the ditch.

A new drug for schizophrenia had been developed that was purported to be eighty percent effective for people with the illness, and there were virtually no side-effects. The name of the new drug, which was not yet available in Canada, was Risperidone. A few weeks later a copy of a newspaper article about the new drug was included in some printed material that had been mailed to our BCSS branch. I happily photocopied the article and mailed it to Bruce.

On May 18th, I received the first of several phone calls from Bruce that concerned a fellow resident named Ralph*. Ralph had hit upon him, Bruce confided, verifying his suspicions that the fellow was gay. "Not that I have anything against homosexuals," my son insisted, then laughingly added, "I'm not bragging, but for some reason or other they seem to find me attractive."

Bruce said he was concerned that Ralph might be a child molester. He had spotted the man's car close to an elementary school playground. Ralph had picked up three young boys aged about twelve or thirteen and driven away. Bruce had voiced his suspicions to others, but felt they did not believe him because he was schizophrenic.

I assured Bruce that I believed him. As far as I knew, he had never deliberately lied to me. Even when he had been deeply psychotic, his perceptions of actual events had usually been consistent with my own. Bruce asked me to phone Jim Draper, the man who was his house parent, and tell Jim that Bruce's concerns should be considered, even if he was schizophrenic.

I had never met Jim Draper. I had talked to him once on the telephone when I had enquired as to whether Bruce was still on medication. His answer had been a trifle short, I recalled, when he told me that Bruce certainly was; he had had his shot on the previous day. I did not want to talk to Bruce's house parent on the telephone.

I wrote a letter instead, and mailed it Priority Post. In it, I explained that I believed Bruce implicitly when he stated he had observed Ralph picking up young boys. But Bruce had also mentioned that Ralph smoked marijuana all the time. It may well be that Ralph's interest in children was to sell them drugs.

I did not hear from Bruce for some time. I was preoccupied with my job and the interesting but time-consuming activities associated with helping to put together another Writers' Group anthology.

Throughout May and June the countryside around Fraser Lake had once again become green and beautiful. Bruce, however, continued to postpone his long awaited visit. I mailed him a pair of designer blue jeans for his birthday on May 5, and suggested he come up at that time. The parcel was returned to me because he forgot to pick it up at the post office. When I phoned, he promised he would come up in time for my birthday on June 26.

Bruce phoned early in June to tell me he had lost his wallet, which contained all of his grocery and cigarette money. He emphasized that he hated to ask me for money, but it was an emergency. I transferred the amount he had lost to a Bank of Commerce branch near his residence.

On the evening of June 29, Bruce called again, this time to inform us that he was about to have a book of poems published. Fern answered the telephone. She said later Bruce was so excited that the phone lines vibrated. When I talked to him, he said the money to publish had come from a government grant that a man named Randy Allen* who was associated with CMHA had obtained. Randy had been the instructor of the desktop publishing course that Bruce had had taken two years earlier in January 1991. He would manage the new CMHA project, which would establish the former contributors to *Voices* magazine with their own publishing company. The company's first publication would be Bruce's book of illustrated poetry entitled *The Ghosts Behind Things*.

"It's what I've always dreamed about," my son exclaimed.

Almost as an afterthought Bruce added that he had been having some problems lately, but was now feeling fine. He neglected to tell me that he had just been discharged from hospital after having been admitted two days earlier. According to hospital records dated June 27, 1993, Bruce had been experiencing voices that were telling him to hurt someone.

For the next few days, Bruce was occupied with the task of going through the several hundred poems he had written in order to select those that were best suited to be included in his upcoming book. And he was busy drawing illustrations to complement his poetry.

Bruce's recovery was to be extremely short-lived. He was readmitted to Nanaimo General Hospital on Sunday, July 4. This time with voices that were telling him to harm himself. Notes from hospital records state the following: "...neat, clean, soft-spoken, pleasant and cooperative on approach. Says he wants to be here to be 'safe'...potential for aggression: no [sic]. Says he would benefit from a more structured, supervised and supported living structure."

Bruce's psychiatrist, Dr. R.N. Molineaux, was more succinct in his diagnosis. On July 5th, he wrote: "...chronic paranoid schizophrenic illness with some situational problems in the inadequately supervised accommodation for the severity of his illness, but without appropriate alternative being available."

According to his July 5th report Dr. Molineaux tended to underestimate Bruce's ability to relate to circumstances in the real world: "...[He has] lots of grandiose plans for publishing [but] none ever comes to anything."

In February 1995, I finally met with Jim Draper who had been Bruce's house parent for almost two years. Phoenix and I interviewed Jim for several hours at the Tally Ho restaurant in Nanaimo. He filled us in on the declining state of Bruce's mental health since he left Fraser Lake in December of 1991: "From the time I first met him until I left Nanaimo in July 1993, he was never off his medication. It just didn't do the trick for him. He was on a drug called Fluanxol which was given by injection every three weeks. I would put a notice up in the house to remind Bruce when his shot was due. Sometimes he would decide he didn't need it. It would not be long, however, before I would receive a phone call from Dr. Walker telling me Bruce was overdue for his injection.

> "Twenty-four hours after his shot, Bruce's eyes would be glazed over. But when the medication leveled off, they'd become focused. A couple of days before his next shot was due, he'd begin to wander around in a daze. He wouldn't eat.

> "Bruce had a bad habit of not eating which I think was counterproductive to the effects of his medication. When he was fasting, he sometimes gave up drinking coffee and even threw away cigarettes. One time he threw away a full carton of cigarettes.

"Then he would run short of money and have to sell something so that he could buy more cigarettes. He would have to take some of his possessions down to the pawnshop.

"He had side-effect pills called Cogentin, but sometimes he would not take them. One day I was on the back porch of the house when two of these pills almost hit me in the face. Bruce had tossed them out from his upstairs bedroom window.

"Bruce sat in the Dairy Queen restaurant next door almost every day, writing his poetry. He also wrote a book of essays called *Twelve Sermons of a Soapbox Preacher.* He told me he wanted to be diversified in his writings; he did not want to be known as mainstream. He hoped to be recognized as a rebel, but not as a radical.

"There were two or three times when I took Bruce to Emergency at the Nanaimo Hospital and he was not admitted as a patient. Each time they gave him some sort of tranquilizing agent. I would take him home and put him to bed. The next morning Bruce would not remember what had happened.

"One episode occurred when the house was still on Victoria Road. Bruce became convinced that he was possessed by a devil or a demon. He was drooling quite a bit and his body was rigid. I took him to the hospital but nothing they gave him seemed to help. Bruce was adamant he needed to see a priest. But I could not track one down at that time of night. Finally the hospital chaplain came in and stayed with him for about forty-five minutes. Bruce did derive a certain amount of satisfaction from the chaplain's visit.

"Bruce talked to me, sometimes for hours. He told me he had good voices in his head but he also had bad voices. When the bad voices became too loud, he said he needed to talk in order to turn the volume down. The voices would then lapse into a state of compromise. He would sometimes talk about that rape that occurred when he was a child. It came up in the conversation three or four times, at least.

"Bruce knew he needed help. But there was a waiting list at Columbian House. There was a respite bed there but it was not always available.

"One time, it must have been in June, Bruce experienced something he never had before. I found him on the floor rolling around. He was curled up in a fetal position and in a confused state of mind. I shook him for 20 or 30 seconds and then took him to the hospital. They kept him in for two days in order to stabilize him. When they released him, he walked home. He said he felt fine.

"One night the voices in Bruce's head began telling him to kill Ralph. I found him standing outside of Ralph's door muttering to himself. I asked him about the voices and he said they were not too intense. They were not strong enough, he said, to cause him to confront Ralph. But he was having really bad feelings about them.

"I told him to tell me about what he was feeling. He said he did not want to do what the voices were telling him to do. But he was afraid they might become so strong that he would be unable to resist them. He told me to yell. Maybe that would appease the voices and they would go away.

"Bruce wanted me to call the cops. He said 'What if I do heed these voices? Maybe they should put me in jail now, in case that happens.' I told him not to worry. 'My door will be open' I said. 'I can easily hear you if you walk past and approach Ralph's room'.

"'Have a cigarette,' I told Bruce, 'and take some side-effect pills if you have not taken any. Put some music on your ghetto blaster and see how things go. If the voices start up again, come back and we'll talk some more.'

"Two hours later there was a knock at the door. Bruce said the voices were back and they were really bad. His eyes were rolled back in their sockets. He was barefoot and seemed to be confused. I told him to put on his shoes and then I took him to the hospital.

"At the hospital there was a female doctor in the emergency room. I got into a verbal fight with her right there at the entrance. She was one of those types who say, 'Just take a pill and go to bed and see your doctor in the morning.' I told her that it was important that Bruce get into the hospital. If she would not admit him, I would get Bruce to slap me–then call the cops so he'd go to jail. She finally let him in."

On July 7, 1993 Jim Draper left his job as house parent of the residence on Bowen Road to take up similar employment in the nearby town of Parksville. Bruce was discharged from hospital one day later into a residence which Dr. Molineau had previously described as being inadequately supervised. The house was now completely unsupervised.

CHAPTER THIRTEEN

The Death Dream

"This dream was more a feeling than a story:
in it, I am being stalked, from lifetime to lifetime,
by an invisible, implacable, evil enemy,
which kills me, over and over, trying in the process,
to damage my soul/body connection badly enough
to kill me permanently...I was so scared when
I woke up that my heart was beating a mile a minute."

From a letter written by Phoenix Ray
to her parents, Leon and Doris Ray.
The envelope was postmarked August 9, 1993.

M y oldest daughter, Phoenix, was enjoying the summer of 1993 immensely despite what was being described as the coldest, wettest July in the history of Hornby Island. In her letter, she wrote that she had discovered the joys of gardening, and the subsequent pleasures derived from eating vegetables which grew from the tiny bit of nothing that she had planted in the spring.

All three of her children were doing well, Phoenix informed us. They were busy flitting back and forth between Hornby and Edmonton, putting in quality time with whatever parent they had not resided with during the school year. Krys had just returned to Edmonton and a part-time job at the annual Klondike Days celebration. The boys would be back on Hornby in a few weeks' time.

Phoenix was optimistic about the future of her astrology business too. She had set up a small office near the ferry terminal and the appreciative feedback she was receiving from her small but growing list of clients, was very encouraging.

During the past year some amazing coincidences had occurred in her life which had my oldest daughter convinced she was being the recipient in a series of miracles as she called them. The first of these miracles had happened when she obtained her computer. Phoenix was only able to afford it because the owner had needed money and was willing to sell it cheap. After that she had lucked into the purchase of a reasonably priced vehicle to replace the ancient Toyota which had died shortly after its journey to Fraser Lake and back in 1990.

Phoenix's most recent miracle was even more astonishing. She had found a lovely and affordable house to rent, something that was almost unheard of on Hornby Island. The trouble was she already had a lease agreement on the humble cottage where she had been living for the past few years. But, only one day after learning about the availability of the lovely house with a view, she received the news that her present home had been sold. The miracle was, Phoenix explained happily, that with places to rent as rare as fish feathers, she had found another place to live even before she knew she needed one.

The one dark cloud on Phoenix's horizon seemed to be that, as the month of August ushered in hotter and drier weather, she found her nighttime slumbers being interrupted by a series of hellish death dreams. Phoenix had not experienced nightmares like these for many years. They were so frightening that she was sometimes afraid to go to bed at night.

Leon and I were enjoying our summer too despite the wet weather. Fern was home from college working as a brusher on a forestry project that provided summer employment to students. It was nice to have her at home again, although she was often dead tired, soaked to the skin and mud from head to toe when she arrived home from her job in the bush.

My vacation leave from work was scheduled for the last part of August because Cheryl, the older of my stepdaughter Diane's two daughters, was being married in Parksville on August 28th. I was busy making travel arrangements so that Leon and I could journey on Via Rail train to Prince Rupert, then ride the Queen of the North ferry to Port Hardy on the following day. On the third day we would take an Island Coachway bus to Courtney where I had made reservations to lease a car. Fern would leave Fraser Lake at a later date to meet up with us there.

On July 19, I was preoccupied with making plans for next month's vacation when the telephone rang and it was Connie. She and Ed were back living in Ladysmith, she told me, after having spent some time living in a construction camp near Lilloet in the BC interior.

Connie said she was phoning to reassure me, in case I was concerned about Bruce. He was fine now and in the hospital, after attempting to cut his wrist with a dull table knife. It had not been an actual suicide attempt, she hastened to explain. Bruce had done this in order to divert anger away from a fellow resident, the man named Ralph. Connie said she had just provided Bruce with all of the essentials for a long hospital stay: cigarettes, his Walkman cassette player and a good supply of batteries.

Before I had the chance to digest this disconcerting information, the phone rang once again, and it was my son on the line. Bruce reiterated what Connie had just told me. "There's nothing to worry about," he emphasized. "The marks on my wrist are almost gone already." The police had been in to see him, he stated ruefully; they usually ask questions when someone shows up at a hospital with marks on his wrists. Bruce had been concerned that I might be notified about the incident and assume that he had actually tried to kill himself.

At the time I was blissfully unaware of the sometimes malevolent nature of Bruce's hallucinations and delusions. His method of using self-mutilation to divert anger away from another person was bizarre, to say the least. But I knew that Bruce was not a violent person. Perhaps, I surmised, it had been an alternative to what would otherwise have been a forceful confrontation.

I had no idea that Bruce had long since resolved his antipathy toward the man named Ralph; or that the anger he had attempted to assuage the previous evening was not his own, but that of his voices. They had been demanding, persistently and vehemently, that he kill his fellow resident.

I asked Bruce if he had been taking his medication and he answered yes; he had just had a shot two days earlier. "In that case," I retorted, "It's obvious to me that the anti-psychotic you're on isn't working."

"That's the reason I'm in the hospital," Bruce answered, "because I want a change of medication." I gave the doctor the information about Risperidone that you sent down. They're going to put me on it, as soon as they can fly some in from Eastern Canada."

I was instantly ecstatic. I told Bruce about the miracles that his sister Phoenix had said were occurring in her life. "I'm so glad you're going on that new medication," I enthused. "It's about time you had a miracle in your life too."

Jim Draper has often maintained that Bruce was never off medication during the time period when he was Bruce's house parent. Dr. Molineax appears to refute that premise in a hospital report dated July 5, 1993: "Flupenthixol [Fluaxnxol] for some time with no adverse affects [but] if he does not take it, it tends not to work." The list of medications at the time of Bruce's July 5th hospital admittance were: Largactil [chlorpromazine] 50 P.R.N. Fluaxnol 3 mg T.I.D. and benztropine [Cogentin] 2 mg. There is no mention of an anti-psychotic to be taken orally.

According to his outreach nurse, Ching Blas Muego, Bruce was also supposed to take Fluaxnol in tablet form to supplement the injections. Ching recalls having her battles with Bruce because of his non-compliance. The pills were sedating, he explained, and interfered with his creativity. Eventually, Ching says, she couldn't help but respect his view about how he thought he could better manage his condition. That was when she began to back off and simply stood by until he asked for assistance.

Ching recalls: "It was not easy to monitor his symptoms and most of the time only Bruce knew he was having a hard time with the voices. His best state, in terms of controlling the symptoms, happened when he was on the injection but even then he argued because of the side-effects.

"I am not sure if having a choice with his anti-psychotics was a point of issue. People who are experiencing acute symptoms sometimes are not able to make sound decisions about their treatment. They are hospitalized so that the professional caregivers are able to give the doctor a feedback about the effects of the change of medications so that adjustments may be made prior to their discharge…"

Bruce sounded pleased with himself when I called the hospital on July 25th. He had just learned that the publication of his book would be going ahead on schedule, despite his being confined to hospital. Tom Morris*, a fellow poet whose book would also be published soon, had been in to see him. Tom had been gathering Bruce's writings and illustrations from the residence on Bowen Road and the computer room of the CMHA building across the street. Randy Allen, who was the editor as well as project manager, would make the final decision on what poems to use in the book.

"I don't care," Bruce said happily. "The only thing I really want input in is the title. I want the book to be called *The Ghosts Behind Things*."

The Risperidone was working well, Bruce assured me, with no sedating side-effects. He'd had some confusion though and been treated with chlorpromazine, which seemed to help. In a week or so he would be discharged from hospital into a new, more monitored residence that the people at CMHA had found for him. When he was all settled in, he planned to come up to Fraser Lake for his long-awaited visit. Bruce promised to let me know when he was to be released from hospital.

On July 30th, I made a phone call to Nanaimo General Hospital and asked to speak to Bruce's nurse on the psychiatric ward. I was curious as to just how well the medical staff considered him to be. The nurse hesitated before telling me that, because of confidentiality, she could only say his voices are less bothersome. She added the information that Bruce was scheduled to be discharged early next week. When I inquired as to whether she thought he was well enough to handle the long bus trip to Fraser Lake, she answered that she did not know. He was okay in hospital but there was no telling just how well he would be able to cope under stress. On August 7th, I phoned once again, this time to talk to my son. I was told that he had been released from the hospital two days earlier. At the time of his discharge Bruce had been in Nanaimo

General Hospital for 22 days. Medical records indicate he was on a prescribed medication of 6 mg of Risperidone daily, and had shown marked improvement. A footnote written by Dr. Molineax states the following: "Discharged in my absence on the 5th of August/93 at which point showing no episodes of aggression but still a number of residual psychotic features."

Bruce was released into the care of the management of a group home facility called the Nanaimo Care Unit. It was a respite care home, providing temporary semi-supervised accommodation and board for people with various mental problems, but who were not considered to be a threat to themselves, or to other members of the community. The residence was administrated by the Nanaimo chapter of the Salvation Army.

It was not until the evening of August 9th that Bruce phoned to let me know of his new address and phone number. His voice sounded low and flat, but he answered yes when I inquired if he liked his new residence and the people who managed it. "Did you buy yourself a watch yet?" I asked. I had sent money down for that purpose. His new medication was in pill form and he would need to keep track of the time to know when to take it. He said he had not, but there wasn't a problem because the people who ran the group home gave him the Risperidone when it was required.

Bruce's thought processes and response time seemed slower than usual. Our conversation soon became stilted because it was so one-sided. I found myself babbling to fill in the gaps. At one point, he muttered something about receiving Thorozine (a brand name for chlorpromazine) to relieve symptoms of anxiety and confusion during his hospital stay. His caretakers had some chlorpromazine tablets on hand as a P.R.N. (prescription required when needed) medication.

Before we ended our conversation I told Bruce about the wedding that Leon and I had been invited to in Parksville at the end of the month. I suggested he accompany us back to Fraser Lake on our way home from that. Bruce sounded pleased. He agreed with me that September is often the most beautiful month of the year in the northern half of the province.

I had almost forgotten about his upcoming book publication. "What did you say the title would be?" I inquired. *Native Tongue* he replied flatly, with no explanation about why it had been changed.

On the morning of August 11th, I was at my client's country home just north of Endako. My husband was usually unaware of where I worked but this particular client was one whom we both had been acquainted with for more than twenty years. She had been a strong energetic woman, not at all adverse to helping her husband on his trapline or skinning out his moose during hunting season. Now she was frail and desperately ill with terminal cancer. Leon drove up to her house around ten a.m. and I strolled outside in the bright sunshine to greet him. I had no idea of the absolutely unthinkable turn of events that had occurred in Nanaimo on the previous evening.

My husband is a man of few words. But the words he spoke that day reflected his compassion and deep personal sorrow. A lawyer from Nanaimo had phoned, he told me. The man, whose name was Stephen Taylor, had spoken to Fern. Bruce had stabbed someone at the group home where he now lived. He was in jail charged with second degree murder.

The word murder hit me like a slap in the face. Emotionally I went numb. I was not able to associate my son, the poet and artist, with that horrible word and its connotations. Possibly, I reasoned, Bruce had defended himself from an assailant. But why on earth was he in jail? Leon answered my unspoken question. "The attack was unprovoked," he said gently. "The lawyer told Fern the man died from a single wound to the abdomen."

"Are you going to be okay driving home?" he inquired. I told him there would not be a problem. I wanted to finish the stint with my client before having to return home and face the painful new reality.

My client understood that something had happened to my mentally ill son and I would soon be travelling to Nanaimo to visit him. She did not as yet know the full story. In our small community, the phone lines would be busy and she would hear it all in a day or two. When I was ready to leave, she placed one bony arm on my shoulder and we hugged each other gently. "I will pray for you," she rasped in her heavy German accent. The tears ran down my face. "I'll pray for you, too," I blubbered. She died two and a half months later on November 2, 1993.

The next few days are a blur in my memory. I recall working at my clients' homes on Thursday and Friday. Everyone was very kind and even diplomatic, but they knew enough about the incident to be curious. I wanted each and every one to know the truth, but I knew very little myself. It would be more than two years before I was able to piece together the full story of what had happened.

On Sunday morning Cathy picked Fern and me up, and we drove the six hundred miles to Vancouver in her brand new mini-van. We had an appointment to talk with Bruce's lawyer on Monday afternoon in Nanaimo. We arrived back home on Thursday night. During that brief time span, a complete reversal of roles in the familiar mother/daughter relationship I had with the girls developed. I found myself trotting along behind in the footsteps of my three daughters, including Phoenix whom we met in Nanaimo. It was wonderfully relaxing, not having to make any decisions on my own.

But when we returned home I had to tackle the painful chore of informing close friends and relatives of what had happened to Bruce and of our subsequent trip to Nanaimo. I had written a fairly lucid letter to Ian Kluge in Prince George, which more or less covered the situation. I decided to expand on that letter and mail, or give out, copies to those who should know. It was easier for me to cope with what had happened if I did not have to talk about it. The letter was not a literary masterpiece but I knew I would be forgiven for that:

> "August 14th: Cathy, Fern and I are going to Vancouver tomorrow and then, on Monday to Nanaimo to talk to Bruce's lawyer and to his dad and, perhaps, some others. At 5:45 p.m. we will go to Victoria to visit, for one hour, with Bruce where he is being detained for murder at the Wilkinson Road Remand Center (Saanich). He is being held there until whenever there is a bed open at the Forensic Psychiatric Institute in Port Coquitlam (next week sometime). Bruce is only allowed two adult visitors at one time, so Cathy made the appointment for both of Bruce's parents: Ed and myself.
>
> "I don't know if you heard on the news (last Wednesday) that Bruce stabbed a 21-year-old-man and, as a result, the man died. The man was killed as a result of a series of tragic errors.

The 21-year-old was the son of a man who works for the city of Nanaimo, but for some reason was down on his luck and had been sleeping at Bruce's new residence, a supposedly structured environment for schizophrenics who were having trouble coping. Bruce had been living for two years at a group home where he was more independent. Jim Draper was the name of the house parent who was there some of the time. Jim phoned the other night to tell me that everyone who knew Bruce and who had seen him at his worst cannot believe what happened. He said, 'The Bruce Ray we know would never have been violent.'

"The thing is: just a month ago Bruce tried to cut his wrist with a dull dinner knife (just scratched). The reason he did this was to direct his anger away from a fellow resident, who may or may not have been a sexual deviant. The potential for violence was there a month ago, at least.

"P.S. August 16 & 17: Now that we have talked to Bruce's lawyer, the pain of it is something that I can handle with an odd one of Dr. Gow's white pills. (Dr. Gow is distressed and cannot believe that Bruce could be that violent). At times I am very angry.

"The boy that Bruce stabbed was not mentally ill. Bruce had been acting irrational and the people in the group home had tried to get him into the hospital at around three or three-thirty in the afternoon. He was not allowed in because the psych ward was full. They would not request that he be transported to Comox Hospital, either, as they sometimes do in emergencies.

"I think the sheriff's report stated that Bruce had appeared to be quiet so they sent him home. But he somehow got a knife and stabbed this 21-year-old boy in the abdomen. He was then heard to say, 'Now I know I am dead.' The lawyer said Bruce was out of control after that, for three days.

"We met Phoenix in Nanaimo shortly before our appointment with the lawyer. Stephen Taylor talked to Ed and I first. (Ed was there with Connie). He said people in Nanaimo are very supportive of Bruce and willing to help him. Even the family do not blame him (the family of the boy he stabbed).

"On September 9th it will be determined if he is fit to instruct his lawyer. Stephen Taylor went into the different scenarios that could happen before and after Bruce's trial. He said he didn't want to sound too confident, but from all evidence he had never seen such a clear cut case of innocent by reason of a disease of the mind. (They don't say insanity anymore).

"To make a long story short: with typical bureaucratic bungling, where there seems to be no communication between the institutional hierarchy, Cathy raced to Victoria (120 km/hr) to arrive on time for the appointment she made for Ed and I to visit Bruce, only to find out he had already been transferred. (Connie had suspected that might happen. She phoned before they left and had been assured that he was still there!) She and Ed will have to see Bruce at a later date."

The sequence of events that occurred on August 10, 1993 would change all of our lives forever. It had started early in the afternoon, when Bruce began to experience what he later referred to as an upheaval of good and evil inside his head. His good voices, some of which he believed originated from within his own soul, were helpful and creative. But the bad voices were revenge-motivated and hurtful. They began to taunt him, saying: "You are damned. We will make you kill someone whether you want to or not."

Bruce was frightened. He informed the caretaker, a man named William McIntyre, about the voices and that he was experiencing a lot of anxiety. Mr. McIntyre gave him an anti-anxiety pill (chlorpromazine) which, Bruce recalls, only made him feel worse.

Shortly after, Bruce told his growing concerns to a fellow resident, who immediately phoned for an ambulance. Bruce explained to the resident and to the perplexed caretaker, that he was hearing voices telling him to kill someone, and he was afraid he might be compelled to do so.

Bruce was attended to in the emergency room of Nanaimo General Hospital by Dr. B. Calvin who noted in his medical report that Bruce suffered from command hallucinations; his effect was flat and his speech slowed. The doctor also noted that his patient was pleasant and obeyed requests. Dr. Calvin recalled later that Bruce told him he was hearing many voices inside his head. The voices were female and they were telling him to hurt someone. Bruce felt he needed to be admitted into the hospital, although he had no specific plan to hurt anyone and recognized that the voices he was hearing were not real.

Accordingly, Dr. Calvin administered to Bruce his prescribed medication and made arrangements for him to be admitted into the hospital. The doctor noted that Bruce was cooperative and appeared to be calm and reasonable throughout.

But there were no empty beds in the psychiatric ward. Dr. Calvin found himself in a dilemma: if Bruce was to receive any further medical help he would need to be transferred by ambulance to another hospital, perhaps as far away as Comox. After his patient had eaten supper, the doctor explained the situation to him. He then telephoned Mr. Philip Orun, the evening caretaker at the Nanaimo Care Home, before making the crucial decision to release Bruce into his care.

In his medical report, Dr. Calvin stated the following: "He is comfortable returning to group home setting...continue on Risperidone as before...increase chlorpromazine 50 mg. See family doctor in 1-2 days to be reassessed. If his condition deteriorates in the meantime, he will be brought back to the emergency or transfer to the nearest available psychiatric bed will be considered."

But Bruce's mental state had deteriorated to the point where he was now out of touch with reality. He believed that the forces of evil were in control of his mind. The voices were warning him that if he should be admitted into a hospital, doctors would perform brain surgery upon him.

At approximately 7 p.m. Mr. Philip Orun arrived at the hospital to transport Bruce back to the residence. My son's paranoia had increased to the point where he no longer trusted the caretaker enough to confide in him. The voices in his head reminded him that the Nanaimo Care Unit was a Christian facility. If Philip Orun suspected that Bruce was under the control of Satan, he would very likely punish him.

Upon reaching the residence, Mr. Orun inquired whether he was in need of anything, and Bruce replied that he was fine. The caretaker then advised him to go downstairs to his basement bedroom and relax. But the voices inside Bruce's head were becoming louder. They proclaimed that he was damned; that he was about to die in the group home.

Bruce slipped into the tiny bathroom that was adjacent to his bedroom. Once in there, he attempted to slash the same wrist that he had injured a month earlier with a kitchen knife. This time he used a razor blade. Once again he hoped to assuage the blood lust of the dark voices, but this time he was not successful. His frantic efforts did not lessen the clamour inside his head, nor did the razor blade puncture any of his arteries.

My son shivered as he watched the blood ooze from his wrist and into the white porcelain sink, then trickle slowly down the drain. "You will die and go to Hell," the voices cackled. When it became obvious that his suicide attempt was a futile one, the noise level became more raucous. "Sacrifice the blood!" they shrieked. "Kill someone and we will spare you!"

The part of him that was still Bruce became weaker and weaker until he was reduced to being a mere observer, crouched in abject terror in one small corner of his own mind. His body was like a robot's as it blindly obeyed the instructions of the mad voices. His right hand reached for a towel to bandage the wounded wrist; cold water effectively erased the stains from the sink bowl.

The bathroom door led into a large recreation area where twenty-one year old Mathew Davis reclined on a loveseat watching television. The other residents had opted for a different channel on the upstairs set, but Mathew did not want to miss this week's episode of his favorite show.

Mathew did not suffer from a mental illness, nor did he have a drug or alcohol problem. Like many young adults he was considered to be too old to remain in the family home, but unable to find a job and make it on his own. A family friend, who was one of the directors at the Nanaimo Care Unit, had offered Mathew room and board at the group home for the summer. In return the high school drop-out would volunteer his services to help out with everyday chores, whenever needed. Staff members were encouraging the young man to return to school in the fall and complete his education.

Bruce trekked along the open hallway, the bloodstained towel still wrapped loosely around his arm. A short flight of stairs led him into the communal living room which was occupied by an after-supper crowd watching television, or just lounging around. No one paid attention when he brushed past and turned off into the kitchen.

The room was empty but evident of the recent after meal cleanup was in the spotless counter spaces and the freshly mopped linoleum. Bruce helped sometimes with the cleanup, but tonight he had been at the hospital.

"The knives...the sharp knives," the voices prompted, and he obediently pulled open the drawer where they were kept. Selecting a large butcher knife, he retraced his steps through the living room and back downstairs. He held the knife out of sight pressed hard against his thigh. The raucous cacophony in his head dimmed slightly upon reaching his bedroom. But there was no escape from their murderous whims. "Now! Now! Do it now!" they cajoled. "It is either you or him!" Bruce's mind slipped into what his doctor later described as a "de-personalized" state. His level of consciousness descended to where his deranged lower self manifested complete control.

Thirty-nine minutes after he had been discharged from the hospital Bruce stepped out of his bedroom doorway and stealthily approached the rear of the loveseat where Mathew Davis watched TV. Positioning himself directly behind his victim, he leaned forward and plunged the knife into the young man's upper abdomen. Mathew screamed in pain and immediately pulled the knife from his chest.

Bruce staggered a few steps before collapsing face down upon the carpet. He believed for the moment at least that he had killed himself. Upon hearing Mathew's scream Philip Orun and several of the residents rushed downstairs to where the young man clutched the bloodstained knife in the palm of his hand. Mathew gestured toward my son who lay motionless on the floor. "The guy behind me did it," he said weakly.

Mathew was taken by ambulance to Nanaimo Regional General Hospital where despite resuscitation attempts he died at 10:23 p.m. The wound had punctured his aorta and his death was due to massive blood loss and shock.

At 7:50 p.m. two RCMP officers arrived at the Nanaimo Care Unit. Bruce did not appear to notice that they were even there at first. One officer noted that he moved very slowly as if he had just woken from a deep sleep. His eyes appeared to be glassy. In the car enroute to the police station Bruce was asked if the person had done something to him. Bruce answered "No! The voices told me to do it."

Later after having received the news that Mathew had indeed died; that he was responsible for having taken the life of a fellow human being, my son plummeted into the depths of a suicidal frenzy. For three days he threw himself repeatedly against the unyielding walls of his jail cell in an unrelieved agony of depression and remorse. He was designated a risk for suicide for more than a month.

Funeral services for Mathew Emerson Davis were held at 2 p.m. on Saturday, August 18, 1993 at the Salvation Army church in Nanaimo.

CHAPTER FOURTEEN

The Wall

"When all is forgotten
And the blade cuts deeply
No god would save me
No will to surrender to
Except the bitterness of defeat
I look at the wall
And no sun shines..."

Bruce Ray 1995

I have hazy memories of that warm August evening in 1993 when my daughters and I ventured, for the first time, along that narrow tree-lined laneway leading to the Forensic Psychiatric Institute in the district of Port Coquitlam. Cathy had been driving through heavy traffic along the unfamiliar Lougheed Highway. Phoenix, who sat beside her, peered intently at a wrinkled outdated map of the Lower Mainland, while I gazed stoically at the passing landscape from my solitary seat behind. Just before we reached the turnoff to Riverview Hospital, the girls spotted a tiny sign indicating that Colony Farm Road veered off sharply to the right through what appeared to be a farmer's field.

The rustic scenery that bordered the quarter-mile entrance to the government-run facility brought to my mind a memory of a similar farm located just south of Prince George where various kinds of trees and plants were grown and experimented upon. My sleep-deprived and sedated brain idly compared the lives of patients confined at the Forensic Institute, to the frail misshapen plants that grew amongst the healthier ones at these horticulture experimental farms. "They are isolated too," I mused. "Their symptoms are researched and experimented upon until it is determined that they can or cannot become productive."

As we approached the main buildings, my reverie was shattered by a posted sign which caused us all to flinch with shock until we had correctly interpreted its intended message. The sign read "Watch Out For Patients On Road." Over the years we had visited wild animal preserves where similar warnings had been posted. Now we envisioned pajama-clad psychiatric patients who might at any given moment attack unwary passersby! We had no idea that to traverse the shadowed distance of the tree-lined laneway to the doorway of the Forensic Institute was far safer than to venture along the side streets of any large city.

I felt a sense of otherworldliness as I gazed at the three-storey, fifty-year-old building where my son was to be confined in custody for the next three years. The flowers, shrubs and trees that grew within the borders of its neatly maintained lawns did little to soften the austere appearance of the structure.

The institution was originally built to house large numbers of shell-shocked veterans returning home to Canada from World War II. For many years it had been the center of a large and productive agricultural development. Local people still referred to the acreage on the south side of the highway across from Riverview, as Colony Farm.

The original property, including what is now the Riverview Hospital grounds, had been cleared out of the wilderness by patients from a New Westminster asylum during the early 1900s. The huge tract of land had been donated by a provincial government which, in the days before medication therapy, believed that hard work and peaceful surroundings would likely be beneficial to mental patients. This was at least partly true because it enabled them to eat hearty and nutritious meals. For decades the efforts of patients who worked at Colony Farm provided the entire hospital complex on both sides of the highway with an abundance of milk, butter, meat and vegetables.

Area old-timers recall the herds of horses, sheep, pigs and cows that grazed in the fields and were contained in pens and corrals at Colony Farm. The farm managers took great pains to raise only prize winning breeds of livestock. Until the 1950s, Colony Farm dairy cows were recognized as blue ribbon animals at agricultural fairs across Canada and the north western United States.

The farm was eventually shut down due to the fiscal restraint policies that marked the early years of the Social Credit government in British Columbia. By the 1950s, psychotropic drugs were used regularly at Riverview Hospital to control patients' most debilitating symptoms. Those patients whose condition was treatment resistant or who had become caught up in the criminal justice system were warehoused–sometimes for decades–at the Forensic Psychiatric Institute building across the road.

During later visits to FPI, I learned that all female patients were housed in dormitories on the main floor. Most male patients began their hospital treatment in one of the two heavily-secured wards located on the third level of the building. Those who have been remanded by the courts for psychiatric assessment are admitted to R3 West. Patients considered to be a danger to themselves or others were ensconced in a ward on the east side.

The sight of my son on the evening of August 17, 1993 when we visited him on the third floor of the Forensic Psychiatric Institute, is blazed into my memory. I had been dreading the moment. It had been a year since I last saw him. After what had happened, I half-expected some kind of radical transformation in his appearance. Possibly he would seem larger or stronger or more brutal looking than I remembered him to be.

But if anything it seemed that Bruce's physical stature had become smaller and frailer. His face was thin and deathly pale. His familiar smile revealed a row of unevenly spaced teeth, from where his gumline had healed after the vengeful attack by a roommate the previous winter.

When Bruce and I embraced I realized that he was, essentially, the same sweet, caring person he always was. He spoke quietly, saying "It's what I was afraid of, Mom. It was the worst possible thing that could happen."

The anti-anxiety pill I had taken at Fern's landlady's home in Surrey left me as animated as a wet dish cloth. I listened placidly while my two older daughters conversed with Bruce. We had been told that only two people at a time could visit him. For that reason Fern had elected to stay behind. After our arrival at the Institute, however, we learned that the rule was often bent for out-of-town visitors.

When Bruce gestured with his hands I could see a deep round wound on his left palm that looked as if it might be a burn mark, possibly caused by a lighted cigarette. It may have been self-inflicted, most likely during the time that he was in custody at the Nanaimo jail. Steven Taylor had told us that Bruce was out of control following the murder. We learned later that he had been in the depths of a suicidal frenzy.

On the inside of his wrist above the barely-healed scar on the palm, I noticed two thin brown lines which looked as if they had been penciled in with crayon. I assumed they were from his so-called suicide attempt a month earlier. It was surprising, I thought, that the scars were still clearly visible. He had described the wounds to me as being mere scratches.

It would be more than two years before I finally learned that Bruce had made a more recent attempt at slashing that same wrist; this last time on August 10, 1993, just minutes before he committed the murder.

When visiting hours were over, we were escorted back downstairs to the tiny office area next to the main entrance. The receptionist collected our personal identification badges and suggested we take a large white canvas bag with us that contained Bruce's belongings.

Out in the car, Cathy rummaged through the bag and discovered an unopened can of tobacco and a cigarette roller, as well as some paper tubes. These, she bundled up with her gift to Bruce, which was a beautiful hand-tooled leather bound Bible and retraced her steps back inside the building. While she was gone, Phoenix and I placed the remaining items back inside the bag. They were mostly books but there were a few articles of clothing. These included the blue sweater that Connie and Ed had given him for Christmas one year, a pair of blue jeans and some well-worn running shoes. I suddenly realized, with a sick feeling in the pit of my stomach, that these were very likely the clothes he had worn on the night of the murder.

At home, it was back to work as usual for a few days until my allotted time off for vacation. I tried hard to ignore the painful ache that I carried inside myself like an oyster harboring a large, misshapen pearl. I was determined that despite all that had happened, Leon and I would enjoy our vacation.

Our long awaited trip to Vancouver Island to attend my step-granddaughter's wedding on August 28 was for the most part, enjoyable. The train ride from Fraser Lake to Prince Rupert was comfortable; the scenery along the ferry route through the Inside Passage was spectacular and the weather consistently beautiful. From our bed and breakfast layover in Port Hardy on the north end of Vancouver Island, Leon and I boarded an Island Coachway bus and travelled south to Courtenay. There we met up with Fern, who had arrived on a bus from Vancouver. We piled our suitcases into a rental car and drove to Hornby Island to visit Phoenix before proceeding on to Parksville for the wedding.

The specter of that previous journey to Vancouver Island, which I had taken only ten days earlier, loomed constantly in the background of my mind. I was able to curb my melancholy thoughts and feelings most of the time. During one of my solitary sojourns on the ferry I experienced a sudden, overwhelming sense of loss. I found myself crouched in the ladies' room with tears oozing down my face. It was as if it had been my son who had died, rather than his having been the cause of a death. I almost wished that it had been so.

Later in the magazine and novelty shop, I discovered a handmade greeting card–pale yellow in color–with matching envelope. It was sparsely decorated with a few dried seeds and tiny leaves. It seemed to be appropriate for me to express my feelings of the moment on the unpretentious card and send it to the family of Mathew Davis. I composed a few paragraphs which I desperately hoped would be of some small comfort to them. I placed the card in an envelope addressed to Stephen Taylor, imploring him to forward it to the Davis family.

At Phoenix's house, the topic of conversation centered upon the horrific turn of events that had occurred in Nanaimo. We did not as yet know all of the facts behind the bewildering question of what had caused Bruce to suddenly behave in such an uncharacteristic manner. The girls and Leon each had a theory which, I noticed, fit in with their own individual life experiences.

"I knew something wasn't right when Bruce phoned to tell us about his book publication," reflected Fern. "He was on such an emotional high that he was almost out of it." Fern had taken drama courses in high school and later in college. She had experienced a gamut of intense emotions while portraying various character roles. "That high level of energy could be hazardous for people with schizophrenia," she surmised.

Phoenix's musings were more esoteric. She had taken math and science courses in college recently: "Bruce may have been aware all along that this would happen," she suggested. "According to the quantum theory of physics, events do not always occur according to our straight line concept of time. If somewhere in Bruce's psyche he knew he was going to–one day–kill someone, the shame and guilt he would have experienced because of that terrible knowledge, might well have triggered his mental illness in the first place."

My husband's hypothesis that the sudden escalation of Bruce's symptoms might compare to a default in an electrical circuit made as much sense to me as anything else did. Leon had repaired motors and mechanical parts of cars and equipment all his life. "I read somewhere that the function of the brain is similar to the way we harness electricity," he stated. "Schizophrenia may be like when there is a loose or damaged electrical wire. It doesn't always cause a short circuit immediately. It can happen randomly–whenever the wire comes in contact with something it shouldn't."

The wedding in Parksville was fun. It was a relief to be with people whom we loved but who apparently knew nothing about Bruce's dilemma. The Nanaimo newspapers had documented the story, and it had been on local radio and television. But although Parksville is only a few kilometers to the north, it might as well have been in a different world. We decided that there was no good reason at all for us to dampen the gaiety of the occasion.

The day we were to leave, I called Brian aside. Of all my stepchildren,

Leon's youngest son was the only one who had known Bruce in recent years. I handed him a copy of the letter I had written two weeks earlier which was to inform friends and relatives about what had happened. I explained to Brian that it was painful for me to talk about the situation. I asked him to share the letter with the others sometime after we had left for home.

Brian is like his dad; he is reluctant to express his feelings. He read the letter and a comforting embrace for me was his only visible reaction.

I had promised Bruce I would write to him at the Forensic Institute at least once a week. The main thing, I believed, was to keep the communication lines open, although I may not always have anything to write that would be of interest to him. I included the price of a package of cigarettes in every envelope. He may not always enjoy reading my weekly platitudes, I thought, but the cigarette money would be a pleasant bonus.

The scheduled date for Bruce's first hearing at the Nanaimo courthouse was on September 9th. This hearing was to determine whether he was fit to stand trial. Ed, Connie, and Stephen Taylor were pleased to inform me later about Bruce's obviously improved state of mental health. He had appeared to be less insane on no medication at all than he had been earlier on Risperidone.

Stephen Taylor later relayed the information that my son was a popular guy in Nanaimo. Several of his friends, including Louis Devoin and Peder Long whom he had played music with at the drop-in center, faithfully attended every one of Bruce's scheduled courthouse appearances. Jim Draper from Parksville, together with the guys at the group home on Bowen Road, forwarded gifts of writing paper and cigarette makings.

I was encouraged that Bruce's lawyer seemed to be taking a personal interest in his case. When we had visited him in his office, Stephen Taylor assured Ed and me that he would do his best to protect Bruce from having to serve time in jail. He assured us that Bruce would get the help he needed at the Forensic Psychiatric Institute. Although people accused of a crime were usually detained there against their will, it was a hospital, not a jail.

Bruce told me later that life on the third floor of FPI was comparable to living inside a pressure cooker. On the day that he was admitted a patient in a bed beside his began freaking out. The fellow ended up with mucus streaming from both nostrils. Another with a toothache, was being driven by the pain into fastening a wire around the tooth in a desperate attempt to pull it out.

The third floor could often be described as a war zone because of the constant fighting between disgruntled patients. Bruce was already experiencing paranoia as a symptom of his illness and the never-ending battles were highly stressful for him. The proximity between his bed space and that of the patients involved in these altercations was quite small. Sometimes Bruce would implore a staff member to place him in the solitary confinement of a side-room in order to escape from the turmoil.

The beds in the huge dormitories were spaced so that staff were best able to control altercations and emergency situations, including threats to themselves. Staff members carried a pen-sized device that when activated, alerted everyone else in the building. Whenever a buzzer sounded it would be immediately followed by the staccato drumming of leather boots and shoes racing up and down the hallways toward the source of the awful noise. Staff members would suddenly be everywhere, grabbing the troublemakers and pulling them into a side-room.

Bruce got along well with the FPI staff because he was always polite. He never got into fights with fellow patients either, although he did come close at least once. The main cause of dissension amongst patients involved some who were always bumming for cigarettes.

At first Bruce was intimidated by these men whom he knew were convicts with long police records. They had broken the law almost all of their lives. But he learned they were not that dangerous, once you understood their tough, street-hardened code of honor.

One fellow was constantly hounding him for cigarettes. If Bruce happened to refuse, he would snarl, "If I ever catch you out on the street, I'll kill you." One day after yet another confrontation, Bruce decided to follow his antagonist into the bathroom, referred to by many as the smoke room. "If you really want a fight," my son challenged, "then go for it." The fellow backed down and after that, was really nice toward him.

Bruce was distressed by some of his roommates attitude toward mindless violence. His own status had actually improved in the eyes of these patients when they learned about his crime. Bruce told me later that one fellow had asked him an extremely stupid question. "He asked me what it was like to kill someone." My son was indignant. "All I could think to say was: none of your damned business!"

His voice filled with emotion: "I should have told that guy the truth. That night, I cried when I realized what I had done. I buried my face in the rug and I wept until the cops came and took me away. I was quite passive. It was not like some Clint Eastwood movie…"

At home in Fraser Lake we had been busily preparing for the upcoming winter. Leon was hauling and splitting firewood. I was canning tomatoes from the greenhouse, and preserving the usual supplies of pickles, jams and jellies. One evening my friend Jeanette of our BCSS group phoned. She inquired hesitantly if I was up to accompanying her on a trip to Vanderhoof where she had made the arrangements to hold our meeting for September. "Most certainly," I replied, "Yes."

At the Vanderhoof Mental Health Center we plugged in the coffee pot and laid out the pamphlets; then basked in the knowledge that there were several more faces in attendance than just our own. Lately our Fraser Lake meetings had been mostly a no-show. But as it turned out, I was not the source of hope and inspiration to others that I had intended to be.

As the meeting progressed my cheerful affectation began to erode. And when the tears threatened, I hurriedly left the room. I spent some time in the rest room, explaining later that it was with intestinal cramps. The truth was I needed to reassess the previous concept I had of myself in relation to the other members of our group. The role I usually assumed was that of a sympathetic advisor, one who had been through the crunch and finally reconciled myself to the reality of my son's illness. The others were still working their way through all the earthly hells that invariably accompany a loved one's schizophrenia.

With a deepening sense of dismay, I realized that there was no one else in our group with a relative who had committed a serious crime, let alone a murder. Suddenly in my own mind, I was reduced to a sniveling shadow of my formerly complacent self. It was a humbling experience.

Lucy Waters, the president of the provincial office of BCSS, mailed me copies of newspaper stories written by a woman named Noreen Flanagan, a staff writer for the *Nanaimo Daily Free Press*. Lucy had told me on the phone that she liked the writings. Unlike most journalists, Noreen was knowledgeable about the disease of schizophrenia because she'd had training as a psychiatric nurse.

Lucy was correct. Noreen had composed an excellent article explaining the disease, in addition to her front page story that concerned Bruce's crime. Her writings reflected obvious compassion for both Bruce and the victim's family. But the headline on a follow-up feature hit me like a bullet through the heart. It was titled "Killing Angers Victim's Friend" and was based upon an interview with a friend of the young man whom Bruce had stabbed to death. I forced myself to study the slightly blurred photocopy of a smiling Mathew Davis which accompanied the article.

Lucy had said that the time-line between when Bruce had been released from hospital, and when he had stabbed Mathew Davis had been approximately 39 minutes. I felt the beginnings to a deep sense of anger. If only Bruce had been confined to hospital or else been monitored—even for a little while—I raged, then the smiling young man in the photograph might still be alive!

A week or so after his first hearing, one of the letters I had mailed to Bruce at the Forensic Institute arrived back at our mailbox. When I phoned the Institute, the staff was only able to inform me that he had not returned to the facility following his court appearance. I made a number of fruitless inquiries. It soon became apparent to me that no one knew where Bruce was and perhaps no one really cared.

I was in the dark as to Bruce's whereabouts for about ten days. During that time, I phoned Ed and Connie, Stephen Taylor's office and the Forensic Institute at regular intervals. "Something must have happened to him," I worriedly told my husband. "Perhaps he escaped and no one has noticed."

On September 21, I penned the first of what turned out to be a series, of angry letters to Lucy Waters at BCSS. I had learned that I could rely on Lucy to be an ever-patient, ever-helpful confidante:

"Dear Lucy…I am becoming angry all over again. At this time,

I do not know where my son is, and no one else seems to know either! Bruce's lawyer's staff gave me the run-around, reluctant to admit they do not know his whereabouts. Finally yesterday someone told me that not even the Crown counsel knows where he is...

"If someone tells me that he managed to walk away and nobody noticed he was gone, I don't think I'd be surprised. If he somehow ended up on the streets of Toronto (he's done that before) I would be the first to know I am sure. He may forget everything else but he always remembers our phone number."

Bruce finally phoned me on September 29th from the Wilkinson Road Remand Centre in Victoria. He said he had previously been unable to get to the one available telephone. He would be confined to that facility, he informed me, until his next hearing on the 29th of October.

The move had been his own idea, Bruce explained. In jail he had access to a typewriter. Also there was more privacy and the noise level was less than at the Forensic Institute.

The big problem at the Remand Centre was that he was isolated from most of the other inmates. Bruce had been assigned to a special security unit, referred to as Protective Custody or PC. "If you are one of the boys in PC," Bruce told me later, "you are despised and vilified by everyone–at every opportunity." PCs were either rats, who had informed on someone, or shinners who were child molesters. "I don't know why I am in Protective Custody" Bruce sounded mystified, "because I'm neither one."

I remembered reading a magazine article that defined the caste system of prison hierarchy. Schizophrenics had also been on the list of the universally despised. Other prisoners very often abuse the mentally ill which is why, in most institutions, they are automatically placed in Protective Custody.

Bruce spent a long, lonely month at the Wilkinson Road Remand Center before being returned to the Forensic Institute. By that time he had decided that the hospital, as nerve wracking as it was, was better than being in jail.

CHAPTER FIFTEEN

The Ghosts Behind Him

"They bicker
And twist phantom Q-tips
Into my ears
Those ghosts behind me
Poke fun
At my sanity
And tap dance
On my patience..."

From "Epiphany" by Fern Ray 1994.
Fern wrote this poem to gain
insight into the bizarre symptoms
of her brother's illness.

Early in October I began assembling what I later referred to as a diary, dating back to January 1991. Using the same process as when I had compiled material for my 1987 *Journey Through the World of Schizophrenia* I painstakingly sifted through scraps of paper, address books and old telephone bills. It seemed to me that Bruce's mental health had progressively declined since that period of time when he had embarked on what was called a "drug holiday." I did not intend to place blame on either Bruce or his doctor for what had occurred two and a half years later. It just seemed important to me that the whole truth leading up to the tragic event be laid out in chronological order. The collect calls from Bruce were itemized on each of the old bills. He had moved fairly often which made it easy for me to match up telephone numbers that were in my address book, to memories and notes which pertained to specific events.

My frustration level reached a new high that month. I received a letter from Stephen Taylor answering my query regarding the possibility of our family and perhaps the Davis family launching a civil suit against the Nanaimo Hospital. But both Ed and I had given up on the idea of initiating legal action. A lawyer friend had advised that the defence actions of members of the medical community in British Columbia were generally supported by the BC Medical Association, which had virtually unlimited financial resources.

Enclosed along with his letter, Stephen Taylor returned the pale yellow envelope with the card inside that I had asked him to forward to the Davis family. He also included a communication from a Nanaimo woman named Sharon Selinger: In his letter, Stephen Taylor explained:

> "...Enclosed [is] correspondence you wished forwarded to the victim's family. I understand that you would like to offer some words of comfort to them but it is not appropriate for either you or I to be in contact with them. As a matter of fact it is against the law. I hope you understand and will not try to contact them on your own as this may jeopardize Bruce's case.

> "I enclose for your information a letter I received from a Mrs. Sharon Selinger which I think you may find of some assistance. If you do consider civil action against the hospital, Mrs. Selinger's information may be of help to your lawyer..."

Sharon Selinger's story which she had documented in a three page letter to the administration of Nanaimo Regional General Hospital, was a true heartbreaker. On the night of April 18th, four months before my son committed a murder, Sharon discovered her 21-year-old son Jeffrey slumped on his bedroom floor with a rope around his neck. He had attempted to hang himself. She rushed him to the Nanaimo Hospital where he died, despite extensive efforts to resuscitate him.

The familiar and extremely disturbing part of Sharon's story was that Jeffrey, who had been exhibiting symptoms of major depression and was suicidal, had been transported by ambulance to the hospital just two weeks earlier. He had been given perfunctory treatment by the Emergency Room physician and released.

Jeffrey Selinger had been in desperate need of monitored medical attention in the early morning hours of April 4, 1993. He had communicated his obsession with suicide to the ambulance attendant on the way to the hospital, and to the emergency room nurse. The attending physician had listened to Jeffrey's comment that life sucks and his confession that two or three months earlier he had examined his father's hunting rifle with the intention in mind of killing himself.

Jeffrey neglected to inform the doctor of the reason why he had been taken in to the hospital via ambulance: he had made a serious attempt to follow up on that intention.

Sharon, and other members of Jeffrey's family, could have informed the doctor of the crisis situation that prompted them to seek help, but they were never consulted. When they had arrived at the hospital after following along behind the ambulance, they were told to stay in the waiting room. Sharon could have informed the doctor that Jeffrey had attempted to cut his own throat with a knife. He would have succeeded except for the timely intervention of his younger sister Leasa, who had wrested the knife from him and telephoned for an ambulance.

As is usual, whenever there has been a suicide attempt, the ambulance dispatcher contacted the RCMP. That morning it seemed as if everyone was aware of the critical state of Jeffrey's mental health. Everyone except his doctor.

The doctor made the decision that Jeffrey was not committable although he did have the option of keeping the young man in the hospital for observation for a period of up to 24 hours. Jeffrey was sent home with a prescription for Nortriptyline, an extremely slow acting anti-depressant which takes up to three weeks to be effective. At no time during the next two weeks, before his successful attempt at suicide, was he referred to a psychiatrist.

Two months later on June 8, 1993 Sharon Selinger sent a letter to Malcolm Telford, Executive Director of Nanaimo Regional General

Hospital. In her letter she recommended that the hospital review their procedures for treating potentially suicidal patients:

> "...Your hospital should have a set procedure that emphasizes total communication with parties who can shed light on a patient's state of mind, and proper consultation with mental health experts who can recommend appropriate treatment.
>
> "Lives depend upon it.
> Sincerely, Sharon Selinger"

When I read the copy of Sharon's letter that Stephen Taylor had sent me, the thought that immediately crossed my mind was: if her recommendations to the hospital had been acted upon, the tragedy that occurred two months later might never have happened.

The hospital's chief of staff Dr. Paul Mitenko replied to Sharon's letter stating, "...I have reviewed Jeffrey's case carefully, and I sincerely believe that, in spite of the tragic outcome, the assessment and management was appropriate and justifiable..."

When the coroner's office released a report of its investigation into the death of Jeffrey Selinger, it made no recommendations whatever.

I mailed a copy of Sharon Selinger's letter and its subsequent reply from Dr. Paul Mitenko, to Lucy Waters at BCSS headquarters in Richmond. I also enclosed a copy of the diary that I had improvised from old telephone numbers. A week later Lucy phoned to tell me that she had faxed everything to Brian Copley, the executive director of Mental Health.

A hearing was held in November to determine whether there had been any criminal intent in regards to Bruce's having committed the crime. Dr. K. Riar, a psychiatrist at the Institute, made the following observations in a letter dated November 12, 1993:

> "...In my opinion, the acute exacerbation of his illness was precipitated by medication change and the stress of moving to a new group home.
>
> "Since his admission to the Forensic Psychiatric Institute, he responded well to Resperidone [6 milligrams]...had a few episodes where he became very restless, anxious and felt that he was losing control. He still actively hears voices but claims

they do not bother him too much and he is able to distract himself from them. The frequency and the duration of these episodes are decreasing everyday…"

In his letter Dr. Riar made several recommendations regarding his patient, Bruce Byron Ray, F.P.I.# 3597:

"1. He suffers from paranoid schizophrenia, chronic type, which has responded significantly, but still has active symptoms of his illness.

"2. He is certified under the *Mental Health Act.*

"3. He meets the test for Not Criminally Responsible Due to Mental Disorder defense as he acted under the influence of command hallucinations and delusional beliefs. Although he knew that stabbing someone was wrong he was compelled to act under the fear, anxiety and confusion from hallucinations.

"4. He should continue to take prescribed treatment and should stay in a secure place until his sickness is under control. For this he should be returned to the Forensic Psychiatric Institute under section 672.29 if there is a delay between his Court appearance on Monday and his trial date."

Despite Dr. Riar's optimism regarding the effectiveness of Risperdone for the treatment of Bruce's symptoms, the medication eventually proved to be useless. In December the disturbing command hallucinations once again began manifesting themselves inside of his head. On one occasion, Bruce cried out to a nurse, "I'm going to kill someone…the voices are really bad…they're telling me to kill myself…I can't stand it…I'm going to lose control!"

These voices seemed to appear suddenly, with no clear-cut warning or known stressors. Although Bruce never acted upon their intrusive demands that he hurt someone or injure himself, he was desperately afraid that he might one day lose control.

Whenever one of his spells as he called them occurred Bruce would immediately notify a staff member that he was in need of whatever medication Dr. Riar had prescribed to be used as a PRN. He would also request that he be secured inside a side room. Hospital reports indicate that Bruce was compliant and cooperative and not involved in any physical aggression towards co-patients and staff.

Toward the end of December Bruce's PRN medication (Loxapine) appeared to be no longer effective in getting him through his acute episodes which were now occurring on a daily basis. At that time Flupenthixol (Fluanxol) was prescribed: 2 mg three times a day along with 5 mg of Haldol every six hours—to be required whenever needed.

In January and February of 1994, I received two handwritten letters from Bruce. In the first of these he addressed me as Mom but in a subsequent communication, I was greeted as Doris. In that letter he explained that he wished to cut the umbilical cord so that we could get to know one another as separate human beings, rather than in our stereotyped roles of mother and son.

When I spotted my first name on my son's letter a memory of that strange encounter I'd had with Dale Olson in 1986 flashed through my mind. I was sure I could detect vestiges of her patronizing attitude between the lines of Bruce's letter. But the other letter, the one in which he addressed me as Mom, I found interesting and enjoyable. He wrote that he was managing to come to grips with the crime that he had committed. Writing in his notebooks was therapeutic, he stated. He had written a few things that dealt with the murder and that had helped a lot.

In his letter Bruce went on to say:

> "By all means have faith in the medication which at its worse is just a sedative and at its best seems to work. I'm on a new medication now, and I have high hopes. The Risperidone just didn't work for me, I guess. I'll have to keep trying whenever a new drug comes out. Meanwhile I'm just trying to behave myself so that I can advance to the second floor where things are easier (I hear). How's everybody up North and all the relatives?

> "Being stuck here is not too hard to take. There's some interesting characters who come and go. I'm trying to observe the way they are, remembering snatches of conversation and keeping it in mind for a story or two. I've been unable to write since I've not had access to a typewriter, but I'm hoping to do so soon..."

He ended his letter by adding a post script: would I please send down some typing paper? He now had access to a typewriter.

Bruce suffered greatly over the next few months. He was given a variety of medications but none provided relief for his symptoms. On the 23rd of January he informed a nurse that he was hearing a lot of voices. "They are telling me to kill someone," he stated worriedly. "This may sound funny to you," he added, "but I would like a lobotomy. I think that's the only thing that will help…"

The one day that Cathy and Fern stopped by, their visit had to be cut short because Bruce suddenly felt one of his spells coming on. Fern recalled later that Bruce's face appeared to be swollen. She assumed that was a side-effect of his medication. What really shocked Fern though was the display of crooked teeth in Bruce's mouth when he welcomed his sisters with his usual easygoing smile. She had not seen her brother since he had been beat up in his Nanaimo group home.

My son was becoming more and more anxious about the outcome of his trial for second degree murder, which was set to be heard at the Nanaimo Courthouse on March 29. I assured him that there would be plenty of us there to lend him moral support. His sisters Fern and Phoenix and I, as well as his dad and stepmother would be there. Cathy was unable to attend, but Phoenix's 16-year-old daughter Krys would be coming out from Edmonton. Krys had become quite fond of her uncle during the years when he lived at her mother's home. Now she was a high school honours student, making plans to attend university and take courses leading to a career in criminal law. Krys was very interested in learning first-hand about courtroom procedure.

Bruce's lawyer sounded vague when I talked to him on the telephone a week before the trial was to begin. More than twenty witnesses had been subpoenaed and he surmised that it could take two or three days for them to testify. But when I phoned two days later, I learned there was to be a radical change of procedure. Because of overwhelming evidence that Bruce suffered from a brain disorder, Crown counsel had agreed to a reading of what was called an Admission of Facts. Mr. Taylor explained that the document would be a condensed version of the information obtained from all of the witnesses.

Stephen Taylor then tried his best to discourage me from attending the trial. I realized later that he was hoping to spare me from what he believed was needless distress. The trial would be extremely short he informed me. Dr. Riar from the Forensic Institute was to be the only witness called to testify. The main evidence following the reading of the Admission of Facts would be the viewing of some graphic photographs of the fatal wound that had killed Mathew Davis.

There was no way anyone would be allowed to visit Bruce, Mr. Taylor warned. He would be held under tight security at the Nanaimo lock-up, both before and after the trial. It was unlikely that we could even communicate with him in the courtroom, either. The prisoner's box was made of glass but it faced the judge. "All that you would see of him in there," the lawyer spoke in what I perceived as a condescending tone of voice, "is the back of his head." "I would not miss my son's trial for the world!" I retorted haughtily. "His sisters and I have promised him that we will be there."

As it turned out, we did miss much of the trial. Phoenix, Fern, Krys, Cory and I had stayed the night in a Nanaimo motel. The trial was to begin at 11:00 the next day. This was confirmed in an early morning telephone call to Stephen Taylor's office. But the lawyer had forgotten to inform his staff that the time had been changed to 9:45. We filed in through the courtroom of Mr. Justice Edwards in time to hear Crown counsel complete his questioning of Dr. Riar. Ed and Connie soon joined us and we sat together on one of the highly polished benches that reminded me of a church pew. About a dozen other spectators were in attendance, scattered throughout the large room.

I had taken an anti-anxiety pill and it had temporarily clouded my mind. A woman on the other side of the center aisle appeared to be slumped over in her seat. Her companion comforted her. "That has to be the groom's side of the room," I speculated idly, my brain locked into the mode of likening the situation to a much happier occasion. I suddenly realized that the woman was probably Mathew Davis' mother. The man responsible for her son's death sat in front of us, inside a glass-walled cage. He had his back to us and had gained a considerable amount of weight but it was definitely Bruce. I felt myself begin to tremble and was immediately grateful for the comforting handholds offered by my two daughters.

Under questioning from Crown counsel Mr. John Blackman, Dr. Riar informed the court that at the time of the incident Mr. Ray suffered from a symptom of acute schizophrenia known as de-personalization. He had lost touch with reality and was unable to understand or appreciate whether the act he committed was morally wrong. Dr. Riar spoke in a quiet tone of voice and he sounded sympathetic toward Bruce.

Mr. Blackman asked if certain physical symptoms noted by police officers who had attended the crime scene were supportive of Dr. Riar's diagnosis that at the time of the stabbing, Bruce suffered from an intense form of schizophrenia. Crown counsel quoted from the Admission of Facts that one officer had stated "...Bruce Byron Ray appeared to be moving very slowly as if he had just woken up from a very deep sleep."

A second officer Cheryl Armstrong noticed later on that "...Mr. Ray's eyes had a vacant look, his eyeballs would disappear rather into the back of his eyes to the extent that no pupils showed and only the whites of his eyes would appear." Constable Armstrong had also observed him rub his eyes and grab his head. She observed him to fall to the ground and curl up in a fetal position and, while in that position, shake his head.

Dr. Riar agreed that the physical symptoms described by the police officers did indeed confirm the diagnosis he had made. The doctor elaborated: "After the stabbing he felt that he killed himself somehow and he was in a very distraught state and people who are in a distraught state have this kind of physical symptoms."

I recalled that in the past Bruce had displayed similar symptoms during those times when he had overdosed on his medication. I wondered if it was possible that the chlorpromazine that was given him to relieve his symptoms had actually brought on or escalated them instead?

Crown counsel concluded the questioning of Dr. Riar by inquiring what in the doctor's opinion were the chances, given Mr. Ray's current condition, of a reoccurrence of the circumstances that had occurred on August 10th, 1993. Dr. Riar replied: "...within the last six months he has not improved even a little bit on very potent anti-psychotic medications and he still gets intense periods of this auditory hallucinations telling him to hurt other people, so the chance…of [it] happening again I think, is extremely high."

Following Dr. Riar's testimony, court proceedings were declared adjourned until 2 p.m. Bruce's wrists were handcuffed together by two uniformed guards. When he rose up from his seat, he turned his head around and peered questioningly about the room. I noticed Bruce wore eyeglasses, something I had not seen him wear for years. When he spotted the seven of us sitting together on our polished bench, his eyes lit up and I noticed he held his head a little higher. My husband was not with us, but I recalled that Bruce often repeated something his stepfather had once said. I could sense Bruce clicking into Leon's matter-of-fact advice: "No matter how bad things get, remember to keep your chin up."

The guards urged my son to proceed quickly up the aisle and away from the courtroom. As they whisked past, Phoenix reached out and patted her brother reassuringly on the shoulder.

Ed worked the midnight shift at a local sawmill, so he and Connie hurried home for him to catch a few hours' sleep. The rest of us were about to leave the building when a smiling middle-aged woman crossed the wide concrete steps toward us. She introduced herself as Ching Blas-Muego. Ching told us she had been Bruce's outreach nurse when he lived across the street from her office, which was in the CMHA building on Bowen Road. She invited us to join her for lunch and meet some of the people who had been acquainted with Bruce. We piled into Phoenix's station wagon and followed Ching across town.

We met several people at the CMHA building who remembered Bruce from when he had spent much of his time downstairs in the computer room. Ching stated–somewhat defensively I thought–that she had been the one responsible for having moved Bruce into the Nanaimo Care Unit after he was discharged from hospital. She said she had no other choice. Jim Draper had left for his new position in Parksville and Bruce was not well enough to live on his own. The people at the Nanaimo Care Unit were willing to provide temporary respite care, until such time as a bed became available at Columbian House.

Ching went on to tell us that everyone who had known Bruce had been severely impacted by the tragedy, especially his former roommates and the people whom he had worked with on the book publishing venture. Randy Allen still had Bruce's poetry and drawings, but that part of the project was now on hold until all the furor generated by the trial had died down. Ching copied down our names and addresses. She assured us that she would mail out copies of Bruce's book as soon as they were made available. But Bruce's book was destined never to be published. The CMHA sponsored endeavor did not receive the full amount of anticipated government funding.

The afternoon session of the trial began with a reading of the indictment against Bruce by Crown counsel. The verdict was then announced by Mr. Justice Edwards. It was documented as follows:

1. Mr. Ray is fit to stand trial.

2. Pursuant to section 672.34 of the *Criminal Code* did commit the offense but he is not criminally responsible on account of mental disorder.

Mr. Justice Edwards concluded: "Mr. Ray is to be detained in custody at the Forensic Psychiatric Institute." The court deferred any further disposition to the British Columbia Review Board which, together with medical personnel at the hospital, would pursue the matter further.

The proceedings concluded with a request by Mr. Blackman: "My Lord, there is just one other matter that I failed to mention. Given the verdict, it is probably of no procedural import as such, but during these proceedings Mrs. Davis, the mother of the victim, Mr. Davis, has been here and, just for completion, as it were, of the sad record of this tragedy, she has provided a Victim Impact Statement, and I ask that it be filed. It will not affect the verdict in any way, but out of deference to her I ask that it be filed."

The court and Mr. Taylor agreed that Mr. Blackman's request was appropriate.

After the trial, both Ed and I were interviewed by the press, which turned out to be the same Noreen Flanagan who had written the previous articles about Bruce for the *Nanaimo Daily Free Press*. Noreen told us that there had been yet another tragedy under similar circumstances, which had occurred just two weeks earlier. A mentally ill man had been released from the Nanaimo hospital to return to his home in Parksville. The following day he punched and stabbed his common-law wife before committing suicide. The woman survived, but that still left a total of three deaths that had occurred during the past year.

Noreen agreed that some degree of accountability should be acknowledged by the hospital for the tragedies. She said advising mental patients to go home, simply because there are not enough beds, is equivalent to telling a heart patient to have your heart attack at another time.

Later I talked to Peder Long and Louis Devoin, who had played music with Bruce and befriended him, despite the fact that he obviously suffered from schizophrenia. The two men had attended every one of Bruce's court appearances and had actually made it to the courthouse at the correct time that morning.

I was still upset with Bruce's lawyer because his office had given me the wrong information about when the trial was to begin. As Stephen Taylor left the courtroom, I accosted the obviously exhausted man: "Some of us travelled more than six hundred miles and only got to see half of Bruce's trial," Mr. Taylor replied that all we had missed was the reading of the Admission of Facts. He thrust his own copy of that document at me and I accepted it as a peace offering. I realized later that we had also missed half of Dr. Riar's testimony. Bruce eventually was able to obtain a transcript of the entire trial for me.

In retrospect, my son told me that he was pleased at the way Steven Taylor had defended him. The lawyer had asked all the right questions when cross-examining Dr. Riar to get at the truth.

We had planned on spending a second night at our Nanaimo motel, mostly because I wanted to talk to Jim Draper who had been too busy that day to attend Bruce's trial. We were all feeling a bit stressed. Especially me. Now that the trial was over, I desperately craved to get out of the city. Phoenix suggested that if I wanted peace and quiet, the best place to go for that was to her home on Hornby Island.

Phoenix was correct. For three days we wandered the length and breadth of the island in the unseasonably warm sunshine. We strolled through beautiful Helliwell Park, and along the nearby rocky shore. It was hilarious watching Krys and her equally citified friend Sandy who had flown in from Edmonton to join us. The two girls tottered over huge boulders in their high-heeled so-called walking shoes, photographing distant sea lions and the starfish that lay in purple clusters against the rocks.

One evening Phoenix and I confessed our deepest feelings to each other about what had happened to Bruce. As we tearfully embraced, I realized her pain was almost as great as my own. It was two years later when Phoenix let me read a poem she had composed the night she received the disturbing news that her kid brother had committed a murder. The following lines are from that poem:

> "...my brother
> who lived through more absurd and terrifying hells
> than Stephen King could fit into a trilogy, my brother
> who always survived and came back to tell us where he'd been
> and how it felt to be lost and find his own way back, my brother
> who returned less often and from further away, my brother,
> who loved the land and danced naked when no one could see him
> then wrote poems about it so others could feel it too, my brother
> whose veins ran green, my brother
> who dreamed he ran with Pan, my brother
> whose hands are forever blooded, my brother
> who is so alien and strange, my brother,
> who is so much like me..."

The following afternoon as the sun beat down as warm as midsummer, I meandered alone along a sandy shore near my daughter's home. The beach was deserted except for a few swooping herring gulls. I had not slept much the previous night. Bruce's trial had reopened emotional wounds that I had thought were almost healed. I lay on the ground and attempted to bury myself, clothes and all, in a layer of clean warm sand.

A wonderful feeling of peace and tranquillity embraced me. The advice I had often given my children, that something good is bound to come out of even the worst situation came to mind. Now I wondered what possible good could ever show itself as a result of Bruce's present condition. Fern had suggested that Bruce might someday write a book which would help others who suffer from schizophrenia. But that was before we listened to Dr. Riar testify at the trial. The doctor had stated before Crown counsel that Bruce's mental health had not improved even a little bit, despite the administration of very potent anti-psychotic medications. There was a strong possibility, I realized, that Bruce might never attain his previously impaired, but reasonably functional, state of mind.

A thought began to crystallize itself in a back corner of my mind. At home I had a drawer filled with notes, letters and newspaper clippings concerning Bruce and about the disease of schizophrenia. There was the story titled *A Journey Through the World of Schizophrenia* that I had completed in 1988 and my more recently compiled diary. In the scheme of things, perhaps it was me who was meant to write the book that Fern had talked about?

CHAPTER SIXTEEN

The Journey of Hope

*"Even when we feel most powerless in the face
of these relentless illnesses, we can work on
our own emotional resolution and find a
way to come to terms with the tragic events
that have changed our lives."*

By Dr. Joyce Burland, Ph.D. author of the
Family-to-Family education program
(formerly called the *Journey of Hope*)
for family members with mentally ill relatives.
This free 12-week course is now available in Canada.

O n April 16, 1994, two weeks after Bruce's trial, Jeanette and I drove
to Prince George to attend the First Northern Conference on
Schizophrenia and Related Disorders which was being sponsored by the
Prince George branch of BCSS. As it turned out the day-long event was
to be the first in a series of learning experiences that would finally allow
me to comprehend and accept the true nature of my son's mental illness.

I arrived at the conference armed with my usual ball point pen and
writing paper. The only way I can keep on track of what speakers are
telling me at public functions is to take notes. My attention wanders
hither and yon. As it was I had no such problem tuning in to what the

keynote speaker of the day, Dr. Phillip Long, a Vancouver psychiatrist, was saying. His speech was anything but dull.

Dr. Long spoke eloquently and humorously for well over an hour. Several of his patients, or consumers as they are now referred to, were in attendance. An attractive young woman named Allison testified that the drug Risperidone had done wonders for her. She said she was now able to get up in the morning without being depressed.

But as Dr. Long emphasized, Risperidone is not for everyone. A young man in the front row had to agree with that statement. For him treatments with the new miracle drug were not at all successful. His condition had only improved after Dr. Long prescribed an older tried and true medication called perphenazine.

My thoughts wandered momentarily to my recent visit with Bruce, a few days after he had been returned to FPI following his trial. Bruce had said Dr. Riar was starting him on some Stelazine–the medication he had been on for several years after being diagnosed with schizophrenia. The drug had been reasonably effective, I recalled, except for the times when he had taken too much.

Dr. Long talked about the recently understood biological basis of schizophrenia. Symptoms appeared to be caused by too much of a chemical called dopamine in the prefrontal cortex section of the brain. Many of the common symptoms including the phenomenon of hearing voices had been pinpointed to originate in specific parts of the brain. Even a normal functioning individual can experience audio hallucinations, Dr. Long said, if a physician were to touch one of his temporal lobes with a probe. He further explained that the temporal lobes were located right behind the human ear.

Following his speech, Dr. Long was inudated by questions from his audience. Jeanette encouraged me to hang in there with my arm in an upraised, dangling position long enough for him to respond to my question, "In your experience do you believe a childhood trauma, such as rape, can induce schziophrenia in later life?"

The answer to that was a resounding and emphatic, "No." It seemed that I had touched a raw nerve in the doctor's psyche. He went on to berate the validity of so-called childhood revelations, which he stated were often based on false memories.

During lunch break I was introduced to Lucy Waters who had been the recipient of my angry letters the previous autumn. She was scheduled to appear on the conference podium later in the afternoon. Lucy told me that she had contacted the BC ombudsman and the health minister Mr. Paul Ramsay, regarding the need for a full public inquiry into the three tragedies that had occurred in Nanaimo during the past year. She said she hoped that the flurry of media interest that had followed Bruce's trial would spur the government into taking action.

An internal review of their own hospital procedures by the Nanaimo Regional General Hospital was already taking place, she said. But according to newspaper articles in the *Nanaimo Daily Free Press,* mostly by the intrepid Noreen Flanagan, there was a growing public demand for an independent inquiry.

The story was gaining widespread publicity. A reporter from the newsmagazine *BC Report* had contacted me and also Bruce. CBC Radio had interviewed Sharon Selinger. Lucy said she had recently talked with Sharon on the phone. The grieving mother confided that she and her husband had put their house in Nanaimo up for sale. She was unable to live with all the painful reminders of their son that were etched in memory inside every room of the family home. I felt a twinge of conscience as I recalled my reflection that it might have been easier for me to bear the news of my son's crime if he had died instead of his victim. Living with Bruce's suicide would have been a horrendous experience, I now realized. As a mother who has often felt that my children exemplify my reason for being, the grief would most likely have been intensified by guilt.

In January 1996, during the time I was researching material for the final chapters of this book, I took the opportunity to correspond with Sharon Selinger. In her letter to me she wrote the following:

"Jeff knew his family loved him very much and wrote it in the letters he left behind. But he talked about the deep pain he had and felt the only way out was to die. If he could have gotten some help, maybe he would still be with us. The last time I saw Jeff alive was in his room and I remember touching his hair and telling him I loved him. 'I know, Mom' were his last words…"

In Dr. Long's lecture he had talked about suicide, which he said was rampant in the city of Vancouver. There were three times as many deaths from suicide, he told us, as there were from AIDS. Because it so often is the cause of death of mentally ill people who are not medicated or perhaps improperly medicated, Dr. Long considered suicide to be the most treatable of all epidemics.

At my request, Noreen Flanagan had forwarded the yellow card and envelope that I had prepared eight months earlier to the Davis family. She also sent me copies of her newspaper articles about Bruce's trial. Noreen suggested in an accompanying letter that I provide input into the Nanaimo hospital's internal review. I mailed a copy of the diary I had compiled to a Dr. K.E. McPherson, who was the chairperson of the review committee.

Dr. McPherson wrote back acknowledging my contribution. She assured me that the diary would be an integral part of the review process.

Shortly after Bruce's trial, an inquest into the death of Mathew Davis was held in Nanaimo. Coroner Jack Harding's report was forwarded to Dr. Barry Morrison, Director of Acute Mental Health Services who ordered a community wide review of all mental health services in the city.

The three day review, conducted by staff members of the health ministry began on May 17, 1994. Representatives from various family and consumer mental health support groups were invited to participate. Dr. Walter Goresky was appointed chairman of the committee. He informed the local press that the review had not been instigated by the three tragedies. Instead, it was a regular part of the health care review process.

Nancy Davis of the Vancouver Island Mental Health Family Advisory Council recalls travelling up to Nanaimo from Victoria to be part of the review team:

> "We reviewed both hospital and community mental health in Nanaimo. We did a lot of interviews and as a committee, evaluated the needs as we saw them. I looked at things from the family perspective, of course. There was a consumer on the committee as well…"

The Review Team came up with a total of 31 recommendations. Although community concerns expressing the need for an investigation into circumstances behind the three deaths involving people with mental illnesses were mentioned, the mandate of the Review Team did not include any specifics.

Their report concluded that the mental health system in Nanaimo had the components of a good system of care, but there was limited coordination or teamwork among the care and service providers. The first priority, the report emphasized, was to develop a Joint Emergency Response Program that would allow for the smooth transition of care through the various emergency services in the Nanaimo area.

In response to that recommendation, an Emergency Response Working Subcommittee was formed. Sharon Selinger was on that committee. The concerns that she had expressed in a letter to Nanaimo Regional General Hospital shortly after her son's suicide, would finally be taken seriously.

Bruce's first BC Review Board hearing was scheduled to be held on May 6th, one day after his thirty-first birthday. I was invited to attend but was unable to do so. At Bruce's request his lawyer Diane Nielsen mailed me copies of the disposition material that had been introduced as exhibits at the hearing.

Dr. Riar had presented a medical assessment dated April 29, 1994, which indicated there was no change in the state of Bruce's mental health. In his report, the doctor made the following recommendations: "We, the treatment team, feel strongly that Mr. Ray should be kept in custody until his mental status is stabilized, at least for six to eight months before considering any other form of status."

Bruce's case management coordinator at FPI, Clem Poquiz, also presented a report to the Review Board hearing. Mr. Poquiz made the following observations: "Mr. Ray continues to experience auditory hallucinations on a regular basis. He does however admit that they are not as intense or as loud as they have been in the past..."

Regarding placement needs Mr. Poquiz wrote: "Mr. Ray continues to reside on R3 East...The treatment team will continue to progress Mr. Ray to the less secure wards throughout the hospital as his mental state and behaviours improve..."

It may have been after Dr. Riar added a prescription for Stelazine to be added to what Bruce called his medication cocktail, that my son's mental health began to improve. That fall he achieved his short term goal which was to be moved into a ward on the second floor. As he had hoped, life on the second floor was easier.

Following his year in hell that was the third floor of the Forensic Institute, Bruce's attitude toward his fellow patients began to change. At first he was wary of the spirit of camaraderie that appeared to exist between second floor patients:

> "I had just come from the third floor and I was pretty paranoid...I started noticing people hugging each other and there was a lot of joking going on...I thought, 'there must be something going on here that I'm not into?' I didn't know what was going on and I didn't know what to do.

> "I started realizing that these guys were joking with each other. They didn't seem to have a problem; it was me that had the problem. So I started to change. That's when I learned what I call brotherhood. I began having this feeling of unconditional love; it was not the least bit sexual; for other patients. It was because we were all in the same boat.

> "One of the guys who was always joking around is a homosexual. Most guys are uncomfortable around homosexuals. But this guy was always making me laugh. For a while he was trying to touch me and hug me. But I kept saying 'go away, go away.' until finally he got the message and quit bugging me. But he has remained my friend.

> "Some are quite isolated from other people because they get picked on [rapists and child molesters]. But I don't believe I should judge anyone for what they've done. You're not going to be close friends with these people but we joke around...You have to acknowledge them. You have to live with them."

My own paranoia regarding Bruce's fellow patients began to dissipate with every visit. At first I made certain that the nurse who was escorting me up the elevator to the second floor interview room where I met with Bruce stayed close by my side every step of the way. After awhile I began to realize that it was not easy to distinguish the people on staff who did not wear a uniform from the patients. Very often the patients were friendlier. Once I asked Bruce about an intense, scary-looking individual whom I had avoided making eye contact with on my way up. It turned out that the fellow was a nurse.

It was during one of my final visits to the main building that I realized how complacent I had become about the intent and purpose of the Forensic Institute. I had packed a jar of my homemade jam before I left home and earlier that day put it inside my roomy purse to give to Bruce. It was wild strawberry–his favorite–and when my son approached, I triumphantly presented it to him. Just then a nurse appeared, seemingly out of nowhere, and with a stern expression on his face, dispatched the jar out of Bruce's hands before he could even say thank you.

Upon seeing the look of abject disappointment on my son's face, the nurse assured him that someone would pour the contents of the jar into a baggy. It would be kept in the coffee-room refrigerator for his use only. The nurse never even looked in my direction. I knew he thought that I was some kind of an idiot. I had completely forgotten about the hard and fast rules pertaining to certain items that must never be brought in to the patients. Anything encased in glass was close to the top of the list.

That same weekend I spent a very pleasant evening with Bruce outside on the grounds, along with a number of other patients. We sat at one of the picnic tables alongside the annex–a long narrow structure attached to the main building that was used by the patients for recreational purposes.

Bruce introduced me to some of the guys and also a few girls who happened to be outside. Everyone else was in the annex; the door was wide open and I could hear music playing from inside. I met a swarthy young man named Gilbert whom Bruce had told me suffered constantly from the delusion that the world was about to come to an end, but who managed to maintain a sense of humour about the whole thing.

Gilbert congratulated me heartily on having a son who was such a nice little guy. Bruce was talented too, Gilbert stated. He pointed excitedly to a sketch, drawn by Bruce, that was in a recent issue of *The Colonist*, a magazine containing contributions by FPI patients. It featured a mustached and muscular young man sitting underneath a tree. The fellow who resembled Gilbert had a serene expression upon his face as he reposed amongst the wild flowers in the grass. "See? That's me!" Gilbert chortled happily.

Almost everyone I met that evening made a point of telling me that my son was a nice guy. A portly middle-aged man said he was from Nanaimo and had been acquainted with Bruce a few years earlier at Columbian House. He did not elaborate further and merely shook his head. I knew he was having a hard time associating my son with the terrible crime that he had committed.

A happy and amazing incident had occurred only a few weeks after Bruce was transferred to the second floor of the Forensic Institute. He had just completed some pen and ink illustrations which he planned to submit to the editorial committee of *The Colonist*. Bruce was at his desk when the director of the facility, Dr. Derek Eves, approached. Dr. Eves peeled off several twenty dollar bills, plus one ten dollar bill from his wallet, and plopped them in front of my son's disbelieving eyes. The genial doctor explained that he wished to purchase three drawings: would Bruce accept fifty dollars for each?

At his January 4, 1994 hearing Bruce received permission from the Review Board that allowed him to commute with an escort to and from the newsroom which was in an adjoining building. A month later when Phoenix and I visited, Bruce gave us each a copy of *The Colonist*. It contained an article written by him entitled "Alive and Well (and getting over it)."

The results of his latest Review Board hearing had been disappointing, Bruce told us. He had expected, at the very least, to be released from the original custody order which was very restrictive. He had hoped to be granted buddy grounds privileges which would have allowed him to go outdoors from time to time in the company of other patients.

Bruce was very soon participating in newsroom activities to the extent that his artwork graced most of *The Colonist* covers, as well as many of the inside pages. He had also become one of the newsletter's most prolific writers. As he had explained to the Review Board panel: having goals and being busy helped him to ignore, and sometimes even block out entirely the voices that he was hearing.

One problem with having schizophrenia is that it is not always easy for others to distinguish paranoia from normal accurate observations. After his January Review Board hearing, Bruce said he suspected his doctor was being somewhat judgmental of him, perhaps because of the enormity of his crime. The episodes of his hearing the dark voices had been few and far between. But it was because of Dr. Riar's recommendations on June 16th, that the Review Board agreed to grant Bruce a conditional discharge from the original custody order. The conditions were that he continue to reside at the Forensic Institute, although it might mean a move to one of the less stringently supervised buildings in the future. All access into the community would be under escort.

During the summer of 1995, Bruce began to attend the group therapy sessions that he had just learned were available to FPI patients. The Tuesday meetings were headed by the hospital chaplain Pastor Tim Fretheim and Dr. Hearn, a psychologist. After he realized that he would not be hung up by his thumbs, Bruce volunteered to be one of the guys on the hotseat.

The first unhappy memory that Bruce divulged to his therapy group occurred during the time when he roamed the streets of Toronto in a state of psychotic confusion in 1986. The sole and heel of his right foot were raw with broken blisters caused by trudging endlessly in worn out and at times soaking wet running shoes. My son's knowledge of first aid was limited. To soothe his painful foot he stole a bottle of Absorbine Jr. liniment and sloshed its contents over the wounds. Bruce recalled that the pain was excruciating until mercifully, his entire foot went numb.

It was good to open up his psyche, Bruce wrote, in one of his rare letters to Leon and me. He admitted he still had a lot of guilt and stuff to deal with. There were seven guys in the therapy group now. They were all becoming more comfortable with it because there was no fear of reprisal. Everything that was said was kept confidential.

I met Pastor Tim Fretheim later that year in November when I spent a pleasant afternoon visiting with Bruce at Hawthorne Cottage on the Riverview Hospital grounds. The charming and completely furnished cottage had been equipped to accommodate patients' relatives who were visiting from out of town. Fern and her brand new baby Julia also visited with us that day.

Tim Fretheim had phoned before I left home. Bruce was only able to leave the facility under escort, he told me, and Pastor Tim, as he is fondly referred to by FPI patients, had volunteered to be the one. He seemed to be as delighted as my son was at the prospect of Bruce's being united with family members at a location away from the FPI premises.

Pastor Tim sat quietly in the background while Fern and I visited with Bruce. After awhile because of his obviously friendly nature, we hardly noticed that he was there at all.

During one of Bruce's smoke breaks outside on the steps of the cottage and while Fern was busy with Julia, I broached the subject of the Christian perception of schizophrenia to Pastor Tim. A well-meaning friend had once confided to Bruce that her entire church group was praying for him. Because of his strange symptoms, they were concerned about the state of his soul. My son's illness had triggered numerous religious conflicts within his own mind over the years. These were caused by hallucinations and delusions, but were very real to him at the time.

Pastor Tim was a good listener. He just nodded his head and smiled while I aired my concerns. I told him how relieved I was that many church leaders and advisors were becoming informed about the medical aspects of schizophrenia. My daughter Cathy had recently taped one of Dr. James Dobson's *Focus on the Family* radio broadcasts. The well-known Christian psychologist had urged family members with loved ones afflicted by the disease to avoid church ministries which continued to preach that the symptoms are caused by demons or evil spirits.

Shortly after my visit, Bruce's treatment team began introducing small amounts of a drug called Clozapine into his daily medication routines. Clozapine was often remarkably effective for treating symptoms of schizophrenia, although there was a slight possibility that it could cause deadly deficiencies in some patients' white blood cell count. Weekly blood tests were therefore mandatory.

By January 15, 1996 it had been determined that Bruce was able to tolerate at least small doses of the drug. In accordance with the latest recommendations of the Review Board panel he was granted his long-awaited buddy grounds privilege.

Three months later Bruce phoned to tell me that he was on top of the world. He had mailed some of his poetry to Susan Musgrave, a well-known Vancouver Island poet and columnist whom he had always admired. The author returned his writings and with them an encouraging critique. She had selected several of his poems as her personal favorites. His work was definitely publishable, she stated.

Although other members on Bruce's treatment team noted an improvement in Bruce's mental health, Dr. Riar's report to the May 23, 1996 Review Board hearing was quite negative. Dr. Riar was concerned because Bruce continued to experience voices inside his head. In his letter to the Review Board, the doctor did concede that for the past several months Bruce had not had any of the acute anxiety attacks that often preceded an onslaught of the bad voices. It was further noted that he had not experienced any command hallucinations since the beginning of January.

In retrospect Bruce said he did not blame Dr. Riar for being cautious. Terrible mistakes had been made in the past. In 1994, a patient who had been given grounds privileges had walked away from the institution. The man had then stalked and killed a Vancouver psychiatrist.

By the same token the Review Board needed to take a position that according to its mandate was the least onerous and least restrictive to the accused. That is, after taking into consideration certain other needs pertaining to the mental state of the accused, particularly the need to protect the public from dangerous persons.

A recent tragedy involving an FPI patient was undoubtedly on the minds of each Review Board panelist. During the previous winter two separate incidents had occurred which resulted in a serious decline in morale among FPI patients. One afternoon when many of the patients were lounging on the grounds outside the annex, a young man named Chris slipped away and managed to climb to the roof of the main building. He was heard to cry out the words, "The Review Board made me do this," before hurtling to his death on the concrete walkway below. Later that winter a patient named Andre also committed suicide by jumping off a building in downtown Vancouver.

In its conclusion the Reasons For Disposition document of Bruce's May 23, 1996 Review Board hearing stated the following:

> "The Review Board is satisfied that it is better from the standpoint of the protection of society, and his own reintegration

into society, to approach his release more slowly, giving him experience living in Hillside or the Cottages before discharging him from the Hospital and placing him in the less supervised setting of a group home…To a large measure the new disposition reflects the contents of its predecessor. However, the Review Board did make one significant change in the terms and conditions. It concluded that there should be a possibility of unescorted access to the community during the term (one year) of the new disposition…"

Shortly after his Review Board hearing Bruce was transferred from the main FPI residence to the Hillside facility. The large white building and the smaller units referred to as The Cottages were located across the highway on the Riverview Hospital grounds. They were all a part of the Forensic Institute system. Patients were transported back and forth to the main building for meals and work therapy which included Bruce's new job as the editor and co-producer of *The Colonist*.

Previous to my next visit, which was in November 1996, Clem Poquiz had made the necessary arrangements that permitted Bruce to accompany me on the first of his unescorted visits into the community. Bruce's new place of residence was just around the corner from Hawthorne Cottage where I had once made reservations.

The first evening of our visit was relatively uneventful. Bruce and I drank coffee and discussed everything under the sun until he had to leave at 9 o'clock. I told Bruce about the BCSS conference I had attended recently that had featured the well-known psychiatrist and researcher Dr. Barry Jones as a keynote speaker. Dr. Jones was a passionate believer in using newer medications such as Closapine, Risperadone and Olanzapine to relieve the symptoms of schizophrenia. The newer drugs were more expensive but they had fewer side-effects, Dr. Jones told us, and they relieved more symptoms.

Dr. Jones acknowledged that the older medications such as Haldol and Stelazine effectively blocked the overproduction of dopamine, which was the cause of hallucinations. "But there is more to schizophrenia than psychosis!" the doctor had exclaimed. "The disease also puts a lot of other receptors out of whack."

The doctor showed us a film projection that displayed two separate

PET scans. One scan was from the brain of a person with schizophrenia. A lack of pale blue markings indicated there was an underactivity of the frontal cortex. When the frontal cortex is not working properly, Dr. Jones said, it can cause emotional and social withdrawal. These symptoms were untreatable before Closapine became available, he informed us: "People woke up, came out of their rooms and socialized."

Bruce had always believed he was at least partly to blame for the escalation of his illness in Nanaimo. Perhaps if he had maintained a caring relationship with friends and family, he might not have become overwhelmed by hallucinations. The notion that his illness may have actually precipitated that isolation was one that he had never before considered.

The following morning a nurse accompanied my son to the door with two sets of medication dosages which she reminded him must be taken at four-hour intervals. I had arranged for Bruce's friend John Burgess to bring a guitar that I had purchased for Bruce. John arrived shortly with the instrument in hand. Fern and my one-year-old granddaughter Julia were next on the scene with the pizza and doughnuts that I had ordered for lunch.

Bruce played the guitar and sang, and little Julia's antics were the life of the party until it was time for her to return home for a nap. Later in the day Bruce and I took the bus into Coquitlam to do some shopping and see a movie. Fern joined us after we were seated in the theatre. During the movie, she would glance at us from time to time and grin. My son and I have a tendency to become soggy-eyed at movies. The storyline of this one, which concerned a man who was in love with the ghost of his dead wife, was very predictable. I enjoyed every minute of it. Unlike similar real life situations, it was obvious from the beginning that there was to be a happy ending.

Bruce had told me he hoped to be released into a group home soon. After the Review Board granted him his conditional discharge, he would be relatively free to carry on with his life. That night my over-stimulated brain wrestled with a question that had never before occurred to me: could what had happened in Nanaimo three and a half years earlier ever happen again?

One aside that Dr. Jones had made during the course of his talk came to my mind. He said that families of people with mental illnesses often have trouble dealing with success; they are so used to dealing with failure. In my heart I knew that my son was a good man. With the help of an effective medication he was fully capable of taking care of his future. I felt a sense of peace within myself as I realized that what had occurred in the past was not mine or anyone else's fault. In the scheme of things there is a reason for everything. I decided to place the whole matter where it belonged. It was now in God's hands–exactly where it had always been.

EPILOGUE

The bleak beginnings of the new year, 1997, brought with it deep levels of snow and forty below temperatures to the Northern Interior. But the news from our kids at the Coast was heartwarming. Fern had enrolled in a college course that would establish her in a future career as a licensed optician. And as for Bruce, the first few ethereal glimmerings of the miracle that I had wished for him back in July of 1993 were beginning to filter through the dark void that was the past three and a half years.

Bruce's treatment team had begun to replace the dosages of Stelazine which had been a part of his medication regime for two years, with elevated levels of Clozapine. Bruce noticed the difference almost immediately. He told Leon on the telephone that he was now able to concentrate much better.

The only voices he continued to hear, he confided to me, were two familiar ones: the one that he had always considered to be his link-up with a higher self and one other that originated on the feminine side of his personality. That voice he sometimes conversed with, Bruce admitted. But only once in awhile.

Before Christmas I had received a letter from him along with copies of the latest *Colonist* magazines. Bruce thanked me for the guitar and wrote that he had really enjoyed my November visit. He referred to a tape recorded interview that I had conducted with him by saying, "If you need any more help [with the book], please let me know. It's hard for me to step outside of myself and look at things with the detachment needed to see the truth. It's hard to be impersonal. I still hurt inside but I am getting better. I know the book is good for you and that you will do a good job at keeping the facts straight. It's been hard for both of us. There's still so much pain when I remember...I try to leave it all behind me (perhaps too much). I live in the present moment and approach everything with as much patience as I can muster.

"I hope to make some progress in the coming months toward establishing a sense of trust between me and the community. You and I know that I am not a violent person, but others hold my fate in hand. Others who do not know me."

Bruce enrolled in a correspondence course in creative writing and received straight "A"s on the first three papers. It was a high school course sponsored by the Ministry of Education. The assignments were an outlet for his creative energy, especially since *The Colonist* was being phased out of existence. The powers-that-be had decided the project was not therapeutic.

During the last week in March I travelled to the Coast on the bus, to spend a few days with Fern and family, and also visit with Bruce. I was able to observe–first hand–the positive changes in Bruce's demeanor. In my diary I noted: "Bruce is the best that I've seen him in years. He's so integrated now, so tuned in. He is an interesting companion and once again displays leadership qualities and concerns about others…"

Bruce had once referred to the voices he experienced when he was very ill, as being shattered portions of his psyche. His conversation had sometimes been slightly out of synch with his gestures. Now as he and I conversed I observed the smooth quick flow of his thoughts, emotions and ideas as they were displayed in facial expression and body language. There was no doubt in my mind that Bruce's psyche was once again whole.

We went shopping and I helped Bruce pick out a stylish black jacket to go with the pants he was wearing. He looked good, I told him, in his new image as the man in black. Bruce smiled sheepishly and said he wondered if his ex-girlfriend would like him in his new jacket. He went on to explain that he had gone out with a girl from FPI for awhile. She had appeared to like him a lot. Bruce assumed that she already knew of the crime for which he had been committed. "Everyone else knows," he said. "But they can see that I am really a mellow guy and not violent."

But Bruce's new girlfriend had not heard the story. "When I told her," he recalled, "she was very upset. Later she said she was afraid to go out with me. I might kill her too. I didn't pursue the issue…I just let her go."

When I left Bruce was about to pack up his belongings and move across the road to the new state of the art multi-million dollar facility. The new FPI complex would replace all existing buildings, including Hillside and The Cottages. The old fortress was destined for the wrecking ball. The surrounding grounds, already populated by coyotes, foxes and rabbits, was to be preserved as a wildlife sanctuary.

Bruce's Review Board Hearing held on May 14, 1997 was quite favorable to him. It reflected the recent positive assessment of his mental health made by Clem Poquiz and the other members of the FPI treatment team. Bruce had a new doctor now. Dr. Riar had left the Forensic Institute in 1996. The Review Board chairperson expressed the pleasure of the panel members upon learning about Bruce's progress. He stated that they were very impressed with the responses that Mr. Ray had given to all of their questions that day.

According to the hearing disposition, Bruce was still to be detained in custody, although he might be granted visiting leaves which might include overnight stays. The chairperson went on to state: "Usually the visiting leave is granted for purposes of placement, but the order mentions other purposes as well, for example, facilitating visits with family and friends. One might contemplate sending Mr. Ray either to Nanaimo or Prince George for a family visit over a period of a few days...One might, I suppose under certain circumstances, even contemplate sending him off to school or programme for a period of a week or so that would assist in his reintegration into society..."

On July 11, 1997 Bruce arrived in Fraser Lake for the first of his visiting leaves as granted by the BC Review Board disposition order. The occasion for which he had received permission to stay overnight with family and friends for a period of four days was the wedding of his cousin LeEtta's son Rodney.

Bruce had a reasonably comfortable trip on the bus, despite a painful bout with gastritis because he forgot to take his anti-acid medication. It was great to be back in Fraser Lake, he stated. As the bus was approaching Prince George, he had revelled in the knowledge that–at long last–he was close to home. When they passed Fort Fraser, he had extolled inwardly upon observing the beauty of the familiar countryside. The incessant rains we had been having had temporarily subsided.

The lush green foliage of the trees and underbrush, and the mirror-bright surface of the lake were now basking in sunshine.

My husband had not seen Bruce since December of 1991. Leon had suffered a debilitating stroke in 1995 from which he had recovered almost completely. The two men shook hands warmly while silently assessing the state of each other's health. Bruce could see for himself that his stepfather had almost fully recovered from effects of his stroke. Bruce's recovery from the effects of his illness was not as obvious.

There were rules to be followed: Bruce needed to notify his ward at the Forensic Institute immediately upon his arrival in Fraser Lake and again on Sunday evening before leaving. I was to contact a man named Rommel at the Forensic Clinic in Prince George. When I phoned, Rommel sounded amiable. He assured me that very likely there would not be a problem with Bruce's mental health. Just in case, he wanted me to know that Dr. Kelly was on call over the weekend, at our medical clinic. The RCMP were also aware that Bruce was here. Rommel gave me his pager number. In case of an emergency, he said, I should call collect.

When Bruce unpacked his bag he handed me the seven or eight vials of medication that he was to take at measured intervals throughout the day. Besides the drugs that controlled his schizophrenia, there were tablets of vitamin C and the prescribed pills for indigestion.

That afternoon we were invited to a barbeque at Cathy and Darwin's on the occasion of Darwin's fortieth birthday. Tyler had grown into a handsome, muscular young man of nineteen. His sister Jennel was now a married woman. If Bruce had felt at all self-conscious around his sister and brother-in-law and their family, it soon wore off in the spirit of jocularity that prevailed. But he did express some trepidation about attending the wedding the following day. He worried about the attitudes of the many aunts, uncles and cousins who would be there. Would they ostracize him because of his crime? I assured him that I had already talked to LeEtta as well as the mother of the bride. There was certainly no problem there.

Bruce need not have worried. At the reception hall he received almost as many hugs and handshakes as did the bride and groom. Our table was almost all Rays and ex-Rays. Bruce's girl-cousins were now married, a few of them more than once. He was particularly pleased to see Teresa looking happier and prettier than when the two of them had been housemates, twelve years earlier. She was with her children, Adrien and Rena, who were now teenagers.

On Sunday afternoon Bruce and I drove to Aunt Marilynne and Uncle Ron's farm, approximately eight kilometers south of Fort Fraser. They had been haying frantically while the sun still shone, which was why we had not seen them at the wedding.

Marilynne was at home. Bruce was also pleased that his favorite cousin Linda was visiting with her mother. Linda had penned a comforting letter to Bruce shortly after his incarceration at FPI. He apologized to her now, because he had never found the words for a reply.

The four of us sat outside in the warm sunshine and reminisced while drinking glasses of lemonade and eating slices of Aunt Marilynne's carrot cake. We were shortly joined by Uncle Ron who was ready for a break from haying.

Linda confessed to having had twinges of guilt following the onslaught of her cousin's schizophrenia. As a child she had been a tomboy and quite willful. Once, following an argument with Bruce she had imprisoned him for hours in her parent's greenhouse. He could not force his way out for fear of damaging the plastic covering. That same weekend, Linda recalled, one of the horses had bitten Bruce right where he sat down. "For years I was convinced it was my fault that you got schizophrenia," she told him.

Shortly after returning from his sojourn to Fraser Lake, Bruce was granted unescorted weekend passes for up to eight hours. His favorite destination was the new public library building in Vancouver. One weekend he attended an intensive updated course in desktop publishing that was being held at the Emily Carr School of Art and Design. In compliance with the Review Board's recommendation that education programs might enhance Bruce's reintegration into society, the Forensic Institute paid half the tuition. I paid the other half.

Shortly before Christmas, Bruce visited his dad and stepmother in Ladysmith. The FPI treatment team had asked where he wished to live in the future and he had decided upon Nanaimo. "Nanaimo was my home for a long time," he told them. "I've been at Columbian House and it is well run."

The lady he had talked to at Mental Health Services had been helpful, Bruce said later. She agreed to consult with the Davis family about how they would feel if he should return to the city. Bruce also implored her to assure the RCMP office that he was no longer dangerous.

He now lived in a minimum security unit at FPI called Hawthorne House. It was to be his final step before leaving the institution and moving into a group home. In preparation the house staff was teaching him how to prepare meals for himself and his fellow residents. This, he may have been too good at, because he gained a considerable amount of weight. During his next visit to Fraser Lake in March 1998 he could barely make it up our kitchen steps without puffing and wheezing. His compulsive eating made Leon and me wonder if he was attempting suicide with a knife and fork.

Clem Poquiz of the Forensic Institute addressed my concerns in a letter: "The treatment team shares your concerns about Bruce's physical health...Certainly the Clozapine has been a factor in contributing to some of the symptoms you described ie. weight gain, puffiness and fatigue, but we have encouraged him to participate in more physical activities and to be more aware of what he eats..."

Bruce's extreme weight gain may have been triggered by depression. A roommate named Carter who had been Bruce's songwriting partner and guitar playing buddy for the past year, had recently been discharged from the facility to his hometown of Victoria. "So many people have been coming and going," Bruce lamented to me on the phone. "And I'm still here."

Bruce was now eligible for temporary leave placements into a selected group home in either Burnaby or Vancouver but there was a long waiting list to get in. The demise of The Colonist had stymied his need to express himself through his writings and illustrations. But after he was encouraged to join the group at the FPI woodworking shop, Bruce discovered a brand new outlet for his creativity.

With a hammer and various-sized chisels my son began to carve faces and three dimensional images out of blocks of wood. The costs of his materials were very soon compensated by sales of these creations to interested patrons. During subsequent visits to Fraser Lake in 1998 he presented both myself and his father, who had recently moved to Fort

Fraser, with pieces of his artwork. In the future if he were ever to make a living from his artistic endeavors, Bruce was convinced it would be from his carvings.

After he had moved into a group home, Bruce took the early morning bus several days a week to the FPI shop. He told me he was constructing a workbench so that he could continue his carving, following his long-anticipated conditional discharge from the Forensic Psychiatric Institute.

His next Review Board hearing, scheduled for the summer, was postponed until September, then October. But Bruce was already enjoying a degree of freedom he had not experienced for many years. He purchased a cheap computer and with my help a few carving tools, and he began to dabble at painting in acrylics at a mental health drop-in center. Bruce was making new friends and reconnecting with old acquaintances.

An FPI acquaintance who now lived in Vancouver was managing to cope without the benefit of medication. He told Bruce that anti-psychotic drugs could lead to brain damage. In early October, after I learned that Bruce had gone off his medication for a period of several weeks, I was surprised and concerned but only because it had happened so quickly. I had thought that his dosages were being monitored at his group home.

I remembered one of the letters I had received from my son during the first year he was incarcerated at FPI. In it he had written: "It has become obvious to me that the medication does not work and in fact never worked. I feel you (as well as me) have been sold a bill of goods. When I killed that man I was on a great deal of medication and [as well] a few mgs of clorpromazine; then I went to the hospital and I think (I'm not sure) I was given more drugs. It's never worked and never will (this gambling as some people call it)."

Without the benefit of medication, Bruce soon became disoriented and confused. He experienced the dark voices, although he said later they were not as strident as before. The group home attendants had been noticing changes in his behaviour. They were not surprised when Bruce requested to be returned to FPI.

Bruce's Clozapine dosages were raised from 150 mgs to 200 mgs three times a day. When I spoke to Clem Poquiz only a few days after my son had been admitted into a ward, I learned that his mental health had already returned to baseline. Bruce told me he had learned at least one important thing from his experiment: FPI was not a place to be feared. The third level of the old facility–reserved for newcomers and backsliders–was gone forever. He was receiving good treatment and good food.

Bruce was up for Christmas. Together with his dad and Connie, as well as Cathy, Darwin and family, we had a bit of a family reunion. Before he left he admitted to having some trepidation about his upcoming Review Board hearing, set for January 6, 1999. The panel members would certainly grill him about why he had gone off his medication. Bruce said he had decided to be absolutely candid about everything. The people in his therapy group were very supportive, he added. That helped a lot.

At the Review Board hearing Bruce read the following statement which reflected his new attitude. "...First of all I've learned that in order to stay functional, I have to make sure my relationship with my doctor and treatment team is mutually conducive. Throughout my therapy with Doctor T....at the clinic, I have come to understand that it is integral I see myself as part of the team, that I have something to contribute to it. Moreover it is useless to be confrontive or even challenging toward a system that I am involved in. It is a matter of trust–both ways. Trust is a lot like money, it must be earned! I see myself as fulfilling the role of a job. In the same way that these professionals do their work, I must contribute.

"I had been told (by other ex-patients) that there's a chance of contacting brain damage from medications, therefore I stopped taking my regular dosages. Afterward as my doctor suggested, I read literature from the orthodox viewpoint. After the consequences, I decided that I had made a mistake. When I had stopped taking my medication, I immediately experienced hallucinations and then volunteered to be returned to FPI to be reassessed. When the dosages were raised I had no more problems and returned to reside [at the group home]. I am of the understanding that if I have a relapse of any sort, I am open to returning to this institution for however long it takes, to be reassessed and treated in any way. I have stated this several times and have no reservations whatsoever–whether I have a custody order, conditional discharge or absolute discharge.

"Thus perhaps I earn the trust that I am given. Now my job as I call it, is to maintain respect for the system and to endeavor to keep myself empowered. To know when I need help and not be too proud to ask for assistance. I am to be honest and not to worry about the consequences.

"I have been as honest as I can be, considering my fears and despite the fact that I lied about the bad voices. They were always present [during the time he was off medication] but were not (as I saw it) debilitating and could easily be ignored through relaxation techniques. Now I can claim honestly that these voices have receded into the background. I feel I am ready to take steps toward a long and healthy rehabilitative return to the community I live in and am a part of."

After much questioning and consultation the Review Board panel members agreed to grant Bruce a conditional discharge from the Forensic Psychiatric Institute.